Cold War Comforts

Studies in
Childhood and Family
in Canada

A broad-ranging series that publishes scholarship from various disciplines, approaches and perspectives relevant to the concepts and relations of childhood and family in Canada. Our interests also include, but are not limited to, interdisciplinary approaches and theoretical investigations of gender, race, sexuality, geography, language and culture within these categories of experience, historical and contemporary.

Series Editor:
Cynthia Comacchio
History Department
Wilfrid Laurier University

For literature and media related projects, send proposals to:
Lisa Quinn, Acquisitions Editor
Wilfrid Laurier University Press
75 University Avenue West
Waterloo, ON
Canada N2L 3C5
Phone: 519-884-0710 ext. 2843
Fax: 519-725-1399
Email: quinn@press.wlu.ca

For all other disciplines, send proposals to:
Ryan Chynces, Acquisitions Editor
Wilfrid Laurier University Press
75 University Avenue West
Waterloo, ON
Canada N2L 3C5
Phone: 519-884-0710 ext. 2034
Fax: 519-725-1399
Email: rchynces@wlu.ca

Cold War Comforts

Canadian Women, Child Safety, and
Global Insecurity, 1945–1975

TARAH BROOKFIELD

WILFRID LAURIER
UNIVERSITY PRESS

This book has been published with the help of a grant from the Canadian Federation for the Humanities and Social Sciences, through the Aid to Scholarly Publications Programme, using funds provided by the Social Sciences and Humanities Research Council of Canada. Wilfrid Laurier University Press acknowledges the financial support of the Government of Canada through the Canada Book Fund for our publishing activities.

Library and Archives Canada Cataloguing in Publication

Brookfield, Tarah
    Cold War comforts : Canadian women, child safety, and global insecurity / Tarah Brookfield.

(Studies in childhood and family in Canada)
Includes bibliographical references and index.
Issued also in electronic format.
ISBN 978-1-55458-623-3

    1. Cold War. 2. Women—Political activity—Canada—History—20th century. 3. Cold War—
Social aspects—Canada. 4. Children—Legal status, laws, etc.—Canada—History—
20th century. 5. Children—Legal status, laws, etc.—History—20th century. I. Title. II. Series:
Studies in childhood and family in Canada

FC613.C64B76 2012   971.063   C2011-907615-2

Electronic monograph in PDF format.
Issued also in print format.
ISBN 978-1-55458-635-6

    1. Cold War. 2. Women—Political activity—Canada—History—20th century. 3. Cold War—
Social aspects—Canada. 4. Children—Legal status, laws, etc.—Canada—History—20th century.
5. Children—Legal status, laws, etc.—History—20th century. I. Title. II. Series: Studies in
childhood and family in Canada (Online)

FC613.C64B76 2012   971.063   C2011-907616-0

© 2012 Wilfrid Laurier University Press

Waterloo, Ontario, Canada
www.wlupress.wlu.ca

RECYCLED
Paper made from
recycled material
FSC® C103567

Cover design by Martyn Schmoll. Front-cover image by iStockphoto; inset photo by Associated Press. Text design by Catherine Bonas-Taylor.

This book is printed on FSC recycled paper and is certified Ecologo. It is made from 100% post-consumer fibre, processed chlorine free, and manufactured using biogas energy.

Printed in Canada

Contents

List of Acronyms and Initialisms

Organizations

ARPO	Air Raid Precautions Organization
CASW	Canadian Association of Social Workers
CAVC	Canadian Aid for Vietnam Civilians
CAWV	Committee Against the War in Vietnam
CBC	Canadian Broadcasting Corporation
CCCRH	Canadian Committee for the Control of Radiation Hazards
CCF	Canadian Commonwealth Federation
CCND	Canadian Campaign for Nuclear Disarmament
CIDA	Canadian International Development Agency
CJC	Canadian Jewish Congress
CPC	Canadian Peace Congress
CPRI	Canadian Peace Research Institute
CWC	Canadian Welfare Council
EMO	Emergency Measures Organization
FCV	Friends of the Children of Vietnam
FFC	Families for Children
FPA	Family Planning Association
FPPI	Foster Parents Plan International
FWIC	Federated Women's Institutes of Canada
ICSC	International Commission for Supervision and Control
IODE	Imperial Order Daughters of the Empire

ISS	International Social Services
KYF	Kuan Yin Foundation
LON	League of Nations
MCC	Mennonite Central Committee
MCSC	Montreal Children's Service Centre
NAC	National Action Committee
NATO	North Atlantic Treaty Organization
NCWC	National Council of Women of Canada
NDP	New Democratic Party
NORAD	North American Aerospace Defence Command
ODS	Open Door Society
QMAV	Quebec Medical Aid for Vietnam
RCMP	Royal Canadian Mounted Police
SANE	Committee for a Sane Nuclear Policy
UN	United Nations
UNA	United Nations Association
UNICEF	United Nations International Children's Emergency Fund
UNKRA	United Nations Korea Reconstruction Agency
UNRRA	United Nations Relief and Rehabilitation Administration
USC	Unitarian Service Committee
VOW	Voice of Women/La Voix des femmes
VWU	Vietnam Women's Union
WILPF	Women's International League for Peace and Freedom
YWCA	Young Women's Christian Association

Archives

AO	Archives of Ontario, Toronto, ON
CEA	City of Edmonton Archives, Edmonton, AB
CTA	City of Toronto Archives, Toronto, ON
DCA	Diefenbaker Centre Archives, University of Saskatchewan, Saskatoon, SK
LAC	Library and Archives Canada, Ottawa, ON
MUA	McMaster University Archives, Hamilton, ON
SWHA	Social Welfare History Archives, University of Minnesota, Minneapolis, MN
UBCSC	University of British Columbia Special Collections, Vancouver, BC
UCOA	UNICEF Canada Office Archives, Toronto, ON

UMA	University of Manitoba Archives, Winnipeg, MB
URIA	University of Rhode Island Archives, Warwick, RI
UWA	University of Waterloo Archives, Waterloo, ON
YUA	Clara Thomas Archives, York University, Toronto, ON

Terms

DEW	Distant Early Warning
ICBM	Intercontinental Ballistic Missile
MAD	Mutually Assured Destruction
Sr-90	Strontium-90

Acknowledgements

I always enjoy reading acknowledgements because authors are usually so giddy that the book is *finally* finished that they are full of glee, love, and good humour. More importantly, acknowledgements are excellent reminders that, although writing and research can feel like a solitary experience, nurturing a book from beginning to end is greatly dependent on the generosity of so many people whom the author encounters on his or her journey. I am incredibly lucky to have been surrounded by wonderful mentors, peers, colleagues, oral history participants, and family from the time this book was only the flimsiest of ideas for a dissertation.

Cold War Comforts began as a dissertation in the Department of History at York University. I am eternally grateful that Kathryn McPherson did not laugh when I suggested a thesis project based on the vague connections between 1950s fallout shelters and international adoption in the 1970s. As my supervisor, Kate pushed me to develop my ideas into something coherent and meaningful, particularly by reminding me that a good story was incomplete without answering the persistent question "So what?" I was joined at York by two indispensable thesis committee members, Molly Ladd-Taylor and Marcel Martel, who went above and beyond to offer feedback, advice, and support on every word written. For future York grad students, I present to you—your thesis committee dream team!

The York History Department was also brimming with encouragement from other faculty members and fellow students. Bettina Bradbury always had time to offer encouragement and guidance. Myra Rutherdale, Craig Heron, Marlene Shore, and Jennifer Stephen were gracious with their wisdom and their interest in my project. The same can be said of my fellow York classmates and friends, particularly Susana Miranda, Kristine Alexander, Greg Kennedy, Sean Kheraj, Natalie Gravelle, Jason Ellis, Sarah Glassford, Jenny Ellison, Christine Grandy, and Lisa Rumiel. I also benefited from the social and professional networking of the Toronto Area Women's Canadian History Group, where I met Samantha Cutrara, Alison Norman, Robin Grazley, and Jennifer Bonnell. I am very lucky to be part of this new generation of historians and genuinely awesome people who are so willing to support each other through graduate work and beyond.

I would also like to acknowledge the substantial funding I received for the dissertation stage of this project from the Social Sciences and Humanities Research Council Doctoral Fellowship, the Avie Bennett Historica Dissertation Scholarship in Canadian History, and the John A. Macdonald Fellowship in Canadian History.

Once I finished my PhD, I was fortunate to have found a similarly supportive environment to continue the research and writing for *Cold War Comforts* at Wilfrid Laurier University. I benefited from the interdisciplinary nature of the Laurier Brantford campus and the company of my fellow historians in Brantford and Waterloo. I am appreciative of the energy and support radiating from my Laurier colleagues, including James Cairns, Rebecca Godderis, Katherine Rossiter, Trish McLaren, Katherine Bell, Stacey Hannem, Charles Wells, Ken Werbin, Lisa Wood, Rob Kristofferson, Geoff Spurr, Peter Farrugia, Terry Copp, and Cynthia Comacchio. Laurier generously provided me with research and travel grants that allowed me to make the transition from dissertation to book. This included the funding to work with two excellent research assistants, Annalise Clarkson and Heather Gauthier.

I am honoured to be included in Wilfrid Laurier University Press's Studies in Childhood and Family in Canada Series, home to so many other books that inspire my teaching and research. From the early stages of my proposal, I had the pleasure of working with series editor Cynthia Comacchio, whose touch always had the effect of immediately improving my words and ideas. Editor Ryan Chynce's patience and advice was much welcomed by this first-time author. I appreciate Rob Kohlmeier's and Benjamin Lefebvre's work putting together the book's final touches. I would like to thank each of the three anonymous reviewers for taking the time to evaluate my scholarship and offer perceptive feedback.

My research only exists because of the foundation laid by other scholars of women's and children's history. Furthermore, Karen Dubinsky, Dominique Marshall, Karen Balcom, Veronica Strong-Boag, Mona Gleason, Franca Iacovetta, Tamara Myers, and Frances Early generously shared their research and offered advice at critical stages of my project's development.

The research and writing of this book was made possible by the assistance of helpful archivists, librarians, and staff across Canada and the United States. Many thanks to the family members and colleagues who gave me access to the personal papers and photographs of the activist women and organizations featured in this book. Most importantly, this research would be incomplete without the personal experiences shared by the oral history participants who trusted me with their stories and memories. It was such an honour to talk to you and include your perspectives in my book. I would like to single out the participation of one person in particular, Julie Medeiros. Many years ago she told me the story of how she came to Canada and included me in her journey to explore her Cambodian roots. I am so grateful that she is my friend and that she allowed me to include her story in this book.

At its heart, this book is about families of all different kinds, those made by blood, marriage, and other circumstances. I am blessed to be part of many families who have welcomed me into their lives as a daughter, wife, sister, aunt, cousin, niece, daughter-in-law, and friend. To the Brookfields, Lunds, Stewarts, Brauns, Whites, Joyces, Marissinks, and Hatchers, thank you for always asking about the book and assuring me it would be a best-seller! My good friend Melissa Stubbs deserves a special mention for being an enthusiastic cheerleader and hand-holder for over twenty years. There are not enough words to describe the encouragement and love (and teasing) I received from my husband, Dennis, throughout this journey. Finally, in a book about mothers and children, it seems fitting to dedicate this book to two important people in my life: my mother, Margaret, and my daughter, Juliet.

Introduction

Vigilant would best describe Ottawa resident Goldie Josephy's state of mind in the 1960s and 1970s. Throughout these decades Josephy could be regularly found on Parliament Hill carrying a nuclear disarmament picket sign, holding a memorial outside the American embassy on the anniversary of Hiroshima, and participating in a march advocating an end to the war in Vietnam. When not actively demonstrating for peace, Josephy, a married mother and recent Jewish immigrant from England, was glued to her typewriter, where she wrote letters almost daily to heads of state and newspapers, expressing her distaste for militarism, imperialistic foreign policy, and nuclear weapons. From the same typewriter she corresponded with her South Korean foster child, Myung Hi, whom she sponsored through the Unitarian Service Committee. Josephy's house was often the site of meetings for peace groups and became the temporary home to several American youths dodging the draft. In between demonstrations and stuffing envelopes, Josephy made time for private reflection, attending the Quaker peace retreat on Grindstone Island with her husband and two sons. She also organized the Ottawa visits of Nobel Peace Prize recipient Linus Pauling and anti–Vietnam War crusader Dr. Benjamin Spock. Josephy's vigilance caused one journalist to remark that it appeared she "worked 80 hours a week for 18 years without pay."[1] When asked to explain her drive, Josephy stated, "I had two beautiful children and decided if I wanted them to grow up with arms and legs attached we can't have another war."[2]

Josephy was one of thousands of Canadian women who mobilized to protect children's health and safety during the nuclear arms race and outbreaks of war between the dropping of the first atomic bomb in Hiroshima and the end of the Vietnam War. Technically Canada was at peace between 1945 and 1975; however, the economic, cultural, and political rivalry between the United States and Soviet Union meant it was a peace that demanded caution and preparation for war. The state of global security (or rather insecurity) was characterized by the existence, evolution, and stockpiling of nuclear weaponry, which, if deployed, promised to end life as it was known. Meanwhile dozens of violent conflicts erupted in Europe and Asia, drawing the attention of foreign allies eager to offer military assistance to protect their economic and political ventures. In this explosive climate, the Canadian government, in both its successive Liberal and Conservative forms, made several investments to keep the Cold War from getting hot, or, failing that, to ensure Canada emerged on the winning side. This meant Canada would continue the course the nation began in the Second World War and remain active in international affairs by helping its allies and monitoring the activities of its enemies. In the diplomatic arena, hope was pinned on the United Nations (UN) becoming the foremost peacemaker, and the Canadian government donated funds and leadership so the fledgling organization had the resources to avert war and build stability through relief, economic development, social justice, and later, peacekeeping. Meanwhile, militarization offered a more familiar solution. Canada helped form the North Atlantic Treaty Organization (NATO) in 1949 and the North American Aerospace Defence Command (NORAD) in 1958, devoting land, troops, and finances to build and maintain defensive perimeters. Throughout the Cold War, the federal government was preoccupied with balancing the nation's security responsibilities with shifting commitments to internationalism, continentalism, multilateralism, and Canada's own sovereignty. As a result, Canada continued to nurture close alliances with Britain and, more importantly, with the United States, with whom Canada aligned their foreign policy and national defence plans, at least until the mid-1960s. On the home front, with an eye to the worst-case scenario, the government implemented a civil defence program to educate its citizens on the rudimentary tools they could use to survive a nuclear war. A system of surveillance was put in place to monitor and persecute communists and other groups construed as threats to Canada's domestic security.[3]

During this thirty-year period the traditional family unit, both in Canada and abroad, was deemed inadequate to survive Cold War threats without new resources and external support. In particular, children's minds and bodies were seen as vulnerable to an assortment of atomic-age dangers as varied as atmospheric radiation caused by weapons testing, communist ideology, and the possibility of a third world war fought with nuclear weapons. To protect their own children from these risks, some Canadian women found solace in following the government-sponsored civil defence program or remained alert for communist insurgents. Another cohort of women believed that security could only be achieved through peace, so they championed diplomacy and cross-cultural understanding through the UN or joined the disarmament movement. Concurrently, armed conflict of a more conventional kind flourished in this era. While many women focused on surviving or diverting a possible nuclear attack on Canada, other women directed their attention and concern towards the welfare of children living in sites of Cold War conflicts. The civil wars, revolutions, and multinational conflicts arising in Greece, Korea, China, and Vietnam were proof that humankind did not need to employ a cocktail of uranium and nuclear fission to cause great destruction. To assist children displaced, orphaned, injured, or otherwise harmed by war, Canadian women raised money for foreign relief, volunteered in overseas orphanages and hospitals, and arranged international adoptions.

These women's varied responses represent divergent paths to securing children's health and safety amid global insecurity. The welfare solutions varied, depending on the time period as well as the activist women's different opinions on the causes of war and Canada's responsibilities at home and abroad. Yet what united these women's activism was their shared concern for children's survival amid actual and imagined Cold War fears and dangers. Projecting their identities as both Canadian citizens and women, this collective demand for war-related child welfare characterized the genuine interest many women had in protecting or improving children's health and safety, as well as offering women a legitimate space in which to operate in the traditionally male realms of defence and diplomacy. Despite pursuing different paths to peace and security, Canadian women from all walks of life, living in all parts of the country, dedicated themselves to finding ways to survive the hottest periods of the Cold War. Their activism directly impacted the lives of children in Canada and abroad, and it influenced changes in Canada's education curriculum, immigration laws, welfare practices, defence policy, and international relations. An analysis of these interconnected social movements offers insight into how women employed maternalism, nationalism, and internationalism in their work, and how it shifted constructions of family and gender in Cold War Canada.

Women Mobilizing for War and Peace

There is a long-established history in Canada of gendered mobilization around issues of war and peace. Despite the unique circumstances of the Cold War, the insecurity it generated and the expectations for civilian engagement were aspects that were familiar from the First and Second World Wars. Research on women's contributions in the First World War, primarily in the field of health and welfare, demonstrates how the majority of middle-class women in English Canada militarized their mothering by caring for lonely, sick, and wounded soldiers and the families they left behind.[4] Meanwhile Ruth Roach Pierson's pioneering book *"They're Still Women After All": The Second World War and Canadian Womanhood* illustrates how amid the influx of women's paid labour in masculine workplaces, the maternalistic spirit persisted in women's unpaid war work during the Second World War.[5] Whatever the form of war work taken on, the dominant view of Canadian women's world war contributions is one of active engagement and patriotism, demonstrated by sending their sons off to fight and their own transition to battlefield nurse, munitions worker, or Red Cross volunteer. Although this mobilization is often the hegemonic view of women's war work, scholars have also called attention to the women who resisted the state's call to arms. These included the pacifist and socialist women who protested their nation's involvement in global conflicts and women living in French Canada who were less moved to sacrifice their sons to distant imperial causes.[6] This established pattern demonstrates how the threat of war and the desire for peace has long provoked communities of women to take a stand and labour toward causes they hoped would improve their world, nation, and family's well-being.

Scholarship on the World Wars helps historicize women's Cold War identities as either warriors or peacemakers or a combination of both. It also demonstrates the effect war has on deconstructing or reinforcing traditional understandings of gender. As Sharon Macdonald notes, the intrusion of war into a society "makes it difficult to maintain traditional social order, and boundaries, such as those of gender, may well break down."[7] Historians have shown how, during the First and Second World Wars, traditional gender roles became flexible, at least temporarily, especially in terms of the division of labour. This occurred most obviously when women replaced enlisted men in factories, on farms, and in non-combatant positions in the armed forces, but also when women became the heads of their households in their husbands' absence. Despite these aberrations, men and women's wartime roles were usually rooted in particular understandings of male and female behaviour, with the ideal man taking on the role of protector in the form of soldiering and the ideal woman acting as a caregiver whose labour reinforced men at the front.

The Cold War challenged the traditional gendered division of labour established in the World Wars. Since the mechanics of the conflict differed greatly, the gender dichotomy was not as simple as men becoming soldiers and women becoming their auxiliary non-combatants, tucked safely behind the front lines. Rather, the superpowers' reliance on nuclear weapons diminished the need for countries to arm themselves with able-bodied men. Instead of sending thousands of soldiers across long distances to defeat an enemy, it became possible over the course of the Cold War to send hundreds of bombs for the same purpose. The change in technology and warfare also served to turn the home front into a battlefield, a concept foreign to Canadians accustomed for more than a century to their wars being fought at least an ocean away. Furthermore, with the exception of the Korean War and Canada's contribution to staffing NATO bases, Canadian men did not leave home in the Cold War, so there was no need for women to replace them in traditionally masculine spaces. Lawrence Wittner concludes that these particularities meant that in the nuclear age "women could no longer protect children by caring for them at home and men could no longer guarantee their safety by soldiering."[8] Therefore, women were expected to defend the new war zone alongside men, and they participated in two main forms of Cold War defence: preventing an outbreak of war and minimizing the cost of war to civilians, particularly children.

Despite the expanded nature of their war work, women's participation in each form of activism featured in this study were usually contextualized in maternalistic terms and performed through acts of caregiving, not unlike their work in the First and Second World Wars. This demonstrates the pervasive spirit of maternalism in Canadian women's activism more than half a century after it was first imbued with political energy in the international suffrage and social gospel movements of the late nineteenth century.[9] Even after the federal franchise was extended to white Canadian women in 1919, female activists continued to rely on maternal identities and rhetoric when seeking social, political, and economic reforms.[10] During the Cold War, politically active women positioned themselves as performing work in accordance with the qualities associated with motherhood—care, nurturance, and morality—especially as the work related to children, who were believed to be the most vulnerable to Cold War threats and violence. Individually and through their work in organizations, they practised maternalism as a humanitarian gesture and as a familiar political strategy that allowed them to claim a legitimate space in which to interact with the public and state. To borrow Seth Koven and Sonya Michel's pre-1950s contextualization, Cold War–inspired maternalist discourses allowed women to transform motherhood "from women's primary *private* responsibility into *public* policy" and exert "a powerful influence in defining the needs of mothers and children and designing institutions and programs to address them."[11] Although the consciousness-raising of the late 1960s and 1970s would culminate in a more expansive view of feminism that focused on combating inequalities in the law, employment, family, and reproductive rights, it is important to recognize that maternal feminism remained a force in women's political participation in the postwar period. Furthermore, demonstrating continuities in women's activism reinforces the need to reconceptualize the history of feminist mobilization, particularly assumptions in the wave theory about stagnant organizing between 1920 and 1960. As Joan Sangster so eloquently states, "One can argue for a women's history that acknowledges waves (or better, streams) of women's equality-seeking organizing occurring over the twentieth century, with these waves ebbing and flowing in intensity, sometimes overlapping but also embodying different—even oppositional—actors, political ideas, objectives."[12]

Expressions of Cold War–era maternalism came in many forms; they were rarely subtle and always complicated. In the coming chapters, it will be clear that this maternalism was implemented by mothers and non-mothers alike, by conservatives and by radicals, and that it was not necessarily attached to an explicit commitment to feminism. It was often used to argue opposing sides of the same argument, such as when women used the language of maternalism to demonstrate support for and protest against the use of fallout shelters.[13] At times maternalism was deployed quite literally, as when Canadian women adopted children from sites of Cold War conflicts, or more hypothetically, as when they became long-distance "mothers" to the children they sponsored through international foster parent plan programs. Moreover the maternalist women did not limit their activism to issues related to the welfare of women and children. As always, women extended their maternalistic activism to broader causes and "searching critiques of state and society."[14] Despite the lack of harmony in its application, maternalism is a useful term to connect with women's Cold War–related child welfare activism. Whether the women were looking homeward at their own children (usually Canadian, middle-class, and white), outward at other children (typically foreign, poor, and/or motherless), or not at children at all, they conducted their activism using maternal rhetoric and actions that were powerful and successful in raising public and state awareness. This allowed individual women and women's organizations to operate sometimes discreetly, sometimes loudly in the masculine worlds of defence, foreign affairs, and diplomacy. Those who questioned the appropriateness of women's presence in these fields could often be pacified or silenced by the response that the women's work was serving the needs of children. It was also useful as a subtle way to steer discussion toward other feminist issues or social justice politics.

Maternalism was not the only ideology or motivation that contextualized women's Cold War concerns. The women's activism was also informed by intersectionality, defined by Cynthia Cockburn as "a term that highlights the way dimensions of positionality cross-cut each other, so that any individual or collectivity experiences several simultaneously. A 'woman' or 'man' is also, always (among other things), ethnically identified and a member of a given social class (and so on)."[15] Particularly close at heart were the activist women's commitments to nationalism and internationalism. Many of the women featured in this study contextualized their activism as being distinctly Canadian, a concept as fluid as maternalism. In this era, being Canadian was often defined as simply being not American and was also highly dependent on the activists' regional and ancestral identities.[16] Regardless of the individualized conceptions of what it meant to be Canadian, activists positioned their work as being in the best interests of their nation and the responsibility of good citizens. For some activists, this meant their accountability ended at Canada's borders; however, a majority of activists chose to look beyond, the consequence of a belief that their nation's fate was intertwined with other nations. Many women recognized that international co-operation provided the widest net for momentum to be built around a cause, especially one that affected the entire world, such as the nuclear arms race.

Internationalism was not a new banner for female activists to fly. It had been present in the women's movement since the late nineteenth century and peaked during women's organizing for peace prior to and after the First World War. Within this movement, solidarity was established around appeals to women's shared experiences of womanhood, sisterhood, and motherhood. These communal identities helped activists transcend cultural, political, and linguistic barriers, and national borders.[17] Women's embrace of internationalism was also influenced by Canada's contributions in the Second World War, which gave the nation a legitimate position from which to involve itself internationally and prompted a national sense of responsibility to preserve Allied victory.[18] Therefore being Canadian after 1945 often meant being a global citizen, though there was no great consensus on what this denoted. For some, internationalism could mean an appreciation for open dialogue, cross-cultural understanding, and equality among nations, while for others it was a medium to spread the idea of the superiority of Canadian values around the world. During the Cold War, some activists restricted their international connections to other Western nations or to those fighting the good fight against communism. To do otherwise, they believed, threatened their patriotism. Understanding that the Cold War was caused by an outdated us-versus-them attitude, other activists purposely extended open arms and made it a point to find common interests with "enemy" women in the Soviet Union, mainland China, and North Vietnam.

The women in this study also contextualized their activism in ways that were deeply personal. Since many of the activists had immigrated to Canada after the Second World War as displaced persons and war brides from Britain and Europe, their experiences in World War II were common starting points for Cold War activism. These women carried with them memories of air raids, rationing, families separated, communities destroyed, and lives utterly transformed; many were refugees, prisoners of war, and survivors of concentration camps. These harrowing experiences made some women determined to avoid another war at all costs, while others were prepared to do whatever it took, be it building a bomb shelter or shunning communists, to ensure their family's survival. There were other important factors that served as women's foundation for activism, such as their faith, ethnicity, politics, class, province of residence, education, and so on. Linking together these personal dimensions were women's shared concern for the fate of their families, their nation, and the world.

From the War Room to the Bedroom: Shaping the History of Cold War Canada

Canada is not normally viewed by historians or even in public memory as a relevant player in Cold War affairs. Scholars who analyze the history of international relations between 1945 and 1991 are most interested in understanding which nations' policies caused and sustained and eventually ended the Cold War.[19] The superpowers and countries whose lands became the site of Cold War conflict dominate global histories. If mentioned at all, Canada is usually included in a list of Western allies, with perhaps minimal attention allocated to the nation's role in the Gouzenko spy affair or Lester B. Pearson's steering of the Suez crisis. Largely Canada's presence is shown to be appreciated, but as an ally or enemy, it is viewed as doing nothing to distinguish itself diplomatically or militarily. Canadian historians do not fundamentally disagree with this assessment; Canada's role in the Cold War mattered primarily to Canada. Yet at the same time, it is valuable to understand how aligned middle-power nations like Canada navigated Cold War currents and how they may have influenced international Cold War culture and politics. As recent studies by Philip Buckner, R. D. Francis, Robert Bothwell, and John Price demonstrate, throughout the twentieth century Canada increased its global footprint in terms of migration, trade, travel, diplomacy, missions, and military involvement, all the while acting as a space for the dissemination of people, commodities, and ideas ranging from imperialism to decolonization.[20] This study will illustrate how, throughout the Cold War period, Canada's responses to global insecurity affected its own domestic landscape, as well as those of the countries with which it interacted. Much like Ruth Compton Brouwer's work on missionary women, *Cold War Comforts* contributes to this field by looking at Canada's global encounters through the labour and ideology of Canadian women engaged in projects designed to save children and change the world.[21]

Looking at the interwoven histories of international relations, defence, diaspora, and ideology through a gendered lens offers a view of the Cold War from rarely seen perspectives—those of women and children. Until recently, the Cold War was seen as the story of diplomats, spies, and military men.[22] Even more than had been the case with the World Wars, the original perspective of Cold War history came from the personalities and politics of world leaders: Eisenhower, Churchill, Stalin, Kennedy, Khrushchev, Mao, and Castro. Conventional Cold War history is the story of these men and their relationships with each other, the weapons they directed to be built, the espionage they ordered, and the territories they fought to control. Emily Rosenberg reminds us that women were not absent from the diplomatic arena, though they may have been viewed as invisible since they typically affected foreign affairs through their involvement in peace groups and international organizations or by performing "women's work" overseas as nurses, teachers, missionaries, and the wives of diplomats.[23] Although at this time women rarely had seats at the tables of power, Cynthia Enloe has shown that women's reproduction, consumerism, labour, bodies, and activism are powerful forces in shaping and supporting global foreign policy from behind the scenes. Furthermore, Enloe argues that if women have so much power in bolstering this system, they also have the power to change it for the better.[24] For the women activists featured in this study, their collective willpower at first built up and then tore down the civil defence program, engaged thousands of women in a worldwide disarmament movement that contributed to the international Test Ban Treaty in 1963, raised millions of dollars in foreign aid, and brought hundreds of war orphans to live in Canada. Alongside politicians, diplomats, and soldiers, ordinary women should be viewed as active political players in managing Canada's Cold War affairs.

In the last two decades, historians have studied Cold War Canada under a much broader lens and have demonstrated the social and cultural consequences of Canada's domestic Cold War politics.[25] Rather than being seen as a series of military and diplomatic events, the Cold War is now being viewed as a phenomenon that occurred on several levels and affected all parts of society. In *The Making of a National Insecurity State*, Reg Whitaker and Gary Marcuse argue that the clandestine nature of Canada's version of McCarthyism made it a more dangerous entity than the highly public anti-communist trials occurring south of the border. Living under "a quasi-McCarthy mentality" had a chilling effect on Canada's commitment to liberal democracy: citizens' rights were violated, police powers spiralled out of control, and some citizens lost their government jobs, were purged from unions, or were deported.[26] Fear arose about certain segments of the population deemed to be "others": communists, radicals, homosexuals, and immigrants. New Canadians, especially those from countries now behind the Iron Curtain, were expected to conform as much as possible to Canadian norms or their claims to citizenship would be contested.[27] Women contextualizing their activism as a noble motherhood cause did not necessarily protect them from state scrutiny. Alongside other suspicious organizations, women's peace and disarmament groups were infiltrated and watched by the RCMP for evidence of subversion.[28]

The family was seen to be at the heart of Cold War society. My research corroborates scholarship that demonstrates how the family—usually conceptualized as the privileged Western family, though sometimes juxtaposed with war-torn families abroad—was an institution whose stability and happiness was considered critical to winning the war. This idea was first analyzed by historian Elaine Tyler May in *Homeward Bound: American Families in the Cold War Era*, an examination of the Cold War influences on American family life and constructions of gender and sexuality in the 1950s. May calls the Cold War an era of "domestic containment," which bound Americans to the home, where "within its walls, potentially dangerous social forces of the new age might be tamed, where they could contribute to the secure and fulfilling life to which post-war women and men aspired."[29] Canadian historians of the postwar family have built on May's idea of domestic containment and applied it to Canada, where the fear of communism and nuclear war positioned families—especially the clean-cut, middle-class nuclear families living in their suburban homes—as the guardians of morals and normality, and as a symbol of Canada's success as a democratic and capitalist nation. Despite a return to stability after the Depression and the Second World War, postwar parents acknowledged the Cold War as, in Doug Owram's words, "a brooding presence that reminded people that their current situation was tenuous [and] children must be preserved from chaos and given security."[30] Veronica Strong-Boag's study of postwar suburbia shows how women were seen as vital to ensuring the survival of strong families. After the mobilization of married women and mothers in the workforce during the Second World War, the state encouraged women to return to the home, to retie the apron strings and nurture their family's fragile security in the face of new global tension.[31]

Of course, not all women were happy to be—or had the opportunity to be—known only as a model homemaker in the postwar period, nor did they wait until the consciousness-raising of the 1970s to protest their containment.[32] The early postwar years show a dramatic increase in working women. Between 1941 and 1961, the rate of married women's participation in the labour force rose from 4.5 percent to 22 percent, while the total number of working women rose over 9 percent. Strong-Boag argues that Canadian women's rising employment was caused by the increase in white-collar and professional-sector jobs, more lenient attitudes toward female labour, and a demand for mass consumption after the barren Depression and war years.[33] In the postwar era, educated women continued to work in caring professions long deemed to be the jurisdiction and calling of women: teaching, social work, and nursing. Due to a high demand for their skills during imagined and real Cold War crises, these workers used fears about global insecurities to increase their expert status in matters related to health and welfare. This opened up opportunities for leadership positions in Canada and overseas. At the same time, women's volunteerism prevailed during Cold War. As in the World Wars, this pitted amateur caregivers against professional workers, causing debates about whether it was women's gendered natures or professional training that defined their expertise. Women's contributions to the postwar labour movement and civil rights in the postwar period also saw working women and minority women fighting for better living conditions, often in the name of their children. Women's Cold War–related activism followed a similar path, involving working women and homemakers who demanded freedom from war as the means to ensure better living conditions for themselves, for other women, and for children around the world.

It is notable that women's focus on children's health and safety during the Cold War corresponded with the baby boom, the creation of Canada's welfare state, and the new international dialogue surrounding child rights. In the postwar period, child welfare captured the imaginations of not only parents but physicians, social workers, economists, psychologists, psychiatrists, politicians, teachers, and women's organizations. This attention was partly due to the fact that children had a larger public presence. In 1947 the birth rate rose from the 1945 rate of 24.3 per thousand to 28.9, and the rate continued to grow, peaking in 1959 and not dropping back to the 24 range until 1963.[34] Family sizes increased as couples wed younger, and improved nutrition and prenatal care lowered rates of maternal and infant mortality. The upsurge in births was attributed to the celebratory zeal following the end of World War II, when economic prosperity and peace encouraged marriages and children the same way years of Depression and war had discouraged them. Coinciding with the baby boom was the postwar emergence of an expanded welfare state offering for the first time universal benefits to all Canadians. The new family allowance program developed in 1945 was the first such program, giving a monthly benefit to all Canadian children regardless of their family's income. This program was seen as a good investment in building stable families and eliminating family poverty, and as a pre-emptive measure to combat problems such as juvenile delinquency.[35] Armed with tools such as *Dr. Spock's Guide to Baby and Child Care* and an expanded welfare system, parents were told it was scientifically and socially possible to nurture Canadian children through infancy, childhood, and adolescence and protect them from any danger, be it an overzealous mother, familial unemployment, or nuclear war.[36]

The term *child welfare* is used frequently throughout this study when discussing the solutions proposed and performed by activist women to buffer children's health and safety against Cold War threats. Undeniably the story I am telling is only a fragment of Canada's child welfare history in this era, and Cold War concerns always remained on the periphery of risks to Canadian children.[37] As depicted in Strong-Boag's two volumes on the history of child welfare in Canada, the "limits of caregiving" occur in "a society dominated by capitalist, colonial and patriarchal power" where social structures, group histories, and personal shortcomings converge and conspire to turn families and children in "society's casualties."[38] To be more specific, on a daily basis thousands of children in postwar Canada were displaced by disadvantages caused by prejudice and oppression and ordinary, everyday crises: unemployment, poverty, death, illness, abuse, and desertion. The majority of child welfare workers worked locally, attempting to heal these wounds and improve the health and safety of Canada's poorest offspring. Yet there were similarities between mainstream child welfare concerns and the atomic age ones featured in this study. In both cases the caring and concern for children disproportionately rested in the hands of women, as mothers, kin, social workers, foster mothers, charitable workers, and other caregivers. We also can see how perceptions of needs and dangers, not to mention understandings surrounding the best interests of the child, were shaped by constructions of race and class, whether the setting was a residential school in Western Canada, an orphanage in war-torn Saigon, or a middle-class home in a Toronto suburb. Furthermore the welfare solutions proposed for saving at-risk or underprivileged children in peacetime and wartime were remarkably similar: providing safe shelter, keeping families together whenever possible, and when that failed, providing substitute parents through fostering and adoption. Just as they did in traditional child welfare settings, some children affected by Cold War interventions flourished, others resisted, and more were betrayed by solutions that did not address the systemic issues that placed children at a disadvantage in the first place.

While the Cold War crusades presented in this study are linked to mainstream child welfare affairs in Canada, they are also connected to a greater postwar awareness about child welfare issues on a global scale. Dominique Marshall has shown that since World War I "the fate of children in times of war has provoked spontaneous movements of sympathy for their rights, across borders and across enemy lines."[39] This sentiment coalesced into serious discussions about the importance of child rights that began in the interwar period. In 1924 the League of Nations produced a Declaration of the Rights of the Child, which began by stating, "mankind owes to the child the best that it has to give" and justified this by explaining "the child, because of his physical and mental immaturity, needs special safeguards and care."[40] By the Second World War it was clear just how severely modern warfare threatened child rights. In the war's aftermath, social workers providing emergency relief estimated that over 13 million children located in Europe, Asia, and the Middle East had been classified as orphaned, separated from, or abandoned by their parents. Additionally, thousands of children suffered from malnutrition and disease, others had been crippled and maimed, and more had been traumatized by living through invasions, bombings, and genocide.[41] Due to media reports, soldiers' stories, and the arrival of refugees, the suffering of these children became well known to Canadians in the postwar period. Dozens of national charities and UN programs were founded to assist war-affected children, and the UN created a more expansive Declaration on the Rights of the Child in 1959. The global dialogue about and promised commitment to child rights gave funds, attention, and new legitimacy to child welfare issues in the postwar period. At the same time, increased Cold War militarism and insecurity further threatened children's health and welfare.

As much as it can, this study attempts to tell the story of real children who became the centre of the activism; however, much more present in my evidence is the symbolic child, a cultural construct whose image and body became imbued with national and international importance. Over time, children's well-being has been commonly used as a measure by which pundits gauged a nation's sense of justice or level of civilization.[42] "Children carry enormous cultural weight on their shoulders," Karen Dubinsky explains in *Babies without Borders: Adoption and Migration across the Americas*.[43] Dubinsky argues that the symbolic child is not a recent invention but grew to prominence in the twentieth century when a sense of "globalized 'childhoods'" created "opportunities for national self-determination through the bodies of children."[44] In particular, from the 1950s through to the 1970s, Dubinsky notes, "children were a product of, and indeed advertising for, Cold War fault lines."[45] In my study, mothers share stories of their own children and real children's voices and bodies are indeed present, yet children most often appear as a concept whose welfare or identity as a "citizen," "survivor," "waif," "cripple," or "orphan" becomes a symbol for something larger than the children themselves. As a result, children become emotionally driven symbols of Cold War successes and failures and act as effective snapshots used to characterized entire wars, condemn or praise governments and UN policies, and fuel multiple forms of maternalistic activism.

Methodology and Organization

The research for this study is based on the oral histories and personal papers of Canadian women involved in Cold War activism. I had the pleasure of conducting eighteen interviews with women activists and their families, including sons and daughters who remember being taken to peace marches and those whose international adoptions were inspired by their adoptive mothers' passion to change the world. The study draws significantly from the archived collections of organizations active in Cold War causes, including the Women's International League for Peace and Freedom, Voice of Women/

La Voix des femmes, the Grindstone Peace Cooperative, Canadian branches of the United Nations Association, Canada's United Nations International Children's Emergency Fund (UNICEF) Committee, the Unitarian Service Committee, Foster Parents Plan International, International Social Services, Families for Children, and the Kuan Yin Foundation. I also consulted documents and correspondence from the Prime Minister's Office, the federal Departments of Defence, Health and Welfare, External Affairs, and Citizenship and Immigration, the Canadian Council for Social Development, the Adoption Desk, provincial Departments of Welfare, Health, Education, and Community and Children Services, and various municipal Emergency Measures Organizations. Daily newspapers from major Canadian cities were examined, as well as *Maclean's*, *Saturday Night*, *Chatelaine*, and *Weekend Magazine*. The CBC's radio and television coverage of women's activism and key Cold War events were another useful resource. These sources were collected and analyzed to discover in what ways Canadian women responded to the Cold War and what their actions represented. This evidence offers the private and public faces and experiences of the activists, the reactions of government officials and the media to their activism, and in some cases, even the voices of the affected children. Please note that, at their request, some oral history participants' names have been changed to protect their identities. Pseudonyms have been given to adults and children named in unpublished private correspondence, including letters to government officials and social workers and letters between foster parents and foster children.

These sources reveal that no one type of woman participated in the movements under study, but that is not to say the activists were representative of all women. The overwhelming majority of leaders were educated, white, and middle-class. The most active women either were full-time homemakers or worked in a "caring" profession, such as teaching, nursing, or social work. They came from a variety of religious backgrounds (Protestant, Quaker, Catholic, Jewish), and many of the women had immigrated to Canada from Britain and Europe before or after the Second World War. The majority lived in Canada's two largest cities, Toronto and Montreal, and their suburbs, and a number came from the Ottawa region, making it a quick journey to mobilize on Parliament Hill. A smaller number of leaders hailed from Western and Atlantic Canada, particularly Vancouver and Halifax. There was strong representation in Quebec from francophone women in the disarmament and peace movement and, to a lesser extent, within the sphere of international adoption. Only a handful of the activists (Cora Taylor Casselman, Margaret Konantz, Muriel Fergusson, Solange Chaput-Rolland, and Thérèse

Casgrain) were elected or appointed to public office; instead most of the women engaged in political action through their membership in long-established or new women's organizations. The women's individual politics ran the gamut from left to right; however, most claimed to be apolitical, despite the overt political nature of their activities. They did so either because they truly believed their work had no political connotations or because labelling it non-political allowed them to operate with fewer limitations and avoid alienating the public. Because of the prejudice against communists, only a few of the women publicly acknowledged any alliance to the Communist Party during this period of their activism, though several had been members in the 1930s and 1940s. Less is known about the women behind the scenes: the low-profile members, volunteers, and donors. Existing records suggest that these women represented a wider cross-section of the country geographically, with representation from small-town, rural, and northern communities, as well as women who identified themselves as workers, immigrants, refugees, uneducated, unemployed, or poor. In all categories of participation, from letter writers to newsletter subscribers, the participants' ages varied considerably. High-school and university students worked alongside mothers with children of all ages, unmarried and married working women, grandmothers, and retirees.

It should be noted that not all Canadian women were drawn to participate in Cold War activism. My own mother, Margaret Stewart, who lived through bombings in World War II as a child in Northern Ireland, immigrated to Montreal as a young wife in 1956. When I discussed my research with her, she admitted that she had no idea Canada had any part in the Cold War. What she remembers from this era were practical and personal concerns: her marriage and divorce, looking for work, and raising my sister, Karen, as a single mother. These anxieties were more relevant to her life than nuclear missiles, the threat of communism, or the war in Vietnam. Although they are not featured in this study, undoubtedly there were many more Canadian women like my mother than there were activist women consumed with Cold War affairs.

Cold War Comforts is divided into seven chapters, each detailing a specific response women had to a Cold War threat related to children's health and safety between 1945 and 1975. The first three chapters focus on various forms of women's activism directed at the fear of nuclear war in Canada. Chapter 1 examines how Canada contextualized the beginning of the Cold War. With the Second World War drawing to an explosive end in 1945, followed by renewed East–West tensions, the Canadian government was forced to consider the nation's vulnerability to atomic age warfare. Nuclear weaponry turned the home front into a front line, and therefore civilians were actively engaged by the state in the 1940s and 1950s to contribute to their communities' defence. Protecting children was viewed by the state as paramount to Canada's survival as a nation, therefore the government collaborated with mothers, women's organizations, and those employed in the health, welfare, and education fields to ensure children's safety at home and school. In chapter 2, civil defence in the late 1950s becomes less of a community-based effort and more of a domestic responsibility. In particular, this chapter focuses on the emergency measures designed for the family home, most notably the backyard or basement fallout shelter that was widely promoted by the Diefenbaker government. While organizations such as the National Council of Women came out in support of the shelter program, there was strong skepticism from women across the country who noted the shelter program's impracticality for childcare and accessibility issues for low-income families. The lack of consensus and criticism from homemakers contributed to the shelter program's ultimate failure to engage Canadian families.

The third chapter analyzes the maternalistic rhetoric and activism of women involved in the international disarmament movement. During the 1940s and 1950s, Canada's peace movement was hampered by the Red Scare, which equated support for peace with support for communism. It was not until the early 1960s, amid the rising threat of nuclear war, that the mainstream Canadian peace movement gained momentum. Part of the new surge in popularity was attributed to the sympathetic and respectable image created by the newly formed Voice of Women, a group of "ordinary" women who viewed Cold War politics as a direct attack on the family. They contextualized their peace campaigns and occasional radical behaviour (violent protests, hunger strikes, and visits with women from "enemy" nations) as the work of concerned mothers.

The last four chapters move the activist scene to the international arena. Chapter 4 analyzes women's roles and experiences working and volunteering with three UN programs with strong commitments to child welfare: the United Nations Relief and Rehabilitation Administration, Canada's United Nations Association, and UNICEF. This chapter considers how the feeding, clothing, healing, and comfort of foreign children was considered a safe populist expression of internationalism and a critical part of Canada's defence plans. This activism, predominantly led by club women and teachers, globalized the *children are our future* message found in civil defence and the peace movement. Chapter 5 explores another popular foreign-relief program, the care of orphaned, ill, or impoverished children living in three sites of Cold War conflict—Greece, South Korea, and Hong Kong—who were sponsored by Canadian individuals, families, schools, church groups, and clubs. As with UN aid programs, foster parent plan programs were positioned as a way to build stability in developing nations. Unlike the universalism found in UN projects, only a specific type of foreign child was considered worthy of Canadian fostering—those who lived in regions that had renounced or escaped communism.

The final two chapters are set primarily in Vietnam, which became the focal point for Canadian women's global child welfare projects in the mid-1960s. Chapter 6 shows women's growing awareness about the toll of the war on Vietnamese civilians and Canada's own complicity in the conflict. These revelations sparked Canadian women's vigorous participation in the anti-war movement and new relief campaigns that offered foreign relief for the first time to children living in a communist regime. Chapter 7 analyzes an alternative and controversial response to the high numbers of war-affected children living in Vietnam and neighbouring Cambodia: international adoption. Between 1965 and 1975 over 700 orphaned and displaced children were adopted by Canadian families. Unlike civil defence or disarmament activists, international adoption advocates considered Canada a haven where children could be raised safely. They also believed foster parent sponsorships and UN aid did not do enough to protect children from immediate danger. Nevertheless, international adoption received considerable criticism from social workers and peace activists, who championed the necessity of local welfare solutions. Regardless, the transfer of children across borders in order to find a new mother and father reinforced the idea that families, even in non-traditional forms, were a dominant feature of Canada's Cold War security plans.

By 1975, the end of the war in Vietnam and a strong commitment to détente shifted the course of the Cold War. Meanwhile, three decades of activism had changed the lives of children in Canada and overseas. At home they were taught to duck and cover, fear communists, hate the bomb, and trick-or-treat for UNICEF, and they grew up to be one of the most politicized generations of youth. Meanwhile, children living in sites of Cold War conflict found temporary and permanent security, love, and disappointment in their new Canadian donors and families. The experiences gained in this wave of Cold War activism opened doors for Canadian women to remain active political players in other causes during the 1980s and 1990s. The Cold War did not empower women in a way that radically altered power structures in the home, workplace, or state; however, just as six years on the front lines of industry and in the military between 1939 and 1945 did make some difference in reframing understandings of Canadian womanhood, three decades of continuous activism influenced the direction of the Cold War at home and abroad and helped legitimize women's presence as political actors.

PART I

At Home

CHAPTER ONE

Cold War Canada
Mobilizing Women for a New War

In a publicity campaign run by the Department of National Health and Welfare in the 1950s, a woman became the spokesperson to warn Canadians of the possibility of a nuclear war and to advise them on preparing for it. "Bea Alerte," a smiling brunette respectably dressed in a suit, hat, and gloves, appeared in a series of illustrated civil defence posters advising Canadians to be prepared because disaster could strike at any time. Featured both alone and alongside her male partner, "Justin Case," calm Bea is depicted as poised and ready to offer advice and a helping hand in a nuclear emergency. Pictured amid chaotic landscapes featuring destroyed homes, Bea, with her air of confidence and strength, is juxtaposed against less-prepared women, including a frightened young girl being chased by a leering cartoon bomb and another dishevelled woman collapsed in a pile of rubble. This series of posters prophesied a doomed destiny for any Canadian woman who chose not to act like Bea, presumably a model citizen in her community, possibly a neighbourhood civil defence warden, most likely trained in first aid. At the very least, she was being alert, just in case.[1]

Making a female character the face of Canada's civil defence program reflects the enormous appeal civil defence had for many women in the early stages of the Cold War, as well as the government's need to tap into women's support and skills. In fact, in the 1940s and 1950s, an army of Bea Alerte look-alikes could be found "invading" the Emergency Measures Organization (EMO), described as "long a stronghold of armed forces and civic

Bea Alerte "Will It Happen Here?" Department of National Health and Welfare, 1950–59. Artifact number 20040030-003 © Canadian War Museum

Bea Alerte "Disaster May Never Occur Here" Department of Health and Welfare, 1950–59. Artifact number 20040030-002 © Canadian War Museum

administration personnel. From church and service organizations, clubs and associations, business and industry, they have trooped to the Davenport Road headquarters to receive special survival tactics or class instruction."[2] In the late 1940s thousands of Canadian women responded to the state's appeal for their labour and dedicated themselves to protecting their nation from the threat of nuclear annihilation. Women continued to have a significant presence in emergency planning throughout the 1950s, the decade that saw the greatest government investment of all time in civil defence, caused by the growing stockpile of atomic weapons and tense relations between the United States and the Soviet Union. By the early 1960s most women had phased out their support for civil defence as a viable solution to Cold War threats, and some women turned to other channels, most notably the peace and disarmament movement. Still, in the program's prime, women were overrepresented in civil defence planning and training.

Civil defence was an attractive form of civic engagement for many women because the specific demands of a nuclear war scenario had much in common with women's work in the World Wars. Just as their mothers and grandmothers mobilized in the First and Second World Wars, postwar women were recruited primarily for tasks related to assumptions about and proven experience with their nurturing personas and domestic skills. Although one civil defence advisor to NATO noted, "It can be said once without fear of contradiction, except perhaps by hardboiled and diehard males, that there is no work in Civil Defence for which women could not be trained,"[3] most women were recruited or volunteered for gendered civil defence work. In a pamphlet called *Where Can You Find Them?* civil defence planners were told to look for volunteers in specific gender-segregated occupations. The armed forces, militia, and police were recruited to assist with the planning of large-scale evacuations. Architects and engineers were hired to design fallout shelters and survey existing buildings for public shelter use. Physicians, dentists, veterinarians, and psychiatrists were asked to comment on the nation's medical needs. Even insurance agents, realtors, office managers, and salesmen were targeted for their initiative, good management, leadership skills, and knowledge of the community, proficiencies required for reorganizing a post-attack city.[4] In the postwar era, these professions were dominated by men, so it can be assumed that in most cases male workers filled those civil defence positions. Meanwhile, women working as librarians, telephone operators, secretaries, and clerks were recruited to work in the EMO's administrative positions. The largest group of women connected to civil defence were those whose knowledge, paid or voluntary labour, and authority in matters of health, welfare, and education placed them in high demand. This included the voluntary members of national women's organizations, considered to be pillars of white middle-class respectability, who had experience doing similar war work in the First and Second World Wars, including the National Council of Women of Canada (NCWC), the Imperial Order Daughters of the Empire (IODE), and the Federated Women's Institutes of Canada (FWIC). Additionally, professional women, particularly nurses, social workers, and teachers, were asked to imagine how their fields could contribute to rehabilitating post-nuclear-war Canada and prepare themselves to perform their regular duties under catastrophic conditions. In most cases, women in these professions were primarily employed in the public sector, thus making their indoctrination into civil defence not only a professional obligation, but a requirement of their employment. These different groups of volunteer and professional women came to staff the EMO's Health and Welfare services and other wings of civil defence dedicated to training, organizing, feeding, sheltering, clothing, and caring for the victims of a nuclear war.

Rather than knitting socks, packing care packages, or treating gunshot wounds, a new war meant facing new dangers and using new tools. Women's Cold War caregiving expanded to include the ABCs of nuclear warfare caused by atomic, biological, and chemical weaponry. Armed with Geiger counters and firehoses, women were trained to counter the blast, fire, and radiation arising from a nuclear attack on a target city, assist any survivors, and maintain order in postwar communities. Since it was understood that conventional means of defence such as soldiering were inadequate to prevent a nuclear attack, civic preparedness and trained rescue workers were considered the most important line of defence. Therefore, women's health and welfare assignments were not ancillary efforts and took place on the front lines. As the *Civil Defence Bulletin* noted in 1951, "The role of women in the Civil Defence organization is of first-rank importance."[5] Moreover, since nuclear warfare had made the home front a battlefield, it was civilians, not soldiers, who would be the targets of an attack. Civil defence was even referred to as the fourth branch of the armed forces. As Laura McEnaney argues, atomic warfare meant that "citizens had to think of themselves as an integral part of military mobilization even more than they had during World War II, for they were now vulnerable as never before."[6] This meant that civil defence workers were expected to save themselves, along with their neighbours, their families, and those most vulnerable, children.

Protecting children was critical to Canada's civil defence plans as it was understood that infants', children's, and teenagers' bodies were more susceptible to the effects of radioactive fallout than those of adults.[7] Furthermore it was understood that young people would require special guidance and supervision, especially if they were separated from their parents, to survive in a chaotic post-attack context. Since Canada's youngest citizens were viewed as the future generation, they were therefore needed in order to rebuild, defend, and repopulate Canada after a nuclear attack. As the anxious narrator in the EMO film *Flowers or Ashes* warned, "Cities can be rebuilt, but we cannot rebuild a fighting population with the will to stand and overcome any force."[8] Since child welfare was an identified priority of civil defence, it was not surprising that the government collaborated with groups of women associated with caregiving and child care on a professional or personal basis to ensure young bodies and minds would have the best chances of survival. As part of their work, female civil defence planners were recruited to anticipate children's basic and emotional needs in a nuclear war disaster and prepare appropriate caregiving that would minimize loss of life, anxiety, and chaos. In cases where children were separated from their parents temporarily or permanently in an attack, female civil defence workers would also be required to act as mother substitutes by providing emotional comfort to displaced children. These responsibilities built on understandings of women's conventional maternal role. While this may have reinforced stereotypes about women's capabilities, the life and death circumstances of civil defence could also be seen as empowering. Women's role in civil defence positioned them on the front lines and made them authorities on critical matters.

Community-based civil defence was one method Canadian women used to establish protection from Cold War insecurity while concurrently demonstrating their right as citizens to actively contribute to matters of foreign policy and national defence. This mobilization presents a different lens through which to view the immediate postwar period, usually presented as the era when women replaced their patriotic war work with housework. If there was a homogeneous reconstruction of what Ruth Roach Pierson referred to as "full-skirted and redomesticated" womanhood after World War II, it did not mean that "for more than a decade feminism was once again sacrificed to femininity."[9] Women involved in civil defence used the opportunity to expand their influence and authority in new and familiar forms of paid and unpaid work. Rather than question the war itself, as the women studied in forthcoming chapters would do, these women fell in line behind the government's Cold War plans because they deemed it patriotic, practical, and a familiar role to play in wartime. Nevertheless, they did not simply accept civil defence as it was presented to them and actively worked to develop and adapt the program. Through civil defence contributions, masses of real-life Bea Alertes played an important part in the government's plan for keeping their nation, community, and families strong in the face of disaster.

Origins and Organization of Cold War Civil Defence

In his history of Canada's EMO, David McConnell traces the origins of Cold War civil defence to the interwar period, when rising tensions in Europe and Asia caused Prime Minister King's government to establish several new defence projects, including the Air Raid Precautions Organization (ARPO), designed to protect the public from the new danger of attack from the sky. Drawing on Britain's non-military civilian protection program, ARPO recommended the need for warning systems, shelters, first aid stations, and evacuation plans for non-essential workers.[10] The government was slow to act on ARPO's proposals until Canada declared war on Germany in the fall of 1939. Immediately King's cabinet granted $150,000 to ARPO, and the provincial and municipal governments called up volunteers, usually men too young or too old to serve in the armed forces, to work as auxiliary firefighters, utility workers, first aid workers, police, and neighbourhood wardens. According to Anne Fisher, civilian support of ARPO was unstable. It waned during the "phoney" war, rose after France's surrender, and peaked at the end of 1941 when the security of North America was breached by the Japanese attack on Pearl Harbor and the sighting of Axis submarines on Canada's east and west coasts.[11] At its height in 1941, ARPO groups existed in approximately 150 communities and almost 95,000 volunteers were registered.[12] Despite the bursts of public enthusiasm, the government withdrew funding for the program in 1943, citing the need to reallocate resources to the military. With industry devoted to producing for Canada's armed forces, there were few opportunities to manufacture the necessary ARPO equipment needed to run local programs. Yet even the tools that were distributed, such as gas masks, were rarely purchased by overconfident (and possibly frugal) Canadians hoping the war would remain overseas.[13] The combination of an ambiguous threat, inconsistent funding, and tentative public support for emergency planning would reoccur during the Cold War period.

The distant threat of bombings and an abundance of other opportunities for paid war work meant that Canadian women were not tremendously engaged in ARPO, especially in comparison to their counterparts living in war zones.[14] Civilians had increasingly become targets in twentieth-century warfare. It is estimated that non-military personnel accounted for 5 percent of World War I's total casualties but as much as half of the total in World War II.[15] In Europe and Asia, women and children lived through the Second World War with the daily threat of air attacks. "Housewife" was the single largest category of air-raid injuries and deaths in Britain, Germany, Italy, China, and Japan, followed by children and the elderly, especially those in working-class neighbourhoods.[16] In these nations, middle-class women volunteered or were conscripted for programs comparable to Canada's ARPO where they worked as ditchdiggers, ambulance drivers, and air-raid wardens. It was not until the threat of an attack by air on a much different scale during the Cold War that civil defence became identified as a concern and a responsibility for Canadian women. The experience of living through the Second World War meant that some of Canada's most ardent supporters of Cold War civil defence were new to the country, having immigrated to Canada from Europe or Britain after 1945, carrying with them memories of the war's devastation and experience with enlisted or voluntary service.

Although 1949 is the year commonly used to designate the start of the Cold War, a power struggle emerged between Western nations and the growing communist bloc for economic and political supremacy even before the Second World War was over. This was followed by a period when each side strove to collect allies, strengthen their economies, and develop the deadliest weapons.[17] In 1949 the Chinese civil war concluded with a Communist Party victory, and in the same year a crisis over Germany's postwar future saw the nation split into East and West factions, closely monitored by their Soviet and American allies. Then on 29 August 1949, the Soviet Union successfully tested their atomic bomb and the United States lost its monopoly on nuclear weapons. Although Canada did not develop its own nuclear weapons, the nation's membership in NATO and later NORAD linked Canada to a nuclear network of heavily armed allies with similar anti-communist ideologies. The 1945 Igor Gouzenko spy affair proved that the Soviets saw Canada as having a strategic intelligence position. Furthermore, geographically, Canada was sandwiched in between the Soviet Union and the United States, with much of the population living near the American border. It was believed that politics and geography made Canada a primary, secondary, or diversionary target of a nuclear attack by the Soviets; at the very least, Canada would suffer from the radioactive fallout arising from an attack on the United States. These factors, combined with increased instability in Eastern Europe, Central America, and Korea in the early 1950s, forced the Canadian government to investigate how they could survive a nuclear war.

Although experts never agreed on the scope of damage from a war in which multiple nuclear weapons were used, scientists and military strategists speculated that in the next world war, civilians would make up over 95 percent of the total losses.[18] Traditional armies and battlegrounds would be obsolete, as unmanned bombs could soar across continents targeting the enemy's weapons caches, launching sites, seats of government, and centres of agricultural and industrial production, locations often surrounded by residential neighbourhoods and farmland. Predictions about the levels of damage grew greater when the Americans and Russians each successfully detonated a new version of the atomic bomb, the hydrogen bomb, in 1952 and 1953. In 1956 an American test of this weapon conducted in the Pacific Ocean produced an explosion 750 times more powerful than the one used at Hiroshima, which had unexpectedly far-ranging and long-term effects on the environment and inhabitants of the region. Coinciding with the development of the hydrogen bomb was the creation of a new delivery system known as Intercontinental Ballistic Missiles (ICBM), which greatly extended the range of these weapons. These developments caused many of those in power, including Prime Minister Churchill, President Truman, and Premier Khrushchev, to conclude that the simultaneous use of these weapons would mean the end of civilization. This consequence became known as Mutually Assured Destruction (MAD), the acknowledgement that devastating retaliation would prevent either side from ever resorting to using their stockpile of bombs. As historian John Gaddis explains, the superpowers on both sides concluded that a limited war was impossible, and because "a war fought with nuclear weapons could destroy what it was intended to defend, such a war must never be fought."[19] Although it was an intellectual determent, MAD was no guarantee. In 1958 *Saturday Night* reporter Harvey Adams gauged Canada's survival prospects in a world where MAD was abandoned and thought the nation might do better than Britain because "our cities are widely scattered. We have lots of wide open spaces. More of our people live in rural areas."[20] Despite this, Adams concluded that a single hydrogen bomb "dropped without warning" on more than one major Canadian city would "wipe out a large proportion of our people and cripple us as a nation."[21] Predictions like Adams's were the main incentive for civil defence, both as an actual means of survival and as a method of reducing panic.

The Soviet Union's possession of an atomic weapon triggered Canada's Department of National Defence to classify Montreal, Toronto, Ottawa-Hull, Windsor, Niagara Falls, Halifax, Vancouver, Hamilton, Winnipeg, Edmonton, Quebec City, Saint John, and Victoria as potential targets of an enemy aerial strike in the fall of 1949.[22] These thirteen cities were selected for their population density and industrial importance. Their municipal governments were instructed to work with the federal and provincial authorities and local citizens to develop emergency measures. Even if they were not at the epicentre of a detonation, municipalities adjacent to target cities were advised to set up a civil defence organization because they would experience the heat, fire, and radiation coming from the blast. More remote communities were designated as reception areas for evacuees coming from target cities. These plans were cemented in the 1951 Civil Defence Act, which outlined the division of financial and educational responsibilities to be shared by the three levels of government.[23] By 1952, all 13 potential target areas and 543 other municipalities possessed some form of civil defence organization, while 128 communities had fully developed programs that included a director, various services, and training facilities for civil servants, emergency personnel, and civilian volunteers.[24] It was hoped that this level of preparedness would not only serve as a direct survival tool, but would also act as a deterrent to an attack, presuming that an enemy would not waste its resources attacking a prepared nation.

Civil defence was structured around civilian volunteers for three reasons: viability, expertise, and cost. No matter how organized the government was to meet a nuclear war, EMO officials acknowledged that the chaos following a nuclear attack would result in a disruption of regular government services. Therefore, civilians needed to develop self-confidence and self-reliance to know what to do in an emergency because government action could be restricted by fallout, debris, or damage to communications.[25] When looking to start a municipal program, civil defence planners depended on local clubs, businesses, and professionals to help build support, recruit volunteers, donate supplies and space, promote its program among their membership and neighbourhoods, and use their expertise to staff programs. This spirit of volunteerism also cut the necessity of hiring staff and arranging expensive publicity campaigns. Throughout the 1950s and 1960s, Canada's civil defence budget fluctuated, ranging from modest to low, so it is not surprising that the government expected Canadians to share the cost of their survival. After 1953 there was a funding shortage, and most provincial and municipal EMO's depended more and more on volunteer participation.[26]

Mobilizing Women's Clubs and Nurses for Disaster Management

Even before the Soviets had their own atomic bomb, Brooke Claxton, Minister of National Defence, encouraged municipalities to engage leading citizens in a discussion about national defence.[27] In Toronto, Mayor McCallum invited 117 leading citizens, including members from five Toronto women's groups: the Local Council of Women (a branch of the NCWC), IODE, the Zonta Club, the Young Business Women's Canadian Club, and the Soroptimist Club to discuss Canada's national defence. Isobel Heideman, President of the Young Business Women's Club responded enthusiastically to the invitation, explaining that "it is one of the aims of our organization to support and promote all things furthering Canadian welfare and progress, [and] we are in full accord with the suggestions as outlined in your letter."[28] (Interestingly, in Heideman's case, being that her club was for working women, she sent regrets explaining that since the meeting would be held during business hours, she could not personally attend.)[29] For several reasons, women's clubs were considered ideal starting points to mobilize large numbers of volunteers to get civil defence up and running. Many women's organizations had previously mobilized in the name of national security and national pride during the First and Second World Wars and were seen as valuable sources of labour, skills, knowledge, and morale. At the same time, these organizations tended to draw from the ranks of educated middle-class and elite women whose activism, while not uncritical of the government, was normally conservative in nature. Consequently, these organizations were considered safe forums in which to recruit volunteers in a process that was becoming more and more guarded due to anti-communist sentiment.[30] Members of these associations were assumed to be respectable and patriotic citizens, unlikely to rock the Cold War consensus emerging in the late 1940s that centred on the idea of keeping Canada pure and strong against its communist enemies.

Those who attended the Mayor's first meeting discussed how to protect Toronto and the region of York in case of an atomic attack and were asked to recommend other potential volunteers.[31] In the second meeting, the committee divided into subcommittees, including one women's committee that was made up of representatives from the above-mentioned organizations as well as women from the Women's Press Club, the Local Council of Jewish Women, the United Empire Loyalists, the Home and School Association, the Girl Guides, and three women's auxiliaries attached to local militia regiments. One seat on the executive committee was reserved for a woman; it would be held by Mrs. A. K. Richardson (1948–1950) and Mrs. D. W. McGibbon

(1950–1955), both members of the IODE.[32] The executive committee oversaw all civil defence planning until the National Defence committee was dissolved and a more formal body, the Metropolitan Toronto Civil Defence Organization, was created in 1955. This committee liaised with federal and provincial planners, prepared budgets, and organized drills. Even after the committee folded, the new organization encouraged the continued involvement of women's organizations, citing them as an interested and inexpensive faction of civil defence planning.[33]

Toronto's recruitment strategy was replicated across the country, where women's organizations took a leading role in civil defence planning and education. In Montreal, when the city council withdrew support for civil defence in 1954, members of the predominantly anglophone Local Council of Women independently continued their own civil defence education, with the help of three francophone groups, Ligue catholique féminine, Ligue de la jeunesse féminine, and Club Wilfrid Laurier des femmes libérales.[34] The federal government recruited women from Winnipeg's Red Cross organization to represent Manitoba on the Canadian Welfare Council's Civil Defence Advisory Committee because of their experience in dealing with emergency preparedness during the 1951 Red River flood.[35] Meanwhile, in Red Deer, Hazel Braithwaite—wife, mother of six, and President of the United Farm Women of Alberta—became the first female director of a local EMO.[36] Members of women's organizations enthusiastically participated in these programs because they fit within the framework of their organizations' existing patriotic, educational, and charitable focus, and women's participation reconfirmed their position as valuable community leaders. In addition to being routes for social networking, charity, and friendship, women's organizations offered access to influence in the community, school, church, and government. In the postwar era, few women held political office or had the opportunity for leadership on school boards or in trade unions. According to Judith Fingard, it was through women's participation in local and national clubs that they became "more of a political constant than an occasional influence."[37] While these clubs often focused on issues related to improving the lives of women and children, they also expressed their opinions and lobbied for reforms on matters related to Canada's culture, economy, and politics. Therefore civil defence fit well within their mandates, and it became a cause that was regularly debated.

A centrepiece of the EMO was its Health and Welfare Services, a branch dedicated to rebuilding Canadian society after a nuclear attack. According to Paul Martin, Minister of Health and Welfare and head of the Civil Defence Planning Group, caring for the sheer volume people injured in a nuclear attack would be civil defence's biggest challenge. Martin predicted a need for a massive nursing auxiliary. In a nuclear-driven emergency, he estimated that a 200-bed hospital would require approximately 68 volunteer nurses trained in first aid and 51 volunteer nurses' aides trained in advanced first aid, working in eight-hour shifts to assist the regularly employed nursing staff.[38] The other major problem would be dealing with the waves of uninjured people who had been displaced by the attack. Civil Defence's Welfare Services would be staffed by nurses, social workers, dieticians, and trained volunteers who would take care of five areas: clothing, lodging, feeding, registration and inquiry (administration and communications within a refugee centre), and personal services (reuniting families, caring for dependents).

Members of women's organizations registered in droves to take courses in disaster management. These classes were taught by nurses, social workers, and other health and welfare workers employed by the state or non-governmental associations. First aid was the most popular type of training, most likely because it could be useful in countless situations independent of a nuclear war.[39] The courses focused on teaching what to do for basic injuries without the aid of professional medical personnel. First aid trainees learned how to treat shock, trauma, burns, and fractures, and were also advised to keep up their patients' morale by acting cheerful and passing out cigarettes and coffee.[40] In addition to basic first aid, women could take specialized courses in home nursing, which required 44 hours of supervised volunteer work in a hospital. Trainees would practise procedures from bed making to bedpan assistance, and learn more advanced procedures like enemas, blood transfusion, and gastric suction.[41] Simulation was a popular way to practise first aid, and civil defence newsletters were full of articles giving examples of women dedicated to training and improving their skills. In one story, Ruth Oxley, an IODE member from Toronto, pretended to be a casualty and was swathed and sewn into a stretcher. She admitted to feeling quite insecure in the device and declined to be lowered from the window in a rescue simulation. The Welfare Services *Bulletin* reported with glee that

> Mrs. Oxley didn't just grouch about our stretcher, she went home [and] designed quite a clever one made out of aluminum, collapsible and with a simple locking system that would eliminate the bales of rope we now use. Chief Rescue Instructor, Eric Scalan, likes her ideas and we plan to send the sketches to Ottawa for perusal soon. Who knows? Some day we may be training on Oxley Stretchers![42]

Promotional material that praised women's contributions served to boost the morale of any volunteer eager to feel useful.

First aid and home nursing courses trained lay women to be professional caregivers, capable of making casualties comfortable physically and mentally at the scene of a disaster or in a hospital. A pamphlet called *What the Home Nursing Auxiliary Should Know about Civil Defence* included an illustration of a homemaker joining a line of uniformed medical personal.[43] This advanced training made professional nurses protective over their occupation's image and keenly aware of the sex-typing that came with their work. As there had been since the advent of the profession in the nineteenth century, there was some concern over the blurry line being drawn between amateur and professional nursing staff.[44] While teaching home nursing and first aid programs, professional nurses insisted that volunteer nurses were on the bottom rung of a hospital hierarchy and were only there to free professional nurses to handle more serious cases. They also made a clear distinction about their specialized skills, which came from years, not hours, of specialized training. Concurrently, these reminders challenged the assumption that nursing came naturally to women.

Of all working women, nurses had the biggest civil defence role to play. In the aftermath of an atomic attack, they were expected to staff emergency hospitals, supervise the army of volunteers they had trained, monitor public health, offer counselling to traumatized survivors, and generally demonstrate medical responsibility above their regular duties. As in previous wars, nurses were seen by the state as critical to the successful planning and deployment of emergency measures. Evelyn Pepper, the former Principal Matron of the No. 1 Canadian General Hospital for the Canadian Forces during the Second World War and postwar nursing consultant for the Department of National Health and Welfare Emergency Health Planning Group, met with nursing leaders from each of the province's Registered Nurses Association in 1951. In her communication with nurses, she explained the potential threat facing Canada and facilitated discussion of nurses' role in national preparedness. Pepper emphasized nurses' professional code and patriotic duty by concluding

> that every professional nurse in Canada must know her country's and her community's plan for emergency health services ... [and] the individual nurse should prepare herself to fulfil her expected professional role in

the event of disaster. This is not only a belief—it is an opportunity—an opportunity to help solve a national problem—and Canadian nurses have seized that opportunity.[45]

Interestingly, Pepper also viewed the matter as a type of self-preservation, noting that 50 percent of registered nurses lived or worked in a target city. It appears nurses did indeed seize the opportunity and rose to the professional and moral challenge. By 1957, 13,000 nurses across Canada had received orientation and information on disaster nursing, and 65 nurses had been trained as civil defence instructors.[46]

To accomplish their new responsibilities, nurses expanded their training and updated their skills. Graduate nurses returned to the classroom for specialized courses organized by provincial civil defence colleges or the federally run college in Arnprior, Ontario. Meanwhile student nurses were introduced to disaster nursing in a revised nursing-school curriculum in 1958. Nurses studied projected casualty numbers and learned how to treat shock, trauma, burns, and radiation sickness. They were reminded that modern nursing practice relied on elaborate and extensive health resources, possibly unavailable in an emergency situation. Nurses were taught to improvise life-saving techniques under less than ideal conditions; however, they were warned, "This need not lead to a lowering of the standard of health care but will necessitate much ingenuity, pre-planning and organization of available resources."[47] Furthermore, nurses, who were traditionally subordinated to doctors, would need to assume leadership without being asked, delegate responsibility, and show faith that an assigned representative, most likely a female volunteer, could manage on her own. Presumably it would be impossible to gather a complete medical team together in a crisis, so nurses were expected to assume medical responsibility far beyond their regular training and perform tasks normally done by a physician. In this way, disaster was seen as an opportunity to gain more authority and status, both by performing new tasks and supervising less-skilled volunteers; however, nurses were still expected to display gender-specific behaviour. In one civil defence training manual the ideal nurse was compared to a mother: "The good nurse is the 'mother figure' during illness. She supplies an atmosphere of confidence—one which says 'all will be well' and 'we are in good hands.' She is reassuring."[48] Despite the emphasis on increased medical knowledge, professionalism, and skills, presenting a maternal persona was considered equally valuable by the EMO.

Mother Figures, Child Welfare, and Stable Families

Viewing the nurse as a mother figure was widely connected to an emphasis in nurses' civil defence training on how to care for children affected by a nuclear war, especially those who were separated from their parents, and unborn babies. When evacuation was still seen as a realistic solution, phase one, the suspicion of an attack, called for the removal of the "non-productive populace" from target cities to reception centres; this group included young children, the old, the infirm, the disabled, and pregnant women.[49] This process would remove those who could potentially slow the later general evacuation. In the case of children and pregnant women, evacuation also protected those whose safety would be necessary to rebuild Canada. In a post-attack scenario, infants and nursing mothers were to receive priority health care and food and milk rations; next in line were expectant mothers and children.[50] Esther Robinson, nursing consultant for the Child and Maternal Health Division of the Department of National Health and Welfare, taught a course on nursing responsibilities where she emphasized the importance of caring for pregnant women, mothers, and children. Although nurses would continue to treat sick or injured people according to the seriousness of their condition, they also had to pay close attention to the special needs of women and children because

> mothers, especially expectant mothers, infants and children are a vulnerable group whose welfare and survival is important to the welfare and survival of the whole community and nation ... Fathers need to know some plan exists for the care of mothers and children before they can assist effectively with the re-establishment of the community as a whole.[51]

One civil defence nursing manual had detailed instructions on how to manage the physical and emotional care of these special patients, ranging from learning the number of calories per ration for each age group to specialized training in emergency obstetrical care. Nurses were also advised to act as mother substitutes for uninjured displaced children because their young charges "can endure stress, providing that they have the support of their mothers or a familiar mother substitute."[52] Nurses were just one of many groups who, in lieu of actual mothers, were directed to prioritize family stability and child welfare in the face of Cold War threats.

While the nurses were in charge of dealing with the sick and injured, social workers were designated to cope with the non-medical side of a nuclear attack. As the nation's most prominent welfare workers, they were trained to manage reception centres, reunite families, and counsel the surviving population. Like nurses, they were recruited not only for their organizational expertise, but also for their people skills and insight into family management. Having experience dealing with people during more traditional crises, such as unemployment, displacement due to a fire, or cases of abuse, the EMO depended on social workers' ability to predict how people would act in a nuclear war scenario and design methods to avoid conflict and hysteria. In this way, social workers were asked to take on a role similar to the nurses' mother figure, someone who would see to a family's basic needs and soothe nerves.

As with nurses, social workers required new training to fulfill this role. In 1955 Gladys Dunn left her position with the Welfare Council of Toronto to join the federal government's Civil Defence Headquarters staff as Commissioner of Public Welfare. Dunn's background was already strong in emergency planning; previously she had been the welfare coordinator for the Hurricane Hazel relief fund in Ontario and unit supervisor of the Canadian Red Cross in Japan and Korea, and she had served with the Royal Canadian Navy. One of Dunn's tasks was to coordinate the civil defence training of social workers.[53] Senior social workers in each province were nominated by their supervisors to receive EMO orientation at Arnprior. The federal government paid their tuition and travelling expenses for a three-day course. In a report on her experience at Arnprior in 1956, Margaret Douglas, assistant director of Toronto's welfare services and a board member of the Canadian Association of Social Workers (CASW), reported to her superiors that the course was worthwhile because it made the attendees "stop and think regarding our personal attitude to civil defence and also our responsibility as professional people and as a professional association."[54] Despite this acknowledgement, an enthusiastic calling for civil defence did not appear to have effectively reached the lower ranks, which included those who would not necessarily have been compensated for extra committee work or training time. Patricia Godfrey, Information Director of the Canadian Welfare Council and former member of the London Auxiliary Ambulance Service during the Blitz, believed any lack of commitment to civil defence had less to do with social workers' interest in helping out and more to do with the fact that "the average Social Worker has a heavy load in her everyday job and there may be a psychological barrier in asking them to volunteer to do the same thing."[55] To assist their underpaid and overworked colleagues, the CASW and Schools of Social

Work used their leverage as critical civil defence workers to get the provincial governments to do more to encourage a career in social work.[56]

Social workers were specifically approached to offer advice on the potential social and psychological problems arising out of a nuclear attack that could disrupt Canada's postwar rehabilitation. On the simplest level, this meant being prepared to calm confused, belligerent, or hysterical victims of a nuclear attack. On a more complex level, they were tasked with avoiding a breakdown in society caused by upsetting normal social conventions and disruptions in the current welfare system. Families were seen to be at the heart of social stability. If families could be kept together, then the hysteria caused by war and displacement could be mitigated by parents, rather than mother figures. As well, if families were all together, then there was one less reason to panic. To make reuniting families easier, the NCWC recommended that the government develop an identification card or disc that would be carried or worn by every Canadian and would list the person's name, address, and blood type. This would assist civil defence health and welfare service workers in providing the appropriate first aid and give them a means of reuniting families or notifying next of kin.[57] This idea was discussed by the Department of Health and Welfare but never implemented due to cost.[58] In lieu of that plan, welfare workers devised elaborate organizational charts to track refugees, provide daycare for displaced children, billet families, and allocate emergency relief. Although families were the focus, some social workers made it a point to provide civil defence services for individuals living outside a family. For example, social workers Frances Montgomery and George Caldwell used concerns about emergency preparedness to raise awareness about the problems of substandard housing of certain state welfare institutions—old-age homes, hospitals, asylums, prisons, and residential schools—which, they argued, were often too debilitated and overcrowded to offer adequate protection in a fire, let alone a nuclear emergency.[59] They wanted to ensure that people without a traditional family to care for them would not be forgotten in the chaos of war. In the meantime their recommended renovations would improve the standards of living in peacetime, too.

Ensuring refugees had access to food was considered central to averting postwar chaos. Emergency Feeding courses did not teach cooking—they assumed women already had that skill—but rather how to modify recipes and improvise cooking tools to feed large numbers of people under challenging environmental conditions. At a meeting of the federal government's Welfare Planning Committee, Edith Walker, Director of Emergency Feeding in Great Britain, lectured Canadians about her experience feeding hungry people during the Blitz. She informed her audience that in Britain "61,000 women, most of them middle-aged matrons with grown children, belong to an army of housewives who are trained to build stoves out of rubble, whip up a hot cup of tea or a two-course meal in the middle of devastation, and serve food to 500 people at a sitting."[60] She warned the planners that "women won't react to vague exhortations. You've to tell them what they can do. [We tell the housewife,] look, you're a good cook, you can cook for five or six; we want you to learn to cook for 500."[61] In the courses, women studied how to cook without the aid of their Frigidaires and Roper Ranges, abandoning their postwar consumer demand for new appliances and instead make "CD Stew" and "EMO burgers" outdoors on stoves made out of bricks, rubble, pipes, and old sheeting. During a training exercise in Scarborough, Ontario, the welfare service group was called "tremendous" for preparing a dinner for 500 people on stoves made out of cement blocks and for being able serve 78 meals in eight minutes.[62]

Generally, social workers advocated for minimal change in the lives of refugee families. Maintaining the status quo was seen as one way to maintain a sense of normalcy. Equating harmony with normal social conventions was found in the recommendations made by three social workers—Margaret Douglas, E. Songhurst, and Jean Graham—as to how Canada should plan emergency billeting for families evacuated from target cities. In their report to EMO director R. B. Curry, they stressed the importance of matching homeless families with host families who shared similarities in language, race, class, religion, culture, occupation, nationality, and the number and age of children. They concurred that "while in an emergency most people are willing to offer accommodation to almost any needy person for a very short period of time, if billeting is necessary for a matter of weeks, minor differences and problems assume major importance."[63] Steering clear of class and racial tensions was a priority:

> It would perhaps be better to avoid placing together people who vary greatly in occupational or social status. We would feel that standards of cleanliness and of homemaking might be quite important ... [therefore] it might be advisable to have a placement principle of not mixing people of different colour.[64]

Additionally, in a different report, an anonymous social worker recommended that if possible a family's "pre-disaster standard of living should be evaluated and related to the post-disaster situation when discussing losses, needs and resources" rather than applying a universal relief formula to all evacuees. It is not clear if this meant allocating better housing to wealthier evacuees or giving more care to those with fewer resources before an attack, but the social worker stressed the importance of making the evacuation experience as normal as possible. The report writer also emphasized the importance of ensuring a system was in place that would make certain that citizens already receiving welfare benefits, such as workmen's compensation, old-age pension, or family allowance, continued to get these after an attack.[65] All of these recommendations stressed that preparation and psychology would ensure that war-devastated Canadians behaved appropriately and predictably. In particular, the careful attention devoted to ensuring no one was unintentionally upset by their billeting arrangements showed how unprepared planners were for the actual chaos of a nuclear war; sentiments that became more obvious as information about the dangers of nuclear fallout was made public in the late 1950s.

Initially information about the effects of the bomb were shrouded in secrecy or misunderstood in the early Cold War. One of the first publications to address surviving a nuclear war was the 1951 United States federal government booklet *Survival under Atomic Attack*. Over 20 million copies were distributed around the United States and Canada, intending to dispel myths and panic about nuclear war. The booklet explained that there was really no difference between an atomic bomb and the conventional weapons used in World War II, and it compared the hazards of radioactivity to a sunburn.[66] Survival scenarios grew grimmer by the late 1950s when scientists had more than a decade's worth of data from explosions in Hiroshima and Nagasaki and hundreds of test detonations of atomic and hydrogen bombs. Many scientists predicted that, if a nuclear war occurred, the majority of any nation's leaders, skilled workers, social institutions, and families would be destroyed. Those who survived would suffer radiation sickness, famine, and climate change. Waves of post-apocalyptic fiction and films accompanied these theories, driving the sensational horrors of nuclear war home to their audiences. Books such as Nevil Shute's 1957 novel *On the Beach* terrified readers with its presentation of a post-nuclear-war Australia where the government had given up on civil defence and was instead issuing free cyanide pills.[67] *The Globe and Mail* referred to *On the Beach* as "the best seller of all best-sellers" and praised Shute, a former engineer, for his detailed research on gamma rays and cobalt bombs but hoped "he was wrong."[68] Despite these scientific and literary predictions, civil defence planners remained publicly undaunted and steadfast in insisting Canada could be saved through planning and preparation.

Protecting Children's Minds and Bodies at School

In addition to being prioritized in civil defence's health and welfare services, children received specialized civil defence training in schools. Since civil defence's inception, the NCWC had urged the federal government on an annual basis to plan "a suitable and effective Civil Defence programme for the safety of the school children of Canada" in every province because "this situation is of great importance not only to parents and teachers but to all citizens."[69] The government agreed and in 1954 developed resources to help school boards create civil defence plans.[70] Teachers were assigned a dual role: increase the children's chances of survival through classroom education and ensure they were safe if an attack happened during school hours.[71] This was no small task given the increased numbers of children entering the school system in the 1950s. Schools struggled to meet the pressures of the first wave of baby-boom enrolments and faced a lack of classroom space, transportation concerns, and a teacher shortage. The postwar demand for teachers paralleled that of nurses and social workers, and resulted in the same elimination of the marriage bar, thus encouraging married women to join or return to the workforce.[72] Over the twentieth century, there was a feminization of teaching—a gradual increase in the numbers of women teaching—though proportionately women dominated teaching less than they did in the nursing and social work fields.

Like their counterparts in women's organizations, nursing, and social work, teachers needed training to fulfill their new EMO duties. Saskatchewan led the way for specialized teacher training programs. The Saskatchewan Teacher's Federation approved the use of non-certified instructors in cases where classroom teachers were not qualified to teach civil defence subjects. With that temporary measure in place, the province developed a civil defence summer school to train elementary- and secondary-school teachers in emergency measures on school property; it also introduced revised curricula that included science lessons about nuclear fission and instruction on how to teach Cold War politics in the social studies classroom. All teachers were invited to take the basic civil defence course, and female teachers were directed to take an additional course in home nursing. High-school students could also take these gender-specialized and segregated summer-school courses for credit, with girls taking first aid and boys taking firefighting.[73] Similar summer-school programs for faculty and students were developed across the country.[74]

By the mid-1950s, civil defence lectures and classroom drills became as common as learning about fire safety. By 1961 *The Toronto Daily Star* joked that radiation had become "the fourth R," next to reading, writing and arithmetic.[75] One popular teaching tool was *Duck and Cover*, a film produced by the United States Federal Civil Defense Administration in consultation with the Safety Commission of the National Education Association. Today this film is often used to mock the assumption that the simple act of ducking and covering could save your life, but at the time it was presented in schools with a straight face. *Duck and Cover* featured the animated Bert the Turtle, who taught children how to take cover from an atomic attack which could occur at any time, he warned—at school, on the school bus, on the street, or while having a family picnic. Instead of ducking into their turtle shell like Bert, children practised getting under their desks or, if no cover was available, then at least crouching and covering their head with their hands.[76] After practising Bert's advice, St. Catharines teachers were praised for drilling their self-sufficient students so well in "Operation Turtle" that they could crawl under their desks and clasp their hands over the back of their necks in less than four seconds.[77]

Throughout the students' training, teachers were expected to keep morale high by creating a reassuring learning environment that would avoid panic, confusion, boredom, and overexcitement. Jennifer Hunter's analysis of Cold War public opinion polls found that respondents, presumably all adults, only admitted to a mild fear of nuclear war.[78] Anecdotal evidence from teachers suggests that children's fear of nuclear war was greater. One Montreal grade-school teacher reported to *Maclean's* that many children in her class drew pictures of mushroom clouds and expressed fear of poisonous rain and snow. A survey of high-school students reported that teenage girls were afraid of having deformed babies and that boys were cynical about their futures because they believed them to be non-existent.[79] One Calgary mother of five complained that all this fear was causing teens to "live it up" because they felt they had no future. "This is happening—and it is eroding our country's honour as much as anything can," the mother fretted.[80] Dr. Sybille Escalona, an American psychologist, claimed that children and youth were well aware of the nuclear threat—both the threat of an actual war and the threat of the environment being poisoned by weapons testing. Not only were children frightened of dying and of being separated from their parents, they believed adults shared these fears, which undoubtedly made their own worse. Alma Laabs, a school social worker, and Virginia Hathaway, a school psychologist, recommended honesty as the best approach to reduce anxiety. They advised teachers and parents that "children must be told the truth at a level suited to their understanding. Young children will be fearful of the need to know what will happen to dad, mother, brother or sister. They need to know these individuals will be taken care of. Older students need to know city-wide plans."[81] They also suggested ways teachers could incorporate civil defence in the classroom that would minimize disruption of normal school activity and maximize discipline and productivity.[82] One voice of contention among specialists was Dr. Benjamin Spock, the popular pediatrician and author who became an anti-war advocate in the late 1950s and was one of the founders of the American disarmament group, Committee for a Sane Nuclear Policy (SANE). Spock felt that exposing children to civil defence was "unwise and unfair" because "there's no safety under a desk so what's the use of alarming the children?"[83] Although Dr. Spock's childrearing advice had been like the voice of God throughout the baby boom, his turn to the radical left was viewed suspiciously and Canadian schools ignored his arguments.

If there was not enough warning of a nuclear attack for children to return home, teachers were expected to remain on school grounds, supervising their pupils' evacuation to the school's basement, gymnasium, or a windowless hallway, where they would take care of them until it was safe to return home, be that hours, days, or weeks later. To prepare for this, municipal planners and school boards expected teachers to "become familiar with the psychological basis for working with children under the stress of emergency situations," and maintain good housekeeping and record keeping, ensuring an orderly response to the crisis.[84] Like nurses, teachers were expected to remain on the job at the first sign of a crisis and act as mother figures to any dependent children. No official emergency plans were laid for the teachers to return home to aid their own families; their professions placed them on the front lines of newly drawn battlefields.

Schools were also part of the Canadian government's hostile response to communism. The 1945 defection of Soviet cipher clerk Igor Gouzenko and the evidence he collected of an Ottawa spy ring had proved that Canada was considered a valuable source for intelligence on its more powerful allies. The shocking (or not-so-shocking) revelation that the Russians were spying on a wartime ally marked a turning point in East–West relations and the breakdown of the World War II coalition. Robert Bothwell characterizes the Gouzenko affair as a "dramatic incident, perched as it was on the bridge between war and peace ... the starting gun to the Cold War."[85] In *Cold War Canada: The Making of a National Insecurity State, 1947–1957,* Reg Whitaker and Gary Marcuse show how the Canadian government mobilized against a fifth column deployed by a wartime enemy, albeit in peacetime, which resulted in the surveillance and oppression of Canadians expressing allegiance to the Communist Party or leftist ideologies, a situation comparable to Senator Joseph McCarthy's witch hunt in the United States.[86]

To combat suspected communist influence, the tenets of democracy, patriotism, and nationalism were to be emphasized in school curricula. Alongside civil defence, social studies and history teachers were instructed to promote security by emphasizing "'the greatness and virtue' of the British Commonwealth of Nations and the democratic ideals upon which they have been founded" and "the dangers of 'the police state' where fascist and communist regimes prohibit the 'free party' and 'free voting' systems."[87] Ensuring teacher loyalty was also an issue during the communist backlash. Across Ontario there were public calls for teachers to take a loyalty oath, a process implemented in Kitchener to prove teachers "were 'sincere' in their democratic ideals and "were 'willing to show their loyalty to Canadian and British Democracy by taking an oath of allegiance to the King.'"[88] Kristina Llewellyn's interviews with women who taught at the high-school level in postwar Toronto reveal that some teachers managed to rebel against the limitations placed on their teaching and sneak in literature deemed too radical, such as *Catcher in the Rye*, or include a fair-minded discussion about communism when studying the history of Russia.[89] Still, teachers' activities inside and outside the classroom underwent more scrutiny than some other state employees because they were children's secondary caregivers.

One woman, Marjorie Lamb, President of the Altrusa Club of Toronto, a service club for business and professional women, provided a "counselling service helping Canadians to equip themselves to meet the propaganda and infiltration efforts of Communists."[90] Lamb was born in London, Ontario, and claimed to have observed communist activity, tactics, and objectives while studying interior design in Paris during the interwar period. Upon her return to Canada, Lamb imagined herself as a Bea Alerte of a different sort. She dedicated herself to creating *The Alert Service*, a newsletter that professed to offer authenticated information on communist activity in Canada. Lamb insisted she did not want to "penalize the individual Communist, but rather should concentrate on exposing the fallacies of Communist doctrine and the methods the Communists use to promote their doctrine."[91] The publication of *The Alert Service* depended on money raised through subscriptions and donations. It was most visibly sponsored by one of Canada's oldest women's organizations, the IODE, whose loyalty was never in doubt, and by a new women's club, The United Women, whose membership was made up of postwar female immigrants from Eastern Europe bent on proving their allegiance to Canada. These organizations purchased copies of *The Alert Service* for their members and passed them on to municipal and school libraries. Both organizations believed that Canada needed protection from the infiltration of communist agents into its political, social, and educational institutions, and they appreciated *The Alert Service* directing attention to obvious agents, such as the Communist Party of Canada and its offshoots, the Canadian Peace Congress, and the Congress of Canadian Women. *The Alert Service* also targeted more subtle threats, such as the Voice of Women, a peace and disarmament organization that will be studied more thoroughly in chapter 3.[92]

As the EMO did with emergency preparedness, Lamb positioned routing out communists as a women's issue because it affected youth. She claimed that communists often targeted children and teens through youth groups that looked innocuous on the surface but were really just breeding groups for revolutionary thought and action. The *Alert Service* included quotes from Lenin about recruiting students and how the support of youth would win the revolution for the Soviets. Lamb also created a pamphlet, appropriate for Canadians fifteen years of age and up, entitled *Canada and Communism—A Talk to Young Canadians.* Overall she concluded that "young Canadians generally will not 'buy' Communism or its phoney doctrine," but they "may be fooled into accepting part of it, or into helping Communist operations."[93] Therefore she warned "everyone concerned with the destiny of young people" to refrain from sending students to international youth conferences, since they would be crawling with Communists.[94] By the mid-1960s, *The Alert Service* subscribers faded to a handful of believers, and in 1967 Lamb regretfully discontinued the newsletter.[95] Although anti-communist awareness and action was not an official arm of civil defence, it is relevant to link these interests together because they both involved mobilizing and educating women for security purposes and focused on insulating Canadian children from Cold War threats, both physical and ideological.

Between 1948 and 1963, groups of women responded to the state's call for help and their own concerns about Canada's security in a world assumed to be teetering on the brink of destruction. They did so in different ways, through different channels. For women already actively involved in their community through membership in women's clubs, it did not require much debate to throw their support behind a program that promised to save their lives and was contextualized as a continuation of their patriotic work in previous global conflicts. Groups such as the NCWC and IODE did this not only by acquiescing to what was directly requested of them, but by initiating their own training and information programs and by lobbying for more resources when they saw gaps. In their quest for knowledge, women's organizations relied heavily on women who dealt with issues of health and welfare for a living—leaving their education and training to their professional counterparts in nursing, social work, and teaching. Once professional associations and employers committed their labour force to the civil defence cause either by choice or default, the work of nurses, social workers, and teachers took on new dimensions during the Cold War. It made them part of a militarized project for Canada's security, in which their experience, knowledge, and ideas were sought and respected. New responsibilities meant increased training to master or adapt new concepts and increased attention to worst-case scenarios where they would be required to stretch the boundaries of their previous labour or at least perform it under new pressures. Although the civil defence work of both voluntary and professional women was predominantly limited to maternalistic caring roles—guardians of the sick, wounded, displaced, and dependent—the consequences of their actions were seen by the EMO as critical to Canada's survival, not merely a sideline to the main action. This helped reinforce the value of these professions in peacetime *and* wartime, which contributed to the state's understanding of the need for their growth in the postwar workforce. It also gave several female leaders in the fields of nursing and social work the opportunity to rise high in the EMO hierarchy, though it appears that most employees involved in civil defence incorporated their new responsibilities without sacrificing their regular workloads or receiving any wage increases.

The voluntary spirit that was pervasive within civil defence exemplifies a gulf in status and motivation between the women workers who participated in civil defence and the representatives from women's organizations. Just as the levels of commitment, patriotism, and incentive were perceived to be different between enlisted women, women workers, and women volunteers in World War II, there appears to have been some competition for a sense of superiority here, as well. On the one side were the generally older and more elite women who formed the backbone of organizations like the NCWC and IODE and volunteered under the banner of good citizenship. On the other side were the generally younger, working women who placed emphasis on their professional code of duty and contributions of skills. For the most part, this divide did not impact women's unity or collective work, and the two groups frequently worked together. It is ironic that, even as the professional women strove to distinguish themselves from volunteer women by delivering services based on their professional expertise, they were also expected to become substitute mothers and exude the familiar sense of calm, security, and trustworthiness. Ultimately, however, these two seemingly disparate groups of women together modelled a vision to protect Canada from annihilation that placed great value on protecting children and maintaining family stability.

Noma Taylor, a female writer for *EMO National Digest*, stated that civil defence depended on "the wholehearted support of all Canadian women" because when it came to matters of home and community, "Canadian women were the most influential group in the country."[96] This statement proved to be prophetic. In terms of community involvement, women's volunteer and paid participation in Health and Welfare Services and the school program was civil defence's greatest success.[97] Because of women's support, expertise, and labour, this side of civil defence managed to reach its emergency preparedness goals. On the other side of the program, however, civil defence planners failed to convince homemakers to bring civil defence into the home. In the late 1950s, the family home was positioned by the government as a sanctuary from nuclear warfare, if properly maintained and organized by prepared mothers. At the heart of this program was the family fallout shelter. It was here that women used their influence and expertise to challenge and eventually disengage from a civil defence program they came to believe was faulty, useless, and immoral.

CHAPTER TWO

The Home Front Becomes the Front Line
Fallout Shelter Madness

In the fall of 1961 Canadians were abuzz over the construction of the Berlin Wall. The wall became a symbol of Cold War ferocity and paranoia, representing the expanding divide between East and West. Suddenly Winston Churchill's iron curtain had a corporeal equivalent, constructed first out of wire and later concrete. As NATO countries debated their response to the construction, ordinary Canadians were forced to wonder if this was the crisis that would finally trigger a military conflict between nuclear powers. Amid these tensions, one Toronto family—John McCallum, his wife Winifred, and their two children, six-year-old Jack and five-year-old Karen—ventured down into a thirteen-by-seven-foot fallout shelter, where they would play, study, cook, and sleep for one week. Their shelter was built on the Exhibition Place fairgrounds and stocked according to Canada's EMO recommendations. This publicity stunt was sponsored by the CBC, where John worked as a news editor, to address concerns that family life in a shelter would be impossible. In the early 1960s, a series of similar experiments were carried out across North America to promote the viability of shelter living. Each night the television program *Newsmagazine* gave updates on shelter life radioed in by the McCallums and provided civil defence tips from the EMO. It was reported that the children kept busy doing their homework by battery-operated lamps and that, in their free time, Karen sewed and knit while Jack played with his construction set. When the subdued family emerged from the shelter after seven days, they were greeted by CBC reporter Norm DePoe,

Toronto Mayor Nathan Phillips and his wife Esther, and approximately 100 demonstrators. Many of the protesters were women, accompanied by their children, and they carried signs that read "Bricks do not stop bombs." They were not interested in the fact that Mr. McCallum insisted his family "not only survived but thrived" or that Mrs. McCallum found cooking in the shelter easy because all she had to use were canned goods.[1] The demonstrators believed civil defence was a farce: not only was it impossible to protect Canadians from nuclear warfare, the program's very existence encouraged such a war, a notion which provoked the protesters to shout, "The only defence is peace!"[2]

The McCallums' experiment represented a new stage of civil defence's plans for family safety. As discussed in chapter 1, civil defence planners had always acknowledged the importance of keeping families safe and together as a means of maintaining a sense of normalcy amid predicted post-nuclear-war chaos. If families remained intact after the bombs had fallen, it would give the impression that not too much had changed for life to go on. The new twist to this rhetoric was that by the late 1950s, emergency preparedness was expected to take place solely in the family home. The initial emergency plan to evacuate families from target cities to reception centres proved short-sighted. It was based on expectations that the Distant Early Warning (DEW) Line, a joint American–Canadian system of radar stations in the Arctic along the 69th parallel, would offer sufficient warning times to evacuate target cities. It was believed that, once complete, the DEW Line would provide Canadians with a three-hour warning before planes leaving the Soviet Union entered Canadian airspace. Yet evacuation drills such as Calgary's Operation Lifesaver proved that three hours was too short to evacuate the entirety of most target cities and there were not enough roads to manage evacuation traffic. Planners predicted that it would take Saint John (population 85,000) a minimum of two and a half hours, Winnipeg (427,000) four hours, and Vancouver (667,000) up to fourteen hours to evacuate—*if* all traffic lanes were clear.[3] Even so, by the time the DEW Line was finished in 1957, ICBMs reduced warning times to a mere fifteen minutes. In response, the EMO changed their plans and encouraged Canadians to remain at home during an attack and seek shelter in a backyard or basement fallout shelter. Here families could take cover quickly and supposedly be protected from the subsequent fires and fallout. These changes turned civil defence from a communal effort into a family venture, with specific roles assigned to each household member.

As the traditional caretakers of the home, wives and mothers were expected to prepare their houses and families to withstand a direct attack.

In fact no woman was asked to play a bigger role in civil defence than the homemaker. In an address to the NCWC entitled "The Role of Women in Civil Defence," Major-General F. F. Worthington announced to the audience, the majority of whom would most likely have been mothers and wives, "The role of women in civil defence is no different from that of men, with the possible exception that women have a greater responsibility in protecting the home and family."[4] Like their counterparts in women's organizations and professions, homemakers were assigned health and welfare roles designed to keep their husbands and children safe, healthy, and calm in a crisis. This responsibility gave new importance to women's daily chores such as cleaning and cooking, while adding new tasks to the to-do list, such as neighbour-hood watch, firefighting, and medical triage. Women's caregiving was positioned as a matter of national security. As Laura McEnaney describes in *Civil Defence Begins at Home*, making civil defence a woman's affair de-emphasized the father's paternal leadership role and favoured the mother's maternal protective role.[5] While the father's authority was still seen as necessary to guide the family to safety, it would be the mother's labour that paved the way to survival. This assumed that with only a bit of fine tuning and preparation, a homemaker's nurturing and domestic skills would be a match for the chaos and havoc that an atomic bomb would wreak. However, despite the priority placed on their participation, civil defence support from homemakers was minimal. In particular, their skepticism toward fallout shelters revealed the great uncertainty women felt about the government's plans for Canadians' safety.

Safeguarding Family and Home

Throughout the Cold War, both the Soviet and American propaganda machines held up happy families as proof of their system's superiority. It is no coincidence that American Vice-President Nixon and Soviet Premier Khrushchev held their infamous impromptu debate while standing in a model kitchen in a mock suburban home at the 1954 American National Exhibition in Moscow. When the two politicians compared their nations' technological achievements in manufacturing affordable domestic appliances and housing, they made families, along with families' wants and needs, an important symbol of national values. "Families," Mary Louise Adams writes in relation to Cold War culture, "were understood to be the primary stabilizing influence on both individuals and the nation as a whole."[6] Prosperous, content, and united families were thought to be the result of and contributors to a strong, flourishing nation. Likewise, if families—meaning those positioned within the respectable and stable middle class—were to be a nation's bulwark, then they could also be its ruin. Therefore it was considered a worthy cause to monitor middle-class-family well-being, a task enthusiastically taken on by social scientists, journalists, government officials, and psychologists, many of whom argued that Canadian families appeared to be hovering on the verge of disaster in the 1950s. Psychologist David Ketchum announced on his CBC Radio program in 1954 that "no Canadian institution, not even education, is viewed with more alarm today than the Canadian family."[7] Perceived threats included the strain of building families when most adults of marriageable age had only known the stressful years of the Depression and Second World War, as well as new tensions associated with postwar life: big families, lack of housing, moves to the isolating and underdeveloped suburbs, managing expanded credit and consumption, and the postwar dislocation of veterans. Parents were warned to be aware of and prepared to combat a variety of dangers threatening their children's healthy development, including polio epidemics, juvenile delinquency, and sexual deviancy.[8] As in the past, experts singled out poor mothering as a potentially dangerous force. Mothers were criticized for being over-vigilant, overindulgent, or simply absent due to their increased presence in the workforce.[9]

Conformity to appropriate gender roles and behaviour was often presented as the solution to the woes of postwar families. Normalcy was the ultimate goal, something Mona Gleason demonstrates was equated with heterosexual, white, middle-class values that insisted families should have

> mothers who stayed at home and raised well-adjusted, bright, industrious children, and white-collar fathers who skilfully divided time between the office and home. In this way, an idealized "every family" became the standard against which the unique needs and circumstances of those outside the ideal, such as immigrant, working-class, non-nuclear, or female-headed families, were measured and judged.[10]

This advice paints a picture of the idyllic and comfortable family life found in the fictional realms of *Leave It to Beaver* or the Dick-and-Jane school readers. It suggests that a home—meaning both a physical dwelling and the people living within it, maintained by a loving, housebound mother and paid for by a dedicated working father—would produce dutiful children with strong characters. These homes would therefore be buffered from external pressures, temptations, and conflicts. Given the power this generic family formula was supposed to have, it is not surprising that the same solution was offered to families confronted with the threat of nuclear war. To paraphrase the McCallum peace protesters, bricks may not stop bombs, but the EMO tried to insist that stable families could.

In order to effectively convey this revised civil defence message to families, planners initiated special self-help campaigns emphasizing the family's ability to easily take care of itself in a nuclear emergency. Mothers were most often the target of this message; however, it was more challenging to reach homemakers than their counterparts in women's organizations or workers in the health and welfare fields. Justine Glass, a mother of four living in rural Ontario, wrote a letter to Health and Welfare minister Paul Martin informing him that "like many other young mothers with small children and living in the country there isn't too much opportunity for attending the [EMO] meetings. I'm hoping your department has a booklet for mothers available, giving this practical advice, and if not, why not?... I'm sure every mother would appreciate such a booklet."[11] Martin thanked Glass for her letter, which he praised as "the correct approach of the young housewife" and informed her of upcoming publications on civil defence that would answer her specific questions.[12] Under Martin's direction there was a flurry of publicity surrounding civil defence in the 1950s directed at the housewife, including pamphlets, posters, films, television and radio ads, and newspaper articles, some placed specifically in the women's section of a paper. *Chatelaine* magazine was another popular source for civil defence information. Articles such as "It's a Tough Time to Be in Love" and "Let's Abolish These Atom Bomb Blues" addressed what Valerie Korinek calls the darker side of *Chatelaine*, a running commentary on "Cold War politics, protagonists and prognostications on the future," amid articles on housekeeping, fashion, and parenting.[13] In order not to rely solely on literacy skills, local EMOs also recruited volunteers known as wardens to go door to door, delivering advice about civil defence and collecting information about each dwelling so rescue and welfare workers would have an easier job tracking casualties and reuniting families.[14] During an actual emergency, wardens were expected to help their neighbours evacuate or take cover, before following their own personal plans.

Wardens were selected by the local EMO for their good health, their good character, and their ability to inspire confidence and lead others. Women were considered especially appropriate for this position because it was presumed that they already had established relationships with their neighbours.[15] One senior civil defence advisor to NATO stated that women performed well as wardens in Britain during World War II and should continue to do so because "the warden is a jack of all trades and must be a most adaptable person, and there is no doubt that women are a very great asset in this field, even though the work can at times be very tough going."[16] Wardens were warned that, although most people would be eager for information and advice, they should also be prepared to handle the neighbourhood skeptic. In all cases wardens were directed to "not adopt a superior attitude to the householder or talk down to himself or his family," but rather give information "factually and calmly."[17] As depicted in the Canadian EMO film *Flowers or Ashes*, this conversation could be a challenging task. In this film a housewife's dire prophecy of disaster comes to pass when her husband refuses to heed the warden's warning to prepare for civil defence and a bomb falls on their house, killing the whole family.[18] One could imagine some female wardens might have encountered resistance discussing matters ranging from home renovations to foreign affairs with the male heads of households; however, civil defence officials did not mention this gendered challenge in their training manual. They did, however, ask every warden, male or female, to identify the most capable woman on every block, who in turn would arrange for two or three other women to help her carry out functions related to the needs of survivors, such as matching foster mothers with orphaned or unaccompanied children.[19] The EMO thought housewives would welcome this volunteer service because they would not need to stray far from their own home or neighbourhood to be of use and their services would help relieve professional welfare workers and police to do other work. Although their main job would be comforting neighbours, Patricia Godfrey, the Information Director of the Canadian Welfare Council, thought that the recruited women should have a minimum five lectures on aspects of civil defence, including one on firefighting. This training would "simply instil in their minds the idea that they had some responsibility."[20] Godfrey and others thought this program could be of use in peacetime, too, and warden's welfare aides became the forerunner of the Block Parent Program of Canada.[21]

EMO brochures and wardens insisted that most homemakers' civil defence work fit their normal routines and could be performed without even leaving the home. Cleaning, cooking, and sending the children to school all took on new meaning in a household devoted to civil defence or even one where only the mother was supportive. Civil defence educational material implied that the best-prepared homes were ones that fit typical middle-class standards of cleanliness, order, and appropriate consumer habits. A tidy home was presented as one step toward emergency preparedness. This message was reinforced by the civil defence film *House in the Middle*, which featured footage of atomic weapons tests conducted in the Nevada desert on a series of mock homes. According to the narrator, all the houses had identical structures and were situated an equal distance away from where the bomb was to be detonated. When the mushroom cloud bloomed, the houses with tidy yards, interiors free of clutter, and exterior walls painted with a heat-reflecting light colour were shown to withstand the blast and fire. Meanwhile the rundown homes with neglected yards and rooms filled with stacks of magazines and news-papers went up in flames. In one of the doomed homes, a doll lying in a baby carriage was shown before the explosion; afterwards, only the charred metal frame of the carriage remained. The narrator asked, "Which of these is *your* house?" putting the onus on homeowners, or more specifically housewives, to ensure measures were taken to protect their children from the vaporization that affected the doll. The film concluded with images of all family members, including children, performing chores to keep a house that reflected "beauty, cleanliness, health and safety."[22] The film was produced by the American National Paint, Varnish and Lacquer Association, an indicator of the middle-class standards of much of the civil defence plans and the connection between civil defence and the larger military-industrial complex.

Careful grocery shopping, food storage, and cooking were also part of a mother's civil defence work. Housewives were advised to purchase a fourteen-day supply of emergency food. This included essentials such as dried milk, baby formula, canned fruits and vegetables, canned meat and fish, packaged cereal, crackers, and soup. All items were to be labelled with the date of pur-chase and replaced annually. Recommendations also called for fourteen gallons of water for each adult member of the family and more for younger children.[23] Appealing to tradition rather than using modern space-age imagery, American civil defence planners referred to this plan as "Grandma's Pantry":

> In Grandma's day, her well-stocked pantry safeguarded the family against such emergencies as floods, blizzards, hurricanes and other devastations that rendered outside food sources inaccessible. Superbomb hazards of today furnish similar reasons for householders to maintain a "Grandma's Pantry" with a 7-day stock of food supplies.[24]

Additionally, women were taught how to avoid the dangers of radioactivity in the kitchen. One family-focused pamphlet, *Hints for Housewives about Food and Drink*, listed a set of guidelines to follow in food preparation after an attack. It assured readers that any food and drink stored inside the fridge in airtight containers would be safe if opened away from radioactive dirt, dust, or moisture. Meanwhile all exposed unpackaged food should be thrown away.[25] Mothers were also advised to ensure that, even in a crisis, infants remained on their regular feeding schedule to avoid becoming dehydrated and ill from lack of water. Breastfeeding was thought to be the ideal sustenance, since milk or formula tainted by radiation could cause vomiting and diarrhea.[26] There was no acknowledgement that a mother's breast milk might be exposed to radiation too.

Maintaining strong, healthy bodies was also seen to be part of a family's civil defence plan. Dieticians associated with Emergency Feeding explained to mothers that serving regular, well-balanced, nutritious meals every day would help build up their children's resistance to infection, so their health would be better prepared to withstand an emergency.[27] Newfangled TV dinners would not cut it; mothers were urged to follow the 1949 Canadian Council on Nutrition's food rules, which advised healthy eating from five food groups: milk, meat and fish, cereals and bread, and fruit and vegetables. The Council recommended that children drink milk at all meals and described a proper dinner (served at noon or in the evening) as one that included a serving of milk, fish, or poultry; a potato or other vegetable; fruit or a fruit dessert; and a piece of bread, if desired. The rules also directed children and pregnant women to take vitamin D supplements and advised all Canadians to avoid excess, even after the lean Depression and war years, because *more* was not necessarily *better*.[28] Mothers were also warned to ensure that their children's inoculations were always up-to-date and to keep a record of their child's health and blood type with them at all times.[29] To make the travels to and from school as safe as possible, on days when an attack was suspected, mothers were advised to send their children to school in light-coloured clothing with long sleeves. Light colours were thought to reflect the heat and bright light emerging from a nuclear explosion and the sleeves were expected to protect a child's skin from heat and burns.[30] Feeding and dressing their children appropriately were responsibilities mothers were supposed to do without the threat of nuclear war hanging over their heads. Presumably the normalcy of these tasks was meant to reassure homemakers about how easy and natural it was to comply with civil defence recommendations and survive a nuclear war.

Although civil defence guidelines outlined how wives and mothers' housework and caregiving could mean the difference between life and death, there was also an unwritten understanding that a mother's most vital function, childbearing, should not be compromised because of Cold War fears. Children were a sign of a family's and nation's stability, and existing and future children were seen as critical to Canada's survival. In addition to prioritizing children's safety in a crisis, planners attempted to reassure women that their childbearing plans need not be thwarted by the threat or actual occurrence of a nuclear war or even weapons testing. Some women expressed concerns that fallout would affect their own or their children's future childbearing ability. A *Maclean's* article by Barbara Moon stoked these fears by claiming, "The world is going into the hottest year for fallout since testing began. Canada is the hottest country in the world."[31] Moon's estimation referred to the fact that, between 1961 and 1962, 300 megatons of weapons were detonated in tests, which was equal to the total number of all preceding tests, the long-term consequences of which would not be known for a decade. Despite reassurances from the Department of Health and Welfare, independent studies measuring levels of iodine showed in the fall of 1962 that Calgary, Winnipeg, Sault Ste. Marie, and Quebec City were in range three, the "red light zone," and the national average of the nine test cities was also in range three for two months. By November all figures dropped to range two; however, none of this was known until December—too late for any countermeasures to be employed, such as taking cows off pasture or advising pregnant women, children, and teenagers to switch to powdered milk.[32]

Concerns over radiation's impact on fertility and fetal development were raised often by mothers. In a letter to the prime minister, Sharon Bradbury scolded Diefenbaker for focusing on civil defence rather than diplomacy. She refused to follow civil defence recommendations because she had no interest in "protecting my children so that they can produce misshapen, subhuman offspring."[33] Other women wrote to Diefenbaker with more personal concerns, hoping for answers about their own private misfortunes. One woman from Stephenville, Newfoundland, site of an overseas U.S. Air Force Base, who identified herself only as "A housewife who is praying" wrote to Diefenbaker in 1961 and asked him to investigate the unusual number of miscarriages and children born with brain damage and other deformities, including her own son, in her region between 1958 and 1959, a time she heard was a bad year for radioactive fallout from weapons tests.[34] Diefenbaker responded to these concerns by creating a special division within the Department of Health and Welfare to study radiation levels, paying close attention to its effect on children by sampling powdered and fresh milk. Their research concluded that there was no danger to Canadians, young or old, as did subsequent studies conducted by Pearson's government under the supervision of Minister of Health and Welfare, Judy LaMarsh.[35]

An early civil defence pamphlet used Hiroshima and Nagasaki as examples of how life went on as usual after the atomic explosions, quashing rumours that exposure to radiation caused cancer and infertility. It insisted that Japanese children born before and after the attack were normal.[36] Still, dramatic images were emerging from Japan in the late 1940s and 1950s that suggested how harrowing childrearing would be in a post-nuclear-war world. In 1946 *The New Yorker* devoted an entire issue to journalist John Hersey's *Hiroshima*, an account of the experiences of six ordinary people in the days after their city was bombed. The story became a bestselling book, a Book-of-the-Month Club selection, and a radio dramatization. The popular narrative provided vivid detail about the terrible effects of the bomb's burns and of radiation sickness. Among the stories of devastated families there were two particularly harrowing accounts of mothers found alive in the rubble holding their dead infants, including one mother who refused to let go of the four-day-old corpse of her baby.[37] The grotesque side effects of the bomb were also brought home to North American audiences in the highly publicized story of the twenty-five young female bomb survivors known as the Hiroshima Maidens. These women had been schoolgirls in 1945 when the atomic bomb was detonated and had suffered greatly from the physical pain and social stigma caused by the burns and scars covering their bodies. In 1957 CBC covered their trip from Hiroshima to New York for multiple reconstructive surgeries arranged for Reverend Kiyoshi Tanimoto, one of the people featured in Hersey's *Hiroshima*, and paid for by donation from the Society of Friends, Mount Sinai Hospital, and American disarmament advocate and literary editor Norman Cousins.[38] These two examples demonstrated the personal cost of war on women and children and helped transform images of former enemies into sympathetic and innocent civilians. In the late 1970s the work of Japanese researchers and international peace activists replaced anecdotal evidence with hard scientific data to demonstrate the arduous long-term physical and mental health consequences of atomic-bomb survivors and their descendants.[39]

Ardent civil defence planners might claim the baby boom was proof of Canadians' refusal to let Cold War fears dominate their lives. Between 1947 and 1966, the time when planning for civil defence was considered a national priority, Canada had one of the highest birth rates in the industrial world, averaging four children per adult woman.[40] The boom is attributed to the economic stability brought by World War II and the celebratory zeal following the war that caused women to marry at a younger age and couples to start their families sooner, allowing more years to conceive. In 1945,

300,000 babies were born in Canada, jumping to 372,000 babies in 1947 and 400,000 by 1952, a figure that did not decrease until 1966.[41] During these years Doug Owram suggests that "it seemed that everybody was pregnant or had a new baby."[42] If women had delayed the birth of children because of the Depression and Second World War, there was no mass trend to postpone births due to Cold War uncertainty. Still, it was in the name of these newly born children that women spoke out publicly against the most elaborate form of home-based civil defence—fallout shelters.

The Fallout Shelter Debate

Vigilance over a family's health and welfare was only one part of the domestic civil defence plan. There was no pretence that anyone could survive living in the blast zone simply by having the right type of groceries on hand or wearing light-coloured colouring. It was always understood that Canadians should seek shelter during a nuclear attack, but the type of recommended shelters grew more elaborate over time. When evacuation was still part of Canada's civil defence plans, residents of non-target areas and evacuees from target sites were told to take cover in a basement. Using layman terms, the 1956 pamphlet *Your Survival in an H-Bomb War* explained the threat of fallout, describing it as invisible "radioactive dust" that would make it "extremely dangerous to leave home."[43] Families were therefore told to descend into the basement, where inhabitants could expect to be exposed to only one tenth of the outdoor dose of radiation, or one fiftieth if the home was made of brick or stone rather than wood. The pamphlet also explained the importance of securing livestock in a separate cellar and of sealing a person in with the animals to water and feed them. Finally, there were instructions as to how to decontaminate one's body, water, clothing, and other objects. *Your Survival in an H-Bomb War* offered no specific time frame as to how long one should stay in a shelter, though it claimed radiation would begin to dissipate within seven hours.

Soon after this advice came out, evacuation plans were abandoned and shelter recommendations were changed to suit the needs of families remaining permanently within a target city. The first official mention of a revised shelter program was in Diefenbaker's statement to the House of Commons concerning the federal government's civil defence policy in November 1959.[44] A simple basement was no longer deemed sufficient unless a special concrete or brick room with walls at least sixteen inches thick was built within it (or dug underground in the backyard). Families were told to stay within their shelter for fourteen days to avoid contamination from radiation. A series of new pamphlets, each subtitled *Blueprint for Survival*, was created in the early 1960s to give step-by-step advice on how to build and stock these new types of shelters. The illustrations in these pamphlets depict men performing the actual construction; women were shown organizing the bedding and food supplies. If an attack happened during the day, women would most likely be the only adults at home, so they were also responsible for using their limited warning time to fireproof the rest of their house by turning off the water, electricity, and gas; filling the bathtubs, sinks, and pails with water; closing all shutters and drawing blinds; and ripping down inflammable curtains and drapes before descending into the shelter.[45] Women wrote to the EMO offering their own household survival tips, such as Elsie Mavor's formula of borax, boric acid, and water to fireproof curtains or Jessica Swanson's idea to use collapsible hammocks in her shelter instead of bunk beds to save space.[46]

EMOs provided instructions on how to construct shelters; however, ready-made ones could also be purchased from catalogues and stores. Some

Toronto City Council Chairman Fred Gardiner inspects a model civil defence fallout shelter, 1960. Photographer Ralph Haymer, *Toronto Daily Star.*

builders included shelters in new housing projects, such as the luxury apartments in the wealthy neighbourhood of Oak Bay in Victoria that came equipped with a basement locker room supplied with blast doors, exhaust fans, and a small kitchen and bathroom.[47] One door-to-door bomb shelter salesman shared his gendered sales pitch with CBC Radio in 1958. He described how he would canvass suburban neighbourhoods, knock on the door, and ask whoever answered, "What would you do if a bomb went off right now?" He claimed men tended to laugh nervously, while women reacted more quietly and thoughtfully, saying they would take shelter in the cellar. The salesman would then launch into his pitch, describing how an improvised shelter would not be safe from radiation, and compared building a proper one to buying car insurance: you invested in it even if you hoped to never need it. And wasn't the protection of your family a worthwhile investment? The salesman claimed wives were more likely to buy than their husbands, who appeared ashamed to admit they were unable to protect their family by themselves.[48] Despite the salesman's obvious enthusiasm for his product, men and women failed to embrace the shelter program. Canadians may have endorsed the health and welfare component of civil defence, but few were keen to hide underground and hope for the best.

Not surprisingly, financial constraints made it difficult for many families to commit to building their own shelter. An average shelter cost between $500 and $1,500 to build and stock, a major expense for the average Canadian family in the late 1950s. Low-interest loans were available from the National Housing Association to build a shelter, but few Canadians took advantage of this financing.[49] Unless you lived in a house that you owned, space and permission to build were also issues. Apartment dwellers were advised to negotiate with their landlords to build a communal shelter for all residents in the basement. If you could not afford to construct a proper shelter, the EMO explained that you could improvise by placing bedsprings or boards against a workbench or heavy table, preferably in the basement, and piling mattresses on each end.[50] The notion that civilians were expected to arrange and pay for their own security appalled women like Natalie Dubois, a mother of seven living in northern Quebec. She wrote to Diefenbaker in 1961 asking where she could find the money to build a fallout shelter when it was difficult enough to make ends meet for her large family.[51] Others, such as Maybeth Winslow, felt that if the government was truly serious about saving lives it would build public shelters in every town and city so all Canadians had a chance to survive, even the "poorer inhabitants of our big centres."[52] Under this self-help system, many Canadians were left out of civil defence. Realistically only able-bodied middle-class and wealthier families living in single-family dwellings with enough land and resources to build and stock a shelter could participate.

Money was only one concern. Building a shelter was also considered a moral dilemma. Should you refuse to let your shelter-less neighbours inside? Would building a shelter encourage war? Would there be any point in living in a post-nuclear world anyway? *Chatelaine* addressed these issues in a 1962 article "Can you Protect Your Family from the Bomb?" that took readers through the imagined steps of what would happen in an attack and informed readers about the EMO's recommended survival methods. The article showed how conflicted women were about this domestic side of civil defence. One Ottawa housewife stated,

> I've changed my mind about building a shelter at least ten times. Some things I read make me feel it's nothing but escapism to imagine having a chance if you retreat into a hole in the ground. The next minute I wonder whether I am doing right by my children, that if there is any chance at all of survival and a lot of experts seem to think there is, I ought to at least try.[53]

Another mother wrote to syndicated advice columnist Ann Landers asking if she and her husband should spend their savings on building a recreation room or a fallout shelter. Landers consulted experts and concluded that it was worthwhile for the family to build a shelter because "I feel the race should not allow itself to commit mass suicide. We must make an effort, no matter how slim the chances of survival may seem, to save ourselves and our young children."[54] Interestingly, she added that, despite her research, she would not build a shelter herself because she had no "desire to live in a world of maimed and sick people ... I would prefer to stay above the ground and try to live each day with dignity—and take whatever comes."[55]

Women also pointed out that child care would be a problem for families considering using a shelter. Some mothers were fearful of an attack happening in the daytime when only women and preschool children could use the family's shelter, leading one woman to speculate they would be rebuilding a world stocked with only mothers and young children.[56] Another letter, from grandmother Jean Darcy, suggested that even if a family were together in a shelter, having to "survive 14 days in a cubby hole—dark—no fresh air, no water to keep clean, no space to move, no plan to work off energy— nothing but fear and terror ... Can't you hear the poor babies crying and driving their parents crazy long before release."[57] For Darcy, shelters were just another example of how out of touch the government was with reality, and in this case their ignorance was putting all Canadian lives at risk. Instead she asked the government to stop relying on the bomb and develop alternative measures that she and other "prudent" Canadians thought were possible.[58] Homemakers' concerns were usually expressed in maternal tones, pointing out the flaws in civil defence planning in relation to their families' needs, but they also demonstrated considerable knowledge of government policies, foreign affairs, and up-to-date scientific data.

Drills such as Operation Tocsin B, a nationally coordinated civil defence exercise that simulated a coast-to-coast attack on Canada in November 1961, stirred up considerable criticism from mothers. Played out live on CBC Radio, Tocsin B's imagined scenario featured 250 Russian bombers attacking the NORAD facility in North Bay along with Vancouver, Toronto, Montreal, Halifax, Goose Bay, Edmonton, Ottawa, Windsor, Niagara Falls, Cold Lake, and Stephenville. The outcome was an estimated 1.5 million Canadians dead and 2.5 million injured, and it was predicted that fallout from Vancouver would have made it all the way to Medicine Hat by noon. Provincial and federal governments called the exercise "enlightening" because it brought attention to faulty equipment, such as some malfunctioning sirens, and the weak links in procedures, such as slow communication between government agencies.[59] Meanwhile female critics of Tocsin B complained in letters to newspapers and letters directly to Diefenbaker that these types of imagined scenarios were farcical since they did not take into consideration the true chaos emanating from an attack or the psychological effect of not knowing what would happen when a person emerged from a shelter. Frances Hill, a mother of four from Ottawa, called shelters the government's way of administering "tranquilizers" to the public in order to lull Canadians (or perhaps more specifically, lull women, given the gendered connotation of tranquilizers) into a "dream-like sense of false security."[60] She also suggested that civil defence tests such as Tocsin B or the McCallum family experiment were faulty. Hill believed a real test of readiness would entail the government grabbing a mother and father at random and giving them

> 20 minutes notice to collect their families (and their wits), [and] herd them into one of these shelters ... and don't give them time to gather their children from the various schools they might attend (our four are at three different ones, not close together), don't give them contact with the outside world ... [but] do assure them that they really have no idea what to expect in the event of a "real" nuclear attack, when they emerge—thirsty and hungry, unwashed and undoubtedly half-crazed with fear and worry for their loved ones.[61]

This was a problem Winifred McCallum had alluded to after leaving the shelter. She called her experimental week "peaceful," but admits that this was only because she was aware a real war was not going on.[62] Another letter came from a group of female university students concerned about the practicality of using shelters. They asked Diefenbaker to "think of pregnant women unable to get medical attention. Think of small children crying, needing diaper-wash, boiling of bottles or the run around child with no outlet for activity for an indefinite period." They begged the government to put aside civil defence because it is "no solution for our children. Peace through disarmament is the only defence. Nothing less can save us."[63] Meanwhile Linda Matheson used her best motherly tone to call Tocsin B "so infantile and inhuman a 'game' … How could the top men of our country act like so many little boys playing at war?"[64] She suggested the time and money wasted on civil defence should have been used to set up a Ministry of Peace, a sentiment echoed by Goldie Josephy, who asked sarcastically if the government planned to follow Tocsin B with "Exercise 'Peace' in which a similar all-out effort was made to tackle the problems arising if peace should breakout."[65]

Diefenbaker was dismayed at the number of mothers who found fault with this form of civil defence, especially since they were the target group he most wanted to reach. In response to the female-dominated protests over Tocsin B, Diefenbaker called women's concerns "well intentioned" but he downplayed their significance by making their criticism appear irrational and emotional. In his public response, he attributed women's annoyance to their children having been awakened from their naps by the warning sirens. Diefenbaker also gave an example of one woman from Ottawa who was so frightened by Tocsin B that she refused to send her children to school the next day for fear of an attack. This rhetoric made the complaining women's fears appear illogical and blamed communist propaganda for encouraging Canadians to feel it was wrong to prepare for nuclear war.[66]

Ironically, Diefenbaker himself was revealed to have his own problems following civil defence orders. During his tenure as prime minister, the federal government secretly began constructing its own private fallout shelter. Nicknamed "the Diefenbunker" and measuring 100,000 square feet, the underground facility would act as the emergency government headquarters, providing safety and resources for the government to continue functioning in the event of a nuclear attack. Located in Carp, 20 kilometres outside of Ottawa, the facility could withstand a five-megaton nuclear weapon detonated 1.8 kilometres away. It was made of 32,000 cubic yards of concrete and 50 tonnes of steel, and it had thirty days' worth of food and water for 500 people, including the prime minister and his cabinet, government officials, and military VIPs, but none of their spouses or children.[67] Although Diefenbaker approved the bunker's construction, he vowed to never use it himself, claiming to prefer remaining home with his wife in their own personal shelter.[68] Members of the Opposition criticized this noble sentiment, implying that the prime minister did not have the luxury of living up to the family values implicit in civil defence planning. He needed to be running the country in his specially designed fortress built with taxpayer dollars, not, as Liberal member of Parliament Judy LaMarsh quipped, "sitting with his dog on his lap and his wife's hand in his hand, in his own home."[69] In modelling what he preached to millions of Canadians, perhaps Diefenbaker truly could not bear to be separated from his family in a crisis, or maybe he thought voters would find his homespun sensibility attractive.

The Decline of Civil Defence

While all twenty senior EMO officials claimed to have built fallout shelters for their own families, a 1964 government survey revealed that, out of a population of approximately 18 million Canadians, only 3,000 shelters were known to be in existence across the country.[70] Even the 1962 Cuban Missile Crisis sparked more of a whimper than an outcry for shelters. When American intelligence reports revealed that there were nuclear missiles under development in Cuba that could reach as far north as Hudson Bay and anywhere in Canada east of Regina, only a handful of Canadians appeared to react to the news by seeking information on civil defence, and not much could be done for those who did.[71] Over the two days when the American military was on its highest alert, 1,700 calls were placed to Toronto's EMO office and 200 to Montreal's. Operators informed their callers, whom they described as "sombre" and "very worried" rather than panicked, that all they could do was mail them a pamphlet because "there was no time to tell [them what to do] over the phone."[72] In Vancouver, EMO officials reported that some callers confessed they felt their best bet was to abandon the city and flee to the interior.[73] Following the diplomatic resolution to the crisis, there was no mad rush to build bomb shelters or a public demand for the government to expand its civil defence plans. If anything, having the nuclear doomsday clock come precariously close to midnight in 1962 seemed to make many Canadians dismiss civil defence as a practical solution. Although some lack of interest can be traced to civil defence plans that were poorly executed (illustrated by, for example, malfunctioning warning sirens), overall, limited support was due to growing public awareness about the destructive power of nuclear weapons and falling public confidence that civil defence could protect even the most prepared Canadians. Driven by this acknowledgement, a year later, the United States, the United Kingdom, and the Soviet Union signed a Limited Test Ban Treaty. This agreement did not decrease the huge stockpile of existing nuclear weapons, but it appeared to diminish the threat of war. This coincided with the election of Prime Minister Pearson, whose Liberal government vowed to cut the federal budget and, in light of the treaty, saw civil defence funding as a low priority. Provinces and municipalities began to reorganize their civil defence organizations to focus on preparedness for peacetime emergencies such as search and rescue and providing food, shelter, and clothing for victims of natural disasters.[74]

Public records document the participation of women's organizations and female workers in civil defence programs, but it is difficult to measure homemakers' commitment to civil defence within their individual homes. Letters to EMO officials and politicians by women identifying themselves specifically as mothers demonstrate their interest in the program, but it is impossible to know how much significance it was afforded in their private, everyday lives.[75] We know many homemakers took courses in first aid and home nursing sponsored by women's organizations, but how many, for example, fireproofed their curtains, designed a family evacuation plan, or dressed their children in light-coloured clothes? Despite not knowing exact figures, the paucity of shelters built and the public outcry (especially by mothers) regarding their proposed use indicate a large gap between the expectations of the EMO, where homemakers were told they were the most critical players in civil defence, and women's actual acceptance of this responsibility. This inconsistency speaks to both flaws in the civil defence plans and the difficulty of engaging homemakers in a program based on what-ifs when they were busy raising their children, running a household, going to work, and making ends meet. Their ambiguous response also suggests civil defence was harder to swallow when the target was directly positioned over your family's head and the armour offered as protection—preparation, organization, and morale—seemed wholly inadequate against plutonium and uranium.

Ironically, the state's promotion of civil defence as a women's issue provided women with a solid education about nuclear issues that contributed to building a loud and active female-driven wing of the Canadian peace movement. Whether they had read a few pamphlets, listened to the drills on the radio, or trained to be a neighbourhood warden, women would be familiar with the physical and psychological side effects of atomic warfare. No matter how optimistic one was about the ability of civil defence to ensure life would go on, it was clear that a nuclear war would radically alter Canada's path. As a result, large numbers of women openly rejected the promises of civil defence, and by doing so challenged the Cold War consensus through their search for peaceful alternatives. Just as civil defence harnessed women's maternal energy in the name of war, peace and disarmament used the same ideology to prevent the Cold War from getting hot.

CHAPTER THREE

In the Name of Children
The Disarmament Movement

In 1965 Dr. Ursula Franklin found herself the recipient of over 45,000 baby teeth donated by Canadian mothers whose children proudly wore stickers that declared "I gave my tooth for science."[1] Each tooth was accompanied by a record detailing the mother's place of residence during her pregnancy, the child's date and place of birth, the number of months the child was breast- or bottle-fed, and the child's age when the tooth was lost. Franklin, a physicist at the Ontario Research Federation, who identified as a Quaker, pacifist, and feminist, was chairwoman of the research committee for the peace organization Voice of Women (VOW). With help from local women's groups, kindergarten teachers, school boards, public health departments, dentists, dental nurses, and dentists' wives, Franklin coordinated VOW's teeth collection for Dr. Murray Hunt, director of dental research at the University of Toronto's school of dentistry, who was conducting a study on how radioactive elements, specifically strontium-90 (Sr-90), were absorbed by the body. It was already known that unborn babies, infants, and teenagers, whose bodies were at critical stages of maximum bone formation, were more vulnerable to radiation. Therefore, there was widespread speculation that the atmospheric radiation produced by nuclear weapon tests put these age groups more at risk than the general population.[2] Franklin was so convinced of the hazards of radiation that she gave her own two children calcium supplements to combat any doses of Sr-90 because she would "rather they had kidney stones [from the extra calcium] at 40 than Leukemia at an earlier age."[3] The concern over the health risks posed by frequent weapons testing by the Americans, British, and Soviets in the late 1950s and early 1960s prompted Canadian mothers to donate ten times the number of teeth Hunt needed. The thousands of loose teeth collected by VOW presented an image both tender and macabre, representing both motherly love and the danger that children could lose more than their teeth.

VOW's tooth project faced criticism from the Minister of Health and Welfare Judy LaMarsh, who suggested that a box of randomly collected baby teeth had no scientific value. This appeared to be a cheap shot from the Liberal government eager to discredit VOW activists who had harshly criticized Prime Minister Pearson for allowing nuclear weapons into Canada. LaMarsh's dismissal of the project's merits implied that VOW's gendered motivations made them unsuitable partners in research.[4] Franklin was confident that their research would stand up; because of the lingering assumption that female activists were emotional rather than rational, VOW had made doubly sure of its facts before taking action. Franklin, who declined to take part in the lab work for fear of being seen as biased, insisted, "We reject the alternative—'Dead or red.' We feel there is a way to achieve peace in the world. But we must be knowledgeable on political, technological and economical aspects so nobody can shout us down."[5] By 1966 Hunt had enough research to conclude that, judging by the teeth they collected, radiation from fallout did not appear to be the hazard they feared. Yet the results demonstrated an increased amount of radiation in soil and milk, and there was a twofold increase in Sr-90 concentration in the bones of young children, especially those who were bottle-fed. There was also evidence of extremely high concentrations of radiation in teeth donated from Inuit communities in northern Canada, where it was suspected the main food source, caribou, had been contaminated with radiation.[6] The tests were most successful in creating a baseline for further study, especially for children born in 1961–1962, the period with the highest number of weapon tests, who had yet to lose their baby teeth.[7]

The understanding that fallout was an invisible and irreversible pollutant drove thousands of women to join the peace and disarmament movement in the 1950s and 1960s. In Franklin's opinion, mothers above everyone else understood that the disarmament crusade was "not something that we can leave to others, this is a common problem, it's not my problem, it's not your problem, it's our problem, it's not my children, it's not your children, it's every child and if we cannot get together and say that it has to stop, God help us."[8] Rather than see civil defence and fallout shelters as protection from the nuclear threat, these women demanded an end to the arms race in the name of their children and children everywhere. The belief that war was inhumane because it threatened children's lives or, at the very least, stole from them a peaceful future had been the cornerstone of women's peace activism for almost a century. Just as there was a long tradition of women mobilizing to support Canada's war efforts, there had always been a parallel effort of women working to end or prevent war. Tired of losing their husbands and sons to war and knowing how women and children had suffered and died from war-related misery, reform-minded Canadian women had been mobilizing against imperialism and militarism in women-only and mixed-gender peace groups since the late nineteenth century. In a peaceful world, they believed the lives of women and children would improve since everything from maternal health to child welfare to human rights would be served better in a culture dedicated to peace.[9]

The impetus for this early mobilization had many origins: religion, humanism, socialism, egalitarianism, and internationalism; however, many women found it inspiring and useful to organize around the tenets of maternal feminism. This ideology was founded on the popular assumption that women were caring, co-operative, and nurturing, qualities that positioned them as natural-born peacemakers and just political participants. Furthermore, their biological capabilities and experiences with motherhood made them inherently opposed to death, violence, and destruction. Therefore if masculine qualities such as individuality, aggression, and competitiveness fostered war, maternal feminists argued that war could be avoided by following feminine qualities.[10] To achieve their aims, Canada's first female peace activists campaigned for suffrage and formed links with women in other nations through the Women's International League for Peace and Freedom (WILPF). Given the contentious nature of peace activism in any era, maternal feminism was viewed as a powerful justification for women's political participation. The maternalistic rhetoric was also a useful tool in uniting women from different nations, backgrounds, and beliefs in the shared interest of making the world safer for women, children, and families. Despite a strong tradition of peace activism in Canada, historian Barbara Roberts cautiously reminds her readers that female peace activists were always outnumbered by those who supported war or at least did not vocally oppose it, since "most women have supported or at least tolerated the policies and outlook of those in power."[11]

The women's Cold War peace movement had much in common with the earlier years of activism, yet there were new dimensions caused by the advent of nuclear technology and Canada's expanded role in world affairs. Even with suffrage gained for most Canadian women, Canada's postwar Parliament remained male dominated. This prompted Cold War peace activists to seek action from outside the government in the security and familiarity of women-only organizations. Through these bodies they lobbied politicians to support peace over war, liaised with women overseas, and relied heavily on maternal rhetoric, imagery, and campaigns to explain their cause. As in the past, the female activists faced charges of disloyalty for suggesting war was not in the best interests of Canada and implying the threat to world peace lay not in communist enemies but in the existence of the atomic bomb. Nuclear weaponry meant that the activists were not only up against centuries of masculine militarism, they were confronted with a weapon that had changed the face of war and threatened to end all life on the planet. The new technology meant that the activists had to educate themselves in the science behind the bomb and in turn use that knowledge to demonstrate its dangers. Another difference was that Canada held more autonomy midcentury than it had fifty years earlier. Although Canadian peace activists still embraced internationalism, they felt that their nation's middle-power status allowed them to play a special role as mediators and role models.

It took the threat of nuclear war to see the largest public mobilization of Canadian women for peace. Even so, women came to the Cold War peace movement from different trajectories, depending on their politics, religious beliefs, and the times in which they grew up. Some activists had been lifelong pacifists. Muriel Duckworth, a teacher and mother born in Montreal in 1908, always had a strong theological commitment to peace, which stemmed from her Quaker faith, her membership in the Student Christian Movement, and her studies at the Union Theological Seminary. Duckworth dedicated her life to social justice and pacifism, although she admits wavering in her faith during the interwar period, when the destructive forces of fascism made her question her commitment to peaceful resistance.[12] Ultimately Duckworth's pacifism held strong in the years leading up to and through the Second World War, and she continued her activism into the Cold War period, when she became a national and provincial leader in VOW. For other women, the Second World War was the starting point in their commitment to peace activism. Duckworth's good friend Ursula Franklin was born in Germany in 1921; she spent part of the Second World War in a concentration camp with her Jewish mother and part living in Berlin repairing buildings destroyed by bombs. Franklin's first-hand experiences with the violence, death, and devastation associated with war led her to conclude that "war doesn't work, even for the winner."[13] Other women, such as Duckworth's friend and biographer, Marion Kerans, a mother of six raising her family in postwar Canada, only joined the peace movement in the late 1950s when she was inspired by the fear of nuclear weapons testing to start a mothers' group to study the effects of radiation on children's health. Together Duckworth, Franklin, and Kerans came together in a chorus of "never again." In these activists' minds, the bomb's existence was the real Cold War problem, and removing it from the equation was seen as the first step toward finding common ground between regimes promoting capitalism and communism.

These old traditions and new impetuses contributed to the vast mobilization of women—young and old, French and English—from across the country, women who were confident enough about their duty and righteousness to face police surveillance, demand meetings with prime ministers, travel to enemy nations, publish articles and books outlining alternatives to war, and raise thousands of dollars to establish the Canadian Peace Research Institute. In the early postwar years amid the Red Scare, peace groups such as WILPF were ostracized over their calls to stop the arms race, recognize China, and give the UN more resources and power. As the nuclear threat rose in the late 1950s, more women formed a vocal female-led wing of Canada's disarmament crusade, most notably through VOW. This activism peaked in the 1960s, when women were inspired not only by the fear of nuclear war, but by the spirit of reform and radicalism evident in the civil rights movement and the New Left. Along with their anti-war crusades, peace-minded women encouraged Canadians to build a culture of peace at home by promoting non-violence through the boycotting of war toys, engaging with local social justice issues such as multiculturalism, and becoming global citizens. For many leaders, peace activism became a full-time unpaid job, causing familial, career, or other voluntary obligations to be pushed aside in the crusade to save the world. This wave of Cold War activism raised public awareness of the risks to children's health and safety associated with testing and using nuclear weaponry, and it was influential in persuading heads of state to pass the 1963 Nuclear Test Ban Treaty. As with pro- and anti-civil-defence interest groups, the peace and disarmament movement was another way women asserted political influence during the first three decades of the Cold War. For many activists, the skills and experience gained through peace activism contributed to their consciousness-raising and should be recognized as an important contributor to the intense wave of feminist activism between 1965 and 1975.

From Red Scare to Nuclear Fear: 1945-1960

Unlike the roar of the 1960s, there was a muted response from women peace activists in the first decade and a half after World War II. Peace became a contentious term in the immediate postwar period, as it was considered by many Canadians to be a concept more in line with communism than democracy. As Steve Hewitt and Reg Whitaker have demonstrated, to talk openly about peace was subversive and those who did were labelled communist or communist sympathizers, because in the minds of Canadian government officials, "the Western camp stood for 'freedom' and the Eastern camp stood for 'peace.'"[14] During this period, the only respectable way to advocate for peace was to support the UN, and even then, that was most safely done in a state-sanctioned organization such as the United Nations Association (UNA), which will be discussed in the following chapter. The damnation of peace activism occurred even though many Canadians admitted to being only cautiously optimistic about global security in the early postwar period. The day before Japan officially surrendered to the Allies in 1945, journalist Dorothy Thompson predicted the upcoming Cold War in a *Globe and Mail* editorial by stating, "If we are no longer at war, we are not at peace." If the new world order and promises of modern science could maintain the peace, she asked, would it be a "peace for the peoples" or a "peace of terror"?[15]

Most peace organizations active in the years immediately following the Second World War agreed that the presence of the atomic bomb would lead to "a peace of terror." In this era WILPF was the most prominent and oldest women's peace organization in Canada and had branches in Vancouver, Winnipeg, Toronto, and Ottawa. Founded during the First World War, WILPF vowed "to bring together women of different political views and philosophical and religious backgrounds determined to study and make known the causes of war and work for a permanent peace."[16] Initially WILPF's peace work was greeted by most Canadian men and women with hostility or dismissed as unrealistic, but it gained some credence in the interwar period when it worked closely with the League of Nations.[17] Meanwhile World War II tore apart WILPF both geographically and ideologically. With borders closed and travel dangerous, women could not meet with their fellow activists in belligerent or neutral states. Furthermore, many members left WILPF, concluding that war might not be noble, but it would be better than what Hitler had planned. This left the remaining members to lament the organization's spiralling momentum after twenty years of work. In Canada, WILPF experienced isolation, and work was hampered by the distances between its four branches and by the nation's tremendous pro-war mentality.[18] In April 1945, the remaining members celebrated WILPF's thirtieth birthday in San Francisco and gathered for the first meeting of the UN, where WILPF members set forth a four-point plan for peace based on international co-operation and "a new concept of 'security,' not based on military power and prestige."[19] Unfortunately, the advent and use of the atomic bomb that summer only enhanced the association of security with military power for most nation states.

As a means of resisting the nuclear threat, Canadian branches of WILPF developed numerous policy reforms that they believed would position the UN as a true peacemaker and Canada as an influential peace-minded nation. Like most peace activist groups, WILPF had great hope for the UN, and it was among the first non-governmental organizations to receive consultative status with the new world body. However, the initial optimism turned to disappointment in 1950 when the UN supported militarism over mediation to settle the dispute between North and South Korea.[20] WILPF called for Canada, as a UN member nation, to bring democracy and peace back to the UN by lobbying for disarmament, banning all nuclear weapons tests, recognizing China, pushing for a permanent UN peacekeeping force, and supporting the UN's plan for a universal language.[21] In order to accomplish these goals and remain a strong voice at the UN, WILPF also outlined what the Canadian government could do at home to improve international relations. It recommended that Canada implement a more independent foreign policy and move away from a close association with the antagonistic United States. Additionally, WILPF asserted that Canada should build a culture of peace at home by developing a Canadian Bill of Rights and should provide better housing and employment options for poor Canadians, immigrants, and refugees.[22] The Canadian government viewed the ideological and structural reforms proposed by WILPF as inherently socialist and potentially traitorous, since they favoured internationalism over national interests and positioned the bomb as the real enemy, not the Soviet Union. The state feared that peace organizations were a front for the Communist Party and might act as fifth-column supporters. Therefore the Royal Canadian Mounted Police (RCMP) was instructed to monitor the behaviour of peace groups and individual activists for subversive activities.

The Canadian Peace Congress (CPC), founded in 1949 by James Endicott, a United Church minister and former missionary to China, and his wife, Mary Austin Endicott, bore the brunt of the Red Scare state scrutiny. According to the federal government, the Endicotts' mission for world peace and international friendship was tainted by the CPC's sympathy to the merits of communism and communist China. Although James Endicott never openly identified himself as a communist, he estimated that the majority of CPC members were Communist Party members. The Endicotts and the CPC spent the 1950s dodging accusations of Soviet infiltration and other forms of harassment, including seizure of material, body searches, and public name-calling.[23] This fate was shared by the CPC's sister organization, the Canadian Congress of Women, a communist-led women's organization that listed peace as one of its aims.[24] Both groups appeared repeatedly in pages of *The Alert Service* blacklist reports described in chapter 1.

Although not as hot a target as the CPC, the Canadian branches of WILPF suffered directly and indirectly from the suspicion facing their fellow peace activists; as a result, they never recovered the membership or public support they had had before World War II. Despite WILPF's endorsement of the UN, the organization's peace rhetoric—especially its support of China—and its ties with women in countries behind the Iron Curtain were worrisome enough for the government to watch WILPF and its members. Sheila Young, the Vancouver branch's corresponding secretary, reported to the WILPF executive in Geneva that "we recognize that 'red smearing,' with its harmful effects falls to the lot of all progressive minds, if they persist in honesty and fearlessness," but she remained confident that "the sacrifice of persecuted individuals would create a better world."[25] Though her eloquent words suggest perseverance in the face of these attacks, Young decided it was better to be safe than sorry, so she destroyed many of WILPF's membership lists and files in an attempt to protect the anonymity of their members.[26] Amid this persecution, low membership numbers forced the Ottawa and Winnipeg branches to close.[27] Meanwhile, activities in Toronto and Vancouver were hampered by dwindling membership and conflicts between executives.[28]

Despite being a women-only organization, WILPF did not employ openly maternalistic overtones. Its arguments for peace were based on what it considered to be rational insights for maintaining equity and balance in international relations. The only WILPF project directly related to children in the 1940s and 1950s was the Vancouver-based campaign to ban toy weapons in Canada. In an appeal to parents and toy stores, WILPF called for an end to the sale of toy guns and other toy weapons of war because they "arouse the desire to kill. They breed ideas of enmity and unfriendliness." It asked parents to buy constructive and educational toys that "develop habits of give and take, co-operation and goodwill" and boycott the stores that sold war toys. WILPF told parents this small gesture would "prepare the innocent minds of your children for a peaceful tomorrow by ending games based upon the horrors of war."[29] Despite the "suspect" nature of the organization, Vancouver police collaborated on the toy gun campaign with the local WILPF branch. This one-time co-operation suggests the police hoped the ban would limit the number of young offenders, but it also implies that one could frame peace as a children's issue and have success in making allies out of enemies. The WILPF toy gun campaign brought peace activism down to a level most Canadians could appreciate and avoided contentious geopolitics. While not precluding frank discussions about foreign affairs and defence, VOW would have great success in generating public awareness and support for their peace campaigns in the 1960s by placing children front and centre in all their campaigns.[30]

The long list of recommended reforms coming out of WILPF and organizations such as the CPC were overshadowed by a new breed of peace groups founded in the late 1950s. Rather than getting bogged down in debates over the merits of different forms of global governance, new organizations were founded on a three-word principle: Ban the bomb. A 1960 poll claimed that 45 percent of Canadians were in favour of nuclear weapons, 21 percent against, and 34 percent undecided.[31] Ban the Bomb groups aimed to woo the undecided faction by proving the dangers of nuclear weapons. With a reasoning not unlike WILPF's motivation for banning toy guns, Ban the Bomb groups believed outlawing such destructive tools of war would immediately increase world security. The ultimate goal was to have nations disarm completely, but an interconnected and perhaps more realistic aim was to have nations stop testing weapons. Dr. Joan Harrison, a mother of three boys and a scientist at the University of Toronto, argued that it was important to combine "ban-the-tests" groups with "ban-the-bomb" groups because they addressed two interlinked threats.[32] Since 1945, dozens of atomic and hydrogen bomb tests had been conducted in the underpopulated islands of the South Pacific, as well as in isolated areas of North America (Nevada, New Mexico, Colorado, Mississippi, and Alaska) and Eastern Europe (Kazakhstan, the Ural mountains, the Ukraine, Uzbekistan, and Turkmenistan). Initially these tests were limited because nuclear powers did not have many weapons to spare; however, by the late 1950s, both the Americans and Russians had stockpiled significant numbers of weapons, and testing peaked between 1959 and 1962.[33] Activists believed eliminating tests would slow progress in weapons development, but they also objected to the tests on the grounds that peacetime explosions were not risk-free.

In an anti-war toy campaign similar to those of WILPF and VOW, the Canadian Campaign for Nuclear Disarmament encouraged parents to buy peaceful toys for Christmas, 1964. Courtesy of The William Ready Division of Archives and Research Collections, McMaster University Library.

Although government officials insisted the tests were harmless, there was lingering doubt among activists as to how that could be possible. Long before the bombings of Hiroshima and Nagasaki, there was an awareness that radiation exposure could lead to birth defects, thyroid disease, and various cancers. How could successive explosions thrusting radioactive particles into the air be safe? Moreover there was concern that it was impossible to control the danger of these tests; they were unpredictable, and the radiation released in supposedly remote areas could find its way to populated regions by human error or unpredictable winds and rain. On the movie screen, this speculation launched dozens of radiated monsters and landscapes as a horror-film staple of the 1950s.[34] The United States' first test of a dry fuel thermonuclear weapon, code named Castle Bravo, at Bikini Atoll in the Marshall Islands in March 1954 proved real-life events could be just as terrifying. The secret test became an international incident when the weapon surpassed expectations, proving to have almost double the scope and power. The international press reported that a change in wind direction caused the radioactive fallout to spread immediately to nearby inhabited islands and eventually make its way to Japan, India, Australia, and even parts of the United States and Europe.[35] Japan complained that radiation from the test had contaminated hundreds of thousands of fish, and it claimed that radiation sickness overtook the crew of a Japanese tuna fishing boat, *Lucky Dragon Number Five*, working in an area of the ocean thought to be safe. The United States initially denied these charges and went so far as to allege that the fishermen were spies until photos and medical reports proved radiation poisoning had occurred. The death of one fisherman and the subsequent increased rates of birth defects and cancers among the Marshall Islands' inhabitants and U.S. military personnel fuelled panic and anger over atmospheric testing.[36]

One of the first Canadian Ban the Bomb groups immediately positioned their goal as a women's issue. In the late 1950s Marion Kerans, a West Vancouver homemaker, started a mothers' study group as an offshoot of her bridge club to spread the word about the effects of atmospheric radiation emitted by nuclear weapons tests on children's health.[37] Kerans was particularly interested in the role weapons testing played in spreading radiation in the food chain. With the help of Camille Mather, a psychiatric nurse and alderwoman from Burnaby, Kerans organized over 800 women across the province into the B.C. Women's Committee against Radiation Hazards. Edmonton housewife Mary Van Stolk started a similar group for Alberta mothers, called the Canadian Committee for the Control of Radiation

Hazards (CCCRH). Fearing that cows or their food sources might be contaminated by airborne radiation, both groups attempted to lobby the Canadian government to test radiation levels in milk. As seen in the work of Julie Guard and Denyse Baillargeon, the availability and safety of milk has long drawn the attention of women activists.[38] In this Cold War example, Van Stolk looked outside her circle of concerned mothers for new allies and gathered together professors, physicians, religious leaders, writers, and other intellectuals to form an energetic campaign against nuclear weapons. Once it was juggling multiple types of professional expertise, the CCCRH became male dominated and moved away from its maternal angle to a more masculine scientific one, which led to Van Stolk being replaced as the CCCRH spokesperson in 1961. Despite the change in direction, Roberts argues it is still important to recognize that Canada's earliest Ban the Bomb groups sprang from the queries and efforts of mothers.[39] By the time CCCRH abandoned child welfare as the rationale for its disarmament crusade, a new organization had filled this vacuum. From its founding in 1960, VOW combined the political, scientific, and religious arguments found in other groups, while emphasizing women's special connection to peace work. Throughout the 1960s and into the 1970s, it was Canada's most prominent and active women's organization.

"Voices" Raised for Children

VOW came into existence in the summer of 1960, its birth sparked by a series of columns by columnist Lotta Dempsey in the women's section of *The Toronto Daily Star*. Dempsey asked women, "What can we do?" in response to the cancelled East–West summit between American president Dwight Eisenhower and Soviet premier Nikita Khrushchev, which dissolved when the Soviets shot down an American U-2 spy plane in their airspace. This event was a return to tense relations for the two superpowers, and in the commotion that followed, the Soviets attempted to make Canada complicit in the spy drama. They argued that Canada was the logical place for American planes to land or refuel on their spy missions to Russia and suggested the Royal Canadian Air Force might be doing their own spying during their frequent polar patrols of the Canadian Arctic. External Affairs Minister Howard Green denied these charges, admitting only to allowing American U-2 planes to fly from Canadian bases for meteorological missions.[40] *The Toronto Daily Star* covered the spy plane incident on its front page for several days, but it was Dempsey's columns about the same events that struck a nerve with women readers, perhaps because she made the story familiar by using maternal rhetoric that compared the abortive summit to a broken family, showing how women were affected by Cold War tensions, and insisting women could bring order to this chaos.

Dempsey, a journalist in her sixties, had written for newspapers and magazines since the 1920s, predominantly about beauty and family issues but occasionally drifting into more worldly matters. As someone who had lived through both World Wars, she felt stirred to speak out about the terror of the Cold War. Appalled at the risk that "hate-mad and missile-happy foreign adversaries" (meaning both the Americans and Soviets) were taking with their spy games and power plays, Dempsey's column on 17 May 1968 seethed with anger at the possibility of what a third world war would do to Canada and the world. While she praised Canada's civil defence director Major-General F. F. Worthington for making "more sense than a good many other brass hats," she did not advise Canadians to seek shelter from the coming storm; instead, she proposed that "as Canadians we raise one united protest against the desecration of our fertile, giving lands and our peaceful people."[41] Her first summit column was buried among four articles on the women's page that day—the others dealing with the plight of working mothers, the annual meeting of the United Church Women's Association, the description of a nurse's wedding, and a list of recent engagements, accompanied by several fashion advertisements. Yet despite its seemingly out-of-place appearance, Dempsey's historic column triggered a flood of letters from women echoing her fears about the sad fate of the world and the role Canadian women should take on behalf of their country and sex to fix it.

Hundreds of letters came from female *Toronto Daily Star* readers across Ontario and in other provinces. There were messages from young mothers with toddlers worrying about never seeing their children grow up; grandmothers cursing the heavens for allowing the world to be on the brink of devastation; working and professional women offering their skills for the cause; young girls volunteering to organize something in their schools; club women describing how they can mobilize members from their organizations; recent immigrants from Europe describing their experiences in the last war; women who had already spoken out on the issues by writing to the prime minister; and others who stated they were contemplating taking action for the first time in their lives.[42] The enthusiasm radiating from the letters spoke of the potential for women's presence on the world stage. For example, Margo Gamsby from Clarkson imagined Dempsey's readers could form a delegation of women united for peace, potentially converging on the

UN to demand change because "thousands of women putting their collective foot down in no uncertain manner, and representing as they would thousands more, might get through to the powers that be that we refuse to have our families destroyed."[43]

In her follow-up columns Dempsey printed excerpts of letters like one from Gamsby proposing not only the union of Canadian women but of all women. Mavis Wiley from Downsview offered to scream along with Dempsey, but suggested, "Let us not scream alone—let us urge the women of the world to join us. I say 'women of the world' and that is just what I mean. Russian women—Chinese women—African women. All the women of the world."[44] Dempsey agreed, and perhaps inspired by the civil rights movement, pleaded with Canadian women to put aside cultural and racial differences and unite on the basis of gender because she had "never met a woman anywhere who did not hate fighting and killing, and the loss of husbands and the terrible tragedy of children dead, maimed or left homeless and hungry. Here lies our strength."[45] This strength would unite women across cultures; it would also present the effects of war at the most individual level. Further, it would be a respectable message, seemingly divorced from divisive Cold War politics. This was a call back to attitudes originating in the international women's peace movement at the turn of the century: the assumption that women's shared experiences allowed them to find a common ground to discuss issues of war and peace, despite being separated by great distances and different ways of life. This is what WILPF, as an international organization, had achieved in the interwar period, only to be weakened by the Second World War and anti-communist politics.

If Dempsey's column implied that women were the solution, she also hinted that men were the problem. She placed blame on the heads of governments, chiefs of international affairs, and state departments for failing to secure peace; not only had the people in these roles put the world through two world wars in thirty years, the Cold War arms race was threatening to destroy civilization once and for all. Although Dempsey did not point out the gender of these individuals, it was clear she meant that men and men's ways were the problem. Other letter writers spoke more plainly of the problem, charging that men concerned themselves with gaining power through military and economic domination, while women, with their less selfish motives, were more concerned with people. Wiley, the Downsview mother, argued that Canadian women needed to take responsibility for their government's actions because it was up to "us women [to] get in and pitch—pushing our men into the doing the right thing, if necessary. For if we don't, we shall

all perish, and, as far as North Americans are concerned, we will deserve our fate."[46] Wiley's comments were reiterated by Eleanor Thompson, a nineteen-year-old mother of a six-month-old baby living outside Sudbury, who said she firmly believed in the expression, "Behind every great man is a great woman" and "perhaps if there is a great woman behind all heads of countries or towns or villages we all might be able to live happily ever after."[47]

While Dempsey's column attracted women such as Gamsby, Wiley, and Thompson who would describe themselves as average homemakers, it also got the attention of more publicly recognized women in Toronto who had connections in local government, media, and women's organizations, including *Chatelaine* editor Doris Anderson; journalist June Callwood; Janet Berton, wife of author Pierre Berton; radio host Kay Livingstone; writer Dorothy Henderson; and Bessie Touzel, executive director of the Ontario Welfare Council. They proposed to build on the momentum arising from Dempsey's column and organize more formally. Working closely with Toronto's Committee for Disarmament, these women organized several private and public meetings in June 1960 that culminated with the founding of what they first called the Women's Committee for Peace, whose name was soon changed to VOW.[48] In their first annual general meeting, it was agreed by members that VOW's purpose was to improve the world through the eradication of nuclear weapons and give women a special space in which to be involved with world issues, described in maternal tones as "a means for women to exercise responsibility for the family of mankind."[49] In VOW's first year of operation, it drew over 2,000 paid members and 10,000 newsletter subscribers; in its second year, the number of paid members more than doubled.[50]

The background and motivation of VOW's first president and vice-president represent the varied backgrounds of the women who made up VOW in its first decade of operation. Helen Tucker—a mother of two grown children, a grandmother, and a special lecturer in speech education at the University of Toronto—became VOW's first president. Tucker had years of organizational experience in the Young Women's Christian Association (YWCA), the Canadian Council of Christians and Jews, and the Canadian Association for Adult Education, and she had sat on the executive of the UNA. Josephine Davis, a mother of two young children and a documentary and television writer, was elected as vice-president. Unlike Tucker, Davis described herself as someone who was not a traditional joiner of organizations but she had recently become inspired to use her media contacts to sponsor a family of Cold War refugees.[51] Davis and Tucker were from two different generations and came to the peace cause with distinct service records. Although some women who joined VOW had long histories of involvement in women's groups and social causes, the organization calculated that over 80 percent of those who wrote to VOW claimed to be "non-joiners" like Davis, inspired by the world's desperate situation to get involved collectively for the first time.[52] This stirred great hope among VOW's organizers, because it meant they had a special opportunity to awaken the public and make effective changes.

VOW's membership records and their letters from members confirmed that they appealed to a wide variety of women. Although the group started in Ontario, soon there were members spread out geographically from the Yukon to Newfoundland, with branches forming in urban, small-town, and rural regions. VOW, also known as La Voix des femmes, had strong representation in French Canada, particularly through the leadership of Thérèse Casgrain, a Quebec feminist, long-time reformer, and active member of the Liberal party, and later, of the New Democratic Party (NDP). Casgrain became the organization's second national president in 1962 and fought to ensure the organization's commitment to bilingualism at conferences and in publications. The organization also appealed to a number of American women who had moved to Canada with draft-dodging partners or immigrated for school or employment. Just as Dempsey's column drew women of all ages, so did VOW. As noted in chapter 1, more and more married women with children were working for wages in the 1960s, making opportunities for volunteering potentially limited. Tucker and Davis also reflected the number of members who balanced part-time or full-time work outside the home with child-rearing responsibilities and their volunteerism for VOW.

When it came to class and race, however, there the organization's diversity ended. Despite some early interest from women trade unionists, VOW's early leadership and most of its leaders were middle-class. Afro-Canadian activist and actress Kay Livingstone was the only visible minority leader. This would change in the 1970s, when VOW became more self-aware of the limitations of its narrow race and class composition and made a conscious effort to recruit working-class and minority women, a time when it also made an effort to promote itself among newly formed lesbian organizations.[53] In the meantime, having members described as "prominent women" or "the wife of the well-known ..." gave the group the ability to claim automatic respectability.[54] VOW leaned heavily on the power that came from using the public and government's positive impressions of maternal feminism and class privilege. As Winnipeg member Ester Reiter recalled, VOW members would dress in good clothes when they went to protests and marches, to show the

VOW Disarmament Demonstration on Parliament Hill, 25 Sept. 1961. Courtesy of Duncan Cameron fonds, Library and Archives Canada.

police and potential critics they were respectable ladies and mothers.[55] If they looked reputable, their gender and class would help cloak their somewhat transgressive activities; however, that strategy had not protected WILPF. VOW's founders knew getting government support and approval for their organization would help avoid accusations of communist infiltration that would prevent women from joining or getting VOW's message heard. One of Tucker and Davis's first duties was to present their cause to the prime minister and party leaders.

VOW emerged at a point when the Canadian government had yet to decide whether or not Canada would become a nuclear power. The question haunting Diefenbaker's government was whether they should arm the Canadian Forces with nuclear weapons. In 1960 Diefenbaker commissioned two Bomarc anti-aircraft missile bases in North Bay as part of its commitment to NORAD; these missiles could be armed with either nuclear or conventional warheads. Amid great pressure from the United States for Canada to go nuclear, Diefenbaker's government debated the issue in terms of what it meant to national security and Canada's sovereignty. Support for Canada to remain nuclear-free came from a number of Conservatives, Liberals, and Canadian Commonwealth Federation (CCF) members, as well as Diefenbaker's own Minister of Defence Howard Green, who passionately argued for disarmament at home and internationally.[56] Given the bipartisan attitude, it was not surprising that Tucker and Davis were greeted enthusi-astically by Diefenbaker, Green, Opposition leader Lester Pearson, and CCF leader Hazen Argue on their first visit to Parliament. Davis claimed the private meetings with each leader went beyond her wildest dreams because she and Tucker were listened to and supported by the country's most influ-ential men and not "laughed at; treated as do-gooders; patted on the head and told to run along home, or chided for being just too, too naïve" as they had feared.[57] Instead they heard high praise during their interviews and received Green's official endorsement in a press conference, where he claimed VOW sounded like "an awfully good idea ... They [women] can do a great deal to help with disarmament and restore sanity to the world."[58] Green also told the press he properly vetted the group on behalf of the government and found there was nothing objectionable or "red" about their plans.[59] VOW also went after the support of key women in the government and the wives of senior politicians. By 1961 Senators Muriel Fergusson, Olive L. Irvine, Cairine Wilson, Elsie Inman, and Marianna Jodoin had joined as honorary sponsors, along with Pearson's and Argue's wives. Maryon Pearson started off as an enthusiastic member, offering to help make connections with women in China and the Soviet Union through diplomatic channels.[60] Olive Diefenbaker declined the invitation to join VOW, explaining that she was honoured but felt her name would be a liability, whether they were seeking support from or wishing to challenge the government.[61]

In the early 1960s VOW's work was divided among disarmament activ-ism, building international ties between women, and peace education.[62] VOW met regularly with the prime minister and other state officials, insisting that Canada become a leader in disarmament. Like WILPF, VOW also rec-ommended that the Canadian government recognize China and reconsider their commitment to NORAD and NATO. Franklin lobbied for Canada to stop selling uranium, even for peaceful purposes, noting how a recent sale to France of 25 percent of Canada's uranium reserves freed up French uran-ium for bomb material.[63] At the regional level, local branches focused on close-to-home issues, with the Halifax branch of VOW protesting the pres-ence of nuclear submarines in the city's harbour, and the Regina branch raising awareness about the nuclear missiles positioned on the United States border shared with Saskatchewan. In addition to lobbying efforts, VOW made its agenda public by frequently picketing on Parliament Hill and hold-ing Mother's Day and Remembrance Day vigils at local war memorials. To spread its message among ordinary Canadians, VOW regularly rented a booth at the Canadian National Exhibition in Toronto, setting up a section of the booth as a place where children could create works of art or writing on themes related to peace. VOW also engaged in peacemaking through cultural internationalism, defined by Akira Iriye as "the idea that world order can and should be defined through interactions at the cultural level across national boundaries."[64] To strengthen the bond of international sister-hood, VOW coordinated international exchanges with Soviet women to discuss children's education and compare textbooks, liaised with the Can-adian and international branches of WILPF, and met with the American peace group Women Strike for Peace. VOW hosted two conferences for international women's group in 1962 and during Expo in 1967. Members were also encouraged to form pen-pal programs and learn Esperanto. In the mid-1960s, VOW proclaimed solidarity with women in North and South Vietnam and coordinated visits and relief efforts, projects which will be discussed more thoroughly in chapter 6.[65]

Interestingly, one of VOW's first projects was a civil defence survey to gauge member's opinion on the national program; however, the topic was dropped almost immediately from the agenda when members com-plained that VOW's involvement in the issue would only give credence to a program that "is a preparation for war not peace."[66] A commitment to

VOW Peace Education Booth at CNE, 1969. Courtesy of Lil Greene fonds, Library and Archives Canada.

internationalism was a critical difference between the women organizing for civil defence and the ones striving for peace. Although both movements positioned women as actively contributing to the Cold War discourse, the two projects could not have been more different. Civil defence was a national security system that did not outwardly prevent war; it only saved lives—Canadian lives. It was as hawkish as the peace movement was dovish, looking inward rather than outward. And while it is true that many peace activists were similarly motivated to act by the thought of their children growing up in a nuclear wasteland or not growing up at all, they were also moved by this happening to any woman, any child, anywhere. For the women who joined VOW, war was an international problem that all countries needed to be engaged in finding a solution to. An emergency system such as civil defence, even if it was successful, was only a step backwards.

As an alternative to civil defence, VOW advocated studying peace, not war. One of the ways it did this was through the Canadian Peace Research Institute (CPRI), a scientific foundation modelled after a similar centre in Norway dedicated to studying the causes of war and the potential for peace through science and social science research. The CPRI was created in 1961 after VOW raised $250,000 for a research centre dedicated to peace. Among the many VOW members active in the CPRI was Hanna Newcombe, a chemist from Hamilton. As a child Newcombe immigrated to Canada from Czechoslovakia with her parents; they were one of the few Jewish families allowed into Canada during the 1930s. Newcombe later learned that out of all her relatives, only one family had survived the Holocaust. After graduating from McMaster University in 1945, she found work assisting with the Canadian wing of the Manhattan Project, then in its final stages of research leading to the development of the atomic bomb. Initially she believed in the project because she thought the weapon was necessary to defeat Hitler; however, after discovering the effects of the bomb in Japan, she felt a personal responsibility to discover peaceful alternatives to conflict resolution. After receiving her doctorate in chemistry in 1950, the newly married Newcombe devoted herself to raising a family with her chemist husband. Once her three children were in school full-time, Newcombe took a staff position at the CPRI, where she wrote thousands of scientific abstracts on global peace research and published them in the journal she created, *The Peace Research Abstract Journal*.[67]

Initially, VOW's peace work took a non-partisan approach, but many members found this ideology impossible to maintain after the Cuban Missile

Crisis in October 1962. The heightened nuclear fear during this showdown prompted VOW to speak out more adamantly against the bomb in all forms, a commitment that made it necessary to openly challenge newly elected Prime Minister Pearson when he agreed to arm Canada's Bomarc missiles with nuclear warheads. The decision to speak out directly against the Liberal Party and the prime minister was a major turning point for VOW. It resulted in Pearson's wife resigning from the group, along with many ardent Liberal Party supporters. The abandonment of non-partisanship caused a split within VOW's members and its allies over the groups' goals and direction. Some members saw working against rather than with the government as a move too far to the left, while others felt VOW needed to be even more revolutionary.[68] Around this time, the CPRI dissolved its relationship with VOW because it did not want to be associated with any backlash or critique.[69] The change in attitude caused membership, which had reached its peak of 6,000 in 1962, to drop to 3,000 by 1964.[70] Those who remained insisted that even though they no longer received a red carpet welcome in Ottawa, their original vision had not changed. "VOW ... has only condensed its thoughts on one precise, moral attitude toward nuclear armament or nuclear tests," Quebec member Solange Chaput-Rolland explained, adding that it was necessary to become more militant because "one day, at one specific hour, one is called to choose one's truth and live by it."[71] From this point forward, VOW increased the radicalism of their activism, believing that desperate times called for desperate measures. This lead to Casgrain and VOW's third president, Kay Macpherson, being arrested in Paris for trespassing on NATO property when they gathered with women from other NATO member nations to oppose the organization's Multilateral Force in 1964.[72]

Whether promoting a moderate or more radical course of action, VOW's dominant message was one of maternal responsibility. Mothers became engaged because to do otherwise would be considered a form of neglect. Simply put, one member summed up this attitude as "Your duty as a decent mother involves saving the world."[73] This message downplayed the potentially alienating partisan, feminist, or radical aims subconsciously or consciously connected with peace activism and buffered VOW with an air of decency and propriety. Although peace activism was still considered a contentious movement and VOW would occasionally face attempts by the press or state to discredit it through red-baiting or other strategies, it managed to weather this by playing up the group's ladylike and motherly image. Macpherson wrote that this allowed VOW to bask "in the kind of acceptance and approval usually given to 'motherhood' causes. What, after all, could be more pleasing than women raising their voices in hymns to peace, international under-standing and goodwill towards most men?"[74] These factors, combined with putting VOW leaders' media connections to good use, helped VOW break down the negative images associated with peace activism that had plagued WILPF. However, in keeping with VOW's spirit of open-mindedness, toler-ance, and international unity with women from communist countries, the organization's leaders also insisted they would never ask about the political affiliation of their members, and they openly allowed Communist Party member Lil Greene to play a leading role. As Macpherson declared, "We are on the defensive if we fall into the trap of trying to prove that we are neither this nor that ... It is for us to ask 'Is she working for peace and international co-operation and against war and the threat of war,' not 'Is she a communist, anarchist or anything else.' In this country we are free to think as we please."[75]

In its first decade of operation, VOW had been quite cagey about defin-ing itself as feminist. Even though the organization's very existence was based on the feminist principle that women had the right to a political voice for reasons both maternal and egalitarian, it was thought that this label might alienate the large cohort of members new to activism. Given the public's divisive attitudes toward both feminism and peace, VOW originally chose to focus on the one they thought was more pressing. When asked if they were feminist, early VOW leaders usually sidestepped the question and replied, "V.O.W. has been designed primarily for women, not because we believe men do not share our concern, but we believe that there is a unique contribution which women can make which has not yet been fully mobil-ized."[76] VOW was correct in stating that men cared about peace, too, but men's gender was less visible because they did not overtly link their activism to their masculinity, preferring to organize around their professions, like Dr. Spock and Dr. Hunt, or politics and religion, like Reverend Endicott. Of course, these identifiers were already markers of their masculinity; con-sequently, men did not have to call attention to their manhood because it was assumed. Women's peace groups such as VOW and WILPF went about it the opposite way, organizing around their gender for guaranteed leader-ship opportunities and because it was a clever mobilization technique locally and internationally. Although VOW relied on maternalist rhetoric and iden-tities, its understanding of womanhood was just as broad as men's under-standing of their manhood. VOW incorporated maternalism into other defining traits: faith, personal experiences with war, notions of service, knowledge of science and politics, nationalism, feminism, and global citizen-ship. One only needs to study the diverse backgrounds of VOW members such as Duckworth, Franklin, Dempsey, Davis, and Casgrain to gain a sense of these layered perspectives. Even though the maternal aspect often dominated the discourse, this was strategic as well as naturally connected to their experiences as mothers. Furthermore, the maternalist spirit gave women's peace work an air of respectability that allowed them to navigate controversial issues. While many of the activists were confident of their feminism from the beginning, for others it was their experience in the peace movement that gave them the skills and knowledge to become a part of the equality-seeking activism often referred to as second-wave feminism.

Motherhood was not only a strategic form of rhetoric to gain acceptance and attention. It was a reality for the members juggling family and activism. Although VOW members came from all stages of life, motherhood was a common experience, whether they had older children and grandchildren, like Tucker, or were in the midst of starting their family, like Davis. VOW was formed not only in a period of great international tension but also at the end of the baby boom, so it is not surprising that women linked child rearing with peacemaking. For example, at one point in the spring of 1961, five members of the executive were pregnant. Doug Owram argues that the Depression, the Second World War, and the Cold War shaped the thinking of parents during the baby boom. According to Owram the threat of these events encouraged a more permissive parenting style that was inspired by an appreciation for democracy and the inclination to view the family as fragile, prone to be torn apart by economic trouble or war.[77] These views could also be used to explain the timing of women's increased interest in peace activism. Mothers who had lived through the 1930s and 1940s wanted to ensure that their children did not experience the same sacrifices, deprivation, and fear that they had in their youth.

In return, involvement in peace work gave housebound mothers something to focus on beyond their husbands and children, something to ease the mental and physical isolation that Betty Friedan would identify in *The Feminine Mystique*. Published in 1963, Friedan's book challenged the assumption that women, especially middle-class suburban women, could only be fulfilled by their role as mothers and homemakers, work that was considered less valuable than men's. The sentiment had long been expressed by the Canadian physician Dr. Marion Hilliard in her *Chatelaine* advice column.[78] Friedan's worldwide bestseller helped ignite the women's liberation movement of the 1960s and 1970s, which became intertwined with the female wing of the peace movement. As civil defence involvement had also done, working for peace bolstered the image of mothers and their labour by taking them out of the home and showing their importance in deferring war, while also giving women the opportunity to become engaged in a project outside their domestic sphere. Macpherson explains:

> One of VOW's strong points was the means it provided for women with time but little money, often tied to their homes and children, to take responsibility for action, to DO something constructive and effective. This lessened the feeling of isolation and, by joining together, they could make the weight of women's concerns felt in the places where decisions were being made.[79]

VOW also attempted to make activism easy for inexperienced or isolated activist women by sending them advice on how to start branches in their community and listing examples of the different ways one person could make a difference. One VOW pamphlet suggested that

> childbearing and housekeeping develop a woman's flexibility and practicality—ad hoc measures—and long range goals. With these she has the rare privilege of planning her work—diaper washing can on occasion give way to writing to the Prime Minister! By taking her share of responsibility among women, she develops and learns to use her abilities and influence.[80]

The pamphlet even included a quote from Dr. Spock encouraging parents to work for peace.

VOW leaders were proud that so many young mothers joined them during a time in their lives when they were most likely busy with cumbersome domestic responsibilities and little free time. Women saw participating in VOW as a relevant labour for mothers, even if it meant adding to their workload. When asked why she joined VOW, Mrs. E. M. Hill said she had four reasons: Michael, Brad, Bryan, and Kerry. Hill wanted her sons to enjoy living in a peaceful world, adding that she "had four brothers in the last war and I don't want to raise my sons to go to another."[81] She also offered another explanation as to why women would be so good at peace work: "Women hold the family together so I'm sure they can help in the same respect nationally and internationally."[82] Hill's statement suggests women could easily transfer their skills as homemakers to be successful peacemakers, putting the same diplomatic tact they use managing family arguments, stretching household resources, and debating controversial issues in the Parent-Teacher Association, and apply them to keeping peace within and among nations. This is similar to the rhetoric that was used to describe women's roles in the health and welfare side of civil defence, but now the same skills women would use in managing a disaster caused by the bomb—caring, educating, and nurturing—could also be applied to preventing such a disaster from ever occurring.

Ironically, Hill's testimony also highlighted the important roles women played in the family, something that might slip once a wife and mother began to spend time on an outside project like VOW. In some cases, women's peace work disrupted family life, especially in circumstances where husbands and children were unused to their wives and mothers joining organizations. After one year of volunteering for VOW as vice-president, Davis spoke of how stressful it was to balance her peace activism, her television career, and motherhood. She was on the verge of quitting VOW when she wrote to Casgrain in the fall of 1961 stating, "My health is gone—my spirit is all but defeated. In writing to you today, I take the last action for the cause [for which] I have nearly destroyed myself and my family life."[83] Davis remained with VOW for two more years, but withdrew slightly from the organization, explaining how she skipped the second annual meeting to spend time with her children.[84] Alternatively, Peggy Hope-Simpson, a Halifax member, believed she managed to balance VOW and family life because her husband and children supported her and were active in their own spheres. She also had the economic means to hire a housekeeper to come in once a week.[85] Meanwhile Franklin spoke candidly of how she and her VOW friends simply "stopped being fussy about ironed sheets or anything" and were prepared to shove the box of newspapers about foreign affairs under the couch if there was ever a surprise visit from a mother-in-law.[86] Macpherson notes that, while no one did a survey on VOW's effect on home life, she knew of "many husbands who were towers of strength and totally supportive, glad to see their women being involved, effective and *happy*. We called them the men's auxiliary."[87] Muriel Duggan, the paid staff member who managed VOW's head office, agreed that it was critical to rope men and children into helping with VOW, not only so they would understand their wives' or mothers' preoccupation, but because all help was appreciated. She frequently recruited spouses and older children to volunteer at the office licking stamps and envelopes. Duggan also recruited VOW members whose only responsibility was to babysit, leaving other members free to travel or attend meetings.[88]

It seems that for every member who claimed her family agreed that VOW came first, there were other examples of frustrated husbands and children, which occasionally led to separation and divorce. In her history of the organization, Macpherson acknowledged some "casualties," the word she used to describe the men "who could not take this unconventional, independent type of wife."[89] Goldie Josephy, the Ottawa mother of two whose active commitment to peace activism was shared in the introduction to this book, admitted that her dedication to peace work wreaked havoc on her personal life.[90] Peace always came first, and she juggled her domestic responsibilities by bringing her children along on marches and picket lines, something bystanders often criticized her for doing, even if it reinforced the maternal image. Her husband was also involved in the movement, but never to the extent that his wife was, and their differing levels of commitment caused stress in their relationship. The Josephys divorced in 1975, something her sons attribute to their mother's intense commitment to her activism.[91] Josephy's passion for peace also affected her health. Throughout the 1960s she experienced great anxiety over the possibility of nuclear war. During the Cuban Missile Crisis in 1962, and again in 1965, she became so overwrought and overworked that she was hospitalized for nervous breakdowns, something she believed also caused a miscarriage. Despite these personal sacrifices, Josephy remained confident that the end justified the means, stating, "What we did was right and I'm totally unrepentive [*sic*]. It cost me my health, it cost me my marriage but we were 1000% right."[92]

Josephy and other VOW members could match personal sacrifices with tangible successes. Campaigns like the baby-teeth survey, combined with lobbying, put pressure on the Canadian and world governments to make changes. As discussed in chapters 1 and 2, public disapproval of the bomb was part of the political process that led to the creation of the Limited Test Ban Treaty in 1963, which banned nuclear tests in the atmosphere, underwater, and in space. In 1968 a Nuclear Non-Proliferation treaty was opened for signature by countries without nuclear weapons that agreed not to acquire them. Although an end to weapons tests was far from VOW's dreams of disarmament, VOW acknowledged that it was a step towards stability, if not all-out peace. As the Cold War eased into a period of détente after 1963, disarmament and radiation research became lower priorities for VOW and other peace groups. Although these organizations still acknowledged the ticking nuclear clock, it was the continuation of a more conventional type of conflict in Southeast Asia that became the focus of their peace activism between 1963 and 1975. This led VOW to shift its lobbying efforts, vigils, peace education, and international co-operation programming toward ending the war in Vietnam, a topic discussed in chapter 6.

Although support for the UN was embraced by peace and disarmament activists, there was a separate cohort of peace-minded women who worked

"Child on Sidewalk," Voice of Women Disarmament Demonstration on Parliament Hill, 25 Sept. 1961, Duncan Cameron fonds, Library and Archives Canada.

directly with the UN, predominantly in its international child welfare programs. These women shared the same faith in internationalism as the women in VOW and WILPF, but they focused more on tangible relief efforts rather than big-picture politics. For these activists, it was not enough to speak about peace when people were dying from the consequences of past and present wars. The women who dedicated their efforts to UN international aid believed that hunger, illness, poverty, and unequal distribution of resources bred war and militarism just as much as politics did. As Canadians, these women felt they had a special responsibility to take care of the needy, not only by donating money and goods, but by giving up their comfort and security to work and live in war-torn communities and developing nations.

PART II

Abroad

CHAPTER FOUR

Seeds of Destiny
The United Nations and Child Welfare

In November 1961 Mrs. Wayne Elwood, a California housewife, mailed a cheque for $1,000 to the UN, explaining in her letter to Secretary-General U Thant that this was the advertised cost to build a fallout shelter, but she preferred to invest her family's safety in the hands of the world organization. She specified that her donation be put toward the UN's non-military operations, such as the Food and Agriculture Organization, the World Health Organization, or UNICEF. Inspired by Elwood's action, several of her friends and neighbours, along with twenty-eight families in North Carolina, agreed to pledge similar quantities because they believed the "United Nations was the only real shelter in a nuclear world."[1] This gesture made headlines across Canada, prompting Canadians to make similar promises. *Chatelaine* editor Doris Anderson applauded Elwood's "simple act" and was inspired by the initiative of an "ordinary citizen."[2] She called it a "positive gesture of faith that mankind will not embrace this final piece of madness" but will find a "sane just way to settle the world's tangled problems" in "these anxious times."[3] Not only was 1961 a time of heightened Cold War anxiety, having witnessed the Bay of Pigs invasion, the erection of the Berlin Wall, and the Soviet detonation of the most powerful thermonuclear weapon to date, it also saw the UN overwhelmed by a debt that put the future of its new peacekeeping responsibilities in question.[4] The fear of a crumbling UN prompted one Toronto woman, Brenda Smith, to follow Elwood's philanthropy with her own donation. She felt it was the obligation of "everyone who believes in the United Nations … [to] send in as much money as they could afford."[5]

It is unknown how many people followed Smith's appeal, but between 1945 and 1975 hundreds of thousands of Canadians raised millions of dollars for UN programs, including over $21 million in private donations for UNICEF alone.[6] Meanwhile hundreds of Canadians joined local branches of the United Nations Association (UNA), an educational service club where members promoted UN initiatives and values. Although the UN was a "boy's club" in this era, the majority of UNA members were women, and UNICEF, the largest and most prolific UNA committee, was always chaired by a woman. Several Canadian women also held prominent staff positions in the United Nations Relief and Rehabilitation Administration (UNRRA) overseas. Presumably it was the UN's overall intention to uphold world peace, in addition to its focus on children and youth, that interested so many women. Using explicit maternalistic language, UNA member (and VOW member) Kay Livingstone explained why women were so drawn to the UN:

> No longer can women afford to let someone else look after the world while they look after their homes. To protect our homes we must look after the world. The UN is the only organization today which attempts to speak for mankind. The UNA is the only association in Canada designed to link the citizen with that organization.[7]

As did women engaged in civil defence, Livingstone considered the home under threat and its defence in the hands of women. Rather than signing up to learn first aid or promote the concept of "duck and cover," Livingstone's version of emergency planning and protection was the UN, where she saw women, referenced in her quote above as both homemakers and citizens, having a strong role to play. The UNA encouraged women's participation not only because they believed that "the objectives of the association appeal most strongly to women" but also because they needed women.[8] Just as businessmen contributed money, women put in the volunteer hours needed to coordinate the special events and fundraisers. The UNA also saw women, in their roles as mothers and teachers, as having a great interest in and influence on one of the organization's main targets, children.

For reasons both practical and political, the UN dedicated many of its financial and educational resources to improving global child welfare. Certainly the consequences of war, poverty, and natural disasters particularly affected young people, making children the natural recipients of relief and development projects.[9] The decision to focus on children was also strategic. As Dominique Marshall has explored in her analysis of the UN's history of child rights, children's innocence and vulnerability generated the biggest sympathy from donors and was a subject that could neutralize Cold War tensions.[10] Widespread concern for child welfare was also an important part of Canada's new postwar welfare system and baby-boom culture. While orphaned, neglected, and sick children had always been the recipients of charity in Canada, programs such as the Family Allowance addressed the universal ideology of the nation's postwar welfare state, funding the development of "normal" children as a pre-emptive measure to avoid developmental, health, or economic problems.[11] In the case of foreign aid, this attitude was expanded on, whereby it was hoped that if all children's basic needs were met, the UN could influence the development of future generations. This attitude made foreign aid an important tool in neutralizing threats and winning allies. As the groundbreaking UN film *Seeds of Destiny* proclaimed, it was critical that postwar children avoid the "ruin, doubt, defeatism and despair [that] will breed Fascism, more Hitlers, more Tojos"; instead, we must encourage the development of "Einsteins, Toscaninis, Manuel Quezons, Madame Curies, and Sun Yet Sens."[12]

Although most of the UN's child-focused campaigns served children in war zones and developing nations, they also involved children living in prosperous and peaceful nations such as Canada. The Trick-or-Treat for UNICEF campaign and model UN clubs were considered to be a form of citizenship "training" for young Canadians, inaugurating them into Canada's new postwar commitment to internationalism and teaching them to be generous, co-operative, responsible, and globally aware citizens. In a sense, these programs were promoted as being just as much about shaping the character of young Canadians as they were about building healthy bodies and minds in their overseas counterparts. Therefore children on both sides of the foreign relief equation, the young donors and the young recipients, were considered by the UN to be "seeds of destiny," future leaders who, if nurtured properly in terms of nutrition, health, education, and democracy, would grow up to be peaceful and productive citizens.[13]

While Canadian and non-Canadian children may have been seen as sharing an intertwined destiny, UN campaigns did not portray them as equal or alike, but rather two sides of a problem/solution binary. Laura Briggs has demonstrated how the image of the "rail-thin waif, maybe with an empty rice bowl" became the standard representation of Third World need since the postwar period.[14] The salvation of these children was positioned as in the hands of the white, heterosexual, middle-class Western family, which was seen as "fundamentally caring and committed to the well-being of local non-white and working class children, as well as infants, youth and families around the globe."[15] In general, the young recipients of UN foreign relief, as well as those sponsored by foster parent plans (discussed in the next chapter), were conceived as weak, vulnerable, and in desperate need of Canadian attention, love, and financial contributions. Additionally, it was implied that any foreign child not helped by Canada could grow up to be a dangerous and destructive force. Meanwhile Canadian children participating in foreign relief projects as volunteers and donors were presented as being blessed with health and wealth, and were shown to be enthusiastic in their quest to assist their underprivileged counterparts. Although Canadian children of all backgrounds were encouraged to participate in foreign relief projects, their efforts were contextualized differently based on their perceived economic and social status within Canadian society. In particular, the participation of First Nations and Inuit children was considered exceptional because they were viewed by many Canadians to be somewhat foreign and needy themselves. Therefore heart-warming tales of their generosity were used to solicit donations from middle-class Canadians of European backgrounds and silence critics who felt Canadians should focus on assisting children within their own borders. Given the intense focus on "Canadianizing" Aboriginal children in this era, one could view their participation in UN charities as the same "seeds of destiny" rhetoric directed toward foreign children.

Like the other examples of Cold War projects related to children's health and safety, UN supporters placed great value on preserving children's futures as a motivating factor for peace; however, unlike civil defence or peace activists, UN followers took this belief a step further by also seeing global child welfare as the direct solution to peace. Here endangered children were not just an abstract symbol used to promote peace; their bodies and minds were the arenas in which peace should be built and preserved. Furthermore, instead of imagining nightmarish what-if scenarios found in civil defence and the disarmament movement, the Canadian women engaged in various forms of UN activism confronted distant but real wars and real devastation. Like their counterparts in the peace movement, UN workers and donors wisely praised internationalism as the necessary foundation for peace, though the UN struck a slightly different internationalist chord than the women organizing for disarmament in WILPF or VOW. UN-driven internationalism placed greater attention on working within the established political system, rather than choosing to only align within a united sisterhood or positioning themselves in opposition to a government's policies. Instead, support for the UN was to be demonstrated calmly and efficiently through boosterism, volunteerism, and financial donations. In the postwar period this was achieved through donations to UNRRA in an attempt to rebuild the lives of European civilians, including millions of displaced children affected by the Second World War. After the Korean War, the UN's failure to foster peace and security dampened some of the initial optimism about the world body's powers. While the fervour for diplomatic solutions wavered in the 1950s and 1960s, female UN supporters remained invested in the UN's child welfare programs, particularly UNICEF. They valued the simple yet promising premise behind these programs: raising children to be healthy in mind, body, and spirit and free from want would be a tremendous step forward in healing the wounds of war and building a peaceful world.

UNRRA: Planting the Seeds of Destiny

As Allied armies liberated countries in Europe during the Second World War, they were followed by an international delegation of relief workers organized by the newly formed UN who were assigned to offer care and coordinate the dispersal of supplies to refugees. The high casualty rates and displacement of civilians became a rallying point in mobilizing support during the last year of the war, and at the same time it demonstrated the new costs of modern warfare. Political ideologies and military strategies that deliberately targeted non-combatants, combined with the collapse of agricultural production and breakdowns in sanitation and housing, caused unseen levels of death, devastation, and disease. It has been estimated that the death toll in World War II was approximately 60 million people, the majority of whom were civilians.[16] Even before the war was over, Allied governments collaborated to raise the necessary resources needed to repair the damage in Europe and Asia. Food, wheat, milk, cattle, poultry, seeds, machinery, medicine, blankets, clothes, and shoes were in high demand, as was construction material for the reconstruction of roads, bridges, and buildings. UNRRA (1943–47) was the first of many UN agencies assigned to cater to the human side of reconstruction. It was hoped that, if successful, UNRRA would be able to "pump into the veins and arteries of stricken peoples around the earth the emergency items of relief and rehabilitation that serve as the plasma of peace."[17]

UNRRA was Canada's first involvement in what historian Adam Chapnick called "shaping the post-war world," a demonstration of the government's and the people's commitment to long-term internationalism.[18] After the Second World War, Canadians liked to emphasize their nation's special destiny in helping other people, significant as Canada spread its wings globally as a respected middle power. The nation's military and financial contributions during the war gave the government a legitimacy to continue acting upon its international interests and prompted a sense of responsibility to preserve what had been fought for. Unlike its European allies, Canada was not faced domestically with extensive postwar reconstruction, so the government had the public and private resources available to assist with large-scale rehabilitation projects abroad. The federal government donated more than $2 billion to European reconstruction, $90 million of which was channelled through UNRRA in the form of wheat, textiles, and farm implements.[19] The UN elected Canada to chair UNRRA's Suppliers Committee, which was responsible for coordinating countries assigned to pay for the relief and to study the needs of receiver nations. Some UNRRA resources were also collected through private donations, such as the campaign led by Canadian actress Mary Pickford. Pickford advised housewives to purchase an extra canned good or package of food every time they went shopping and place it in a specially marked UN bin found in the major grocery chains. At the end of the day, the grocery stores would calculate the value of the donations, return the items to the store shelves, and use the equivalent value to purchase food in bulk quantities for UN relief.[20] Polls taken during and after the war suggest that the Canadian public supported UNRRA and their nation's continuing internationalist efforts, even if it meant the continuation of food rationing and conserving in the postwar years.[21]

In addition to sending agricultural resources, Canadians with experience in welfare service, administration, and health care, especially those with foreign language skills, were recruited to work for UNRRA. Hundreds of Canadian nurses joined UNRRA's nursing divisions, and several Canadian women rose high in the organization's administration, which proclaimed itself an equal opportunity employer.[22] The mobilization of women working overseas is reminiscent of an earlier form of women's international work, the missionary movement. In the late nineteenth and early twentieth century, women could be found at the heart of Canada's overseas missions in India and China. Overseas charity work was considered a respectable occupation for pious (and adventurous) women looking for a vocation or leadership opportunities they could not find at home. According to Ruth Compton Brouwer, the women who joined foreign missions had a "uniquely authoritative source of information and opinion about life in non-Christian lands and a congenial object for philanthropic zeal" as well as "a siren call to a vocation and to a larger life than any could contemplate in Canada."[23] As seen in the UNRRA careers of two Canadian women—Mary McGeachy, UNRRA's Director of Welfare, and Elizabeth Brown, UNRRA's Chief of Mission for the Middle East—this earlier missionary spirit was paired with the secularized form of internationalism.

McGeachy had been a long-time advocate of Canada's internationalism, a belief she cultivated as a member of the Student Christian Movement and YWCA in Toronto. She wove this interest into a career with the League of Nations (LON), where she was employed as an information section officer in Geneva between 1928 and 1940. After the dissolution of the LON, McGeachy found new work with the UN, where she became the most senior Canadian and the only woman to hold a high-level executive position. In her biography of McGeachy, Mary Kinnear recounts the challenges involved in managing UNRRA's welfare division, whose role was to administer care to the 150 to 160 million refugees living in displaced persons' camps across Europe. This work won the unmarried and childless McGeachy the title "Europe's no. 1 Foster Mother."[24] Kinnear notes that, throughout McGeachy's time with UNRRA, her authority was questioned by other UN officials who were uncomfortable with a woman holding such a senior position; however, she felt the bigger frustration lay in the fact that her "vision of relief could not be adequately measured in the terms of the budgets and personnel."[25] Whatever UNRRA's successes and failures, McGeachy believed it represented the greatest undertaking in international cooperation to date. After the agency folded, she left the UN to get married, but remained involved in international work through her membership in and later presidency of the International Council of Women. Kinnear concluded that "McGeachy's accomplishments were unusual because she was Canadian, not rich or well connected, and female" and that her life showed the "opportunities, and the limitations, that the idea of international cooperation could offer to a woman."[26]

Brown's reflections on this period support Kinnear's contention that international co-operation projects offered a woman-friendly working environment. In 1943 Brown left her position as an employment advisor with the Department of Labour, citing disappointment in the lack of respect shown to federal women employees. She applied to UNRRA because she yearned to "do something in the present world situation" and had an "itchy foot" and the "wanderlust bug."[27] At age forty-two Brown thought there was little chance she would be accepted, yet she passed the medical screening and four weeks of training at the University of Maryland. Just as McGeachy experienced some gender prejudice, so did Brown. Her original UNRRA posting was changed from Yugoslavia to Jerusalem when it was made known that President Tito preferred male UNRRA workers in his country.[28] Between 1944 and 1947 Brown supervised the administration of food supplies, education, medical services, housing, and repatriation programs in refugee camps in Egypt, Palestine, Lebanon, and Syria and opened UNRRA's first Jerusalem office. Brown felt the Middle East was one of the most challenging UNRRA regions due to the high number of legal and illegal entries to the region and the considerable tensions connected to partition. Despite this, "Miss UNRRA Brown," as the locals called her, found great satisfaction in her work and accomplishments, something she found lacking in her work in Canada. She referred to her time with UNRRA as "a miracle," explaining that

> this type of assignment, to organize and administer a program to help people, to carry the responsibility for relationships in the community, with the government, the military and any private groups touching on our work, to have the freedom of planning and carrying UNRRA's chart … was a tremendous challenge, yet one I knew I could handle.[29]

Brown was forced to leave UNRRA in 1947 when the British pulled out of their commitments in Palestine, and she continued her relief work for the UN's International Refugee Organization in Turkey and Germany. In 1954 she was offered a position with the UN relief administration in postwar Korea, but she turned it down, acknowledging the agency's temporary nature and fearing as a single woman in her fifties, responsible for her own support, she needed more secure employment.[30] Instead Brown spent eight years working for an American nursing association before returning to work abroad in 1963 as director of the Saigon Foster Parents Plan International (FPPI) office during the height of the Vietnam War, an experience that will be explored in chapter 6.

Interestingly, experience with UNRRA was viewed by other women as a stepping stone not only to additional international work, but also to leadership opportunities in parallel Cold War movements seeking peace or security. In 1956 the Canadian Welfare Council recruited Molly E. Christie, a social worker with UNRRA's European program, for a position with the Emergency Measures Organization. The committee had put a specific call out to former UNRRA employees, explaining to recruiters that these skilled workers might not be aware of how much their experience in disaster management was needed to manage emergency preparedness in a nuclear war scenario.[31]

UNRRA workers were also sought by the peace movement for their international experience and commitment to the UN. Ethel Ostry, a Jewish social worker and teacher, was a founding member of VOW. One of the reasons she was selected to participate in VOW's 1963 peace mission to ten European countries in honour of International Co-operation Year was her postwar experience working for UNRRA in Germany, Austria, and Italy. Living abroad, being a witness to the consequences of war, and having experience in a workplace dedicated to cross-cultural understanding made Ostry a strong representative for Canada.[32] Although UN service work, peace activism, and civil defence shared different politics, each were contextualized as organizational leadership and professional opportunities for women in fields related to caregiving.

One of the significant tasks facing Brown and other UNRRA workers on the ground was the overwhelming responsibility of caring for the millions of children suffering from malnutrition and disease, those who had been crippled and blinded by shrapnel and other weaponry, and those traumatized by living through invasions, bombings, and the Holocaust. Amid the casualties were an estimated 13 million unaccompanied children who had been orphaned, abandoned, or accidently separated from their parents.[33] UNRRA had a special division devoted to child welfare, which provided care to mothers and their children, devoted resources to improving national child and maternal services, and attempted to reunite displaced children with relatives.[34] Generally there was great sympathy for all children affected by war, although Canadian UNRRA worker Marjorie Bradford recalls how in France she confronted social prejudice towards and the denial of citizenship rights of illegitimate children who had been fathered by Germans and children who parents were accused of being French collaborators. Furthermore UNRRA workers felt the pressures of Zionism and strict Soviet repatriation policies when determining where to resettle displaced children. Whenever possible, Bradford tried to ensure the children's interests were placed first, above political or legal considerations.[35]

A handful of displaced children had been cared for during the Second World War in special nurseries in England financed by FPPI and supervised by psychologists Dr. Anna Freud, daughter of Sigmund, and Dr. Dorothy Tiffany Burlingham. These war nurseries offered residential child care for European refugee children who had been evacuated to England without their parents and British children whose parents were engaged in war work or whose homes had been destroyed in the Blitz. The nurseries were staffed by refugees trained in social work, health care, or education, who under

Freud's and Burlingham's supervision strove to ease the children's separation anxiety and minimize the impact of stress on their social development.[36] Research performed in the war nurseries provided analytical tools and guidelines for social workers and administrators working with young refugees. In 1943 Freud and Burlingham published *War and Children*, the first academic study about the effects of war on children. Their work represented the growing importance of child psychology, which recognized childhood as being a unique and fragile time in a person's life, a time when one needed to be nurtured and protected by parents. They concluded that "the care and education of young children should not take second place in wartime," arguing that "adults can live under emergency conditions and, if necessary, on emergency rations. But the situation in the decisive years of bodily and mental development is entirely different."[37] Freud and Burlingham's research demonstrated the physical and psychological malformations found in children under severe stress from air raids, evacuations, and the shock of separation from their parents, especially their mothers. To minimize the impact of war on children, they believed there should be a concentrated effort to ensure that normal routines were not broken and that there were replacement forms of security (family, home, and school) available if the original ones vanished. The theories in *War and Children* would become a guide for UNICEF, whose programs promised to intervene when parents and communities were unable to offer these elements alone, buffering the care with items of relief and the provision of schools, hospitals, and orphanages. UNICEF agreed with Freud and Burlingham that the "wartime care of children has to be more elaborate and more carefully thought out than in ordinary times of peace."[38] Chapter 7 will discuss a more radical solution—the permanent removal of children from war zones to the safety of Canada, where their needs were met not by organizations and long-distance donations, but by new Canadian parents.

War and Children was considered a landmark achievement among professional child welfare workers working with war-affected youth, but it was the documentary *Seeds of Destiny* that generated a tidal wave of response from the general public. In 1945, eight cameramen from the United States Army Signal Corps were assigned to film daily life in cities and refugee camps in fourteen European countries. (Although Asia is mentioned in the film, it is not visually represented because filming started before the war in the Pacific was over.) What struck the filmmakers was the staggering number of children affected by war, or to lay specific blame, affected by the madness of Axis power leaders Hitler, Mussolini, and Tojo. The film focuses on the lifestyles of children who had survived the war and were now languishing in peacetime.

The Corps footage was edited into a nineteen-minute documentary by Corporal David Miller, a Hollywood director before the war. Miller described the experience as "heart rending" and claimed filming paused at times because the crew were too shaken to continue.[39] The black-and-white film featured image after image of children whose appearance and behaviour challenged the ideals of a modern "normal" childhood favoured by most Canadians. Instead there are scenes of children missing limbs and eyes, or staring blankly into the camera. In other scenes, dirt-smeared urchins dressed in rags scurry around like rats, stealing, begging, and even smoking. A narrator translated the shocking images for viewers, explaining how the baby seen lying in a crib was really a malnourished three-year-old. None of the children are portrayed living in homes or shown with families; instead they appear in public spaces or in institutional care. The film contrasted these experiences with the images of peaceful middle-class suburban homes and schoolyards in North America, and it placed the burden of responsibility for fixing this problem on "ourselves," those whose imaginations, "no matter how vivid, cannot convey the full meaning of what others have endured and still endure."[40]

Still from *Seeds of Destiny*, 1946. United States Department of War, courtesy of Harry S. Truman Library.

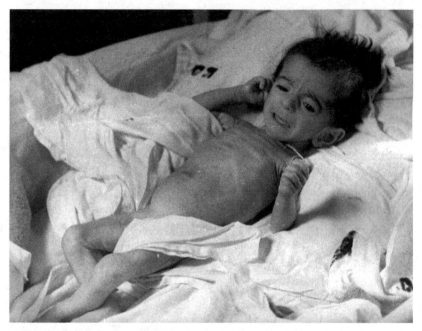

Still from *Seeds of Destiny*, 1946. United States Department of War, courtesy of Harry S. Truman Library.

Seeds of Destiny applauded UNRRA's accomplishments, yet its presentation of sad images proved more support was needed. For example, the narrator argued, the annual UNRRA budget of $2 billion was equal to only 1 percent of the participating countries' gross domestic product, which worked out to be less than the cost of five days of war. *Seeds of Destiny* concluded with a buoyant piece of hyperbole, suggesting that peace must be financed equally to war in order to "preserve the victories won by the fighting men of the United Nations, the hard way, and establish once and for all, that even stronger than the atomic bomb is the human heart."[41] Presumably the comparison between UNRRA and the atomic bomb was meant to suggest that the outpouring of transnational charity had the power to produce peace and stability, much as the Allies argued the bomb had done by ending the war. It did not acknowledge that the people behind UNRRA were the same people who invented such a destructive weapon and contributed to the very human consequences of war that UNRRA hoped to eradicate.

Seeds of Destiny premiered at the White House in the spring of 1946. UNRRA's director, Fiorello La Guardia, announced that the film must be shown everywhere; however, the National Association of Theater Owners deemed the shocking footage of emaciated and wild children too "gruesome" to be shown in public cinemas across North America, so Miller and La Guardia circulated the film among church groups, parent-teacher associations, unions, women's clubs, and other service groups.[42] Within two years, *Seeds of Destiny* was shown to 11 million Americans and Canadians whose private screenings generated $200 million in donations toward UNRRA, with donors giving on average $15 dollars each.[43] As the recognition spread that much more needed to be done beyond the temporary framework of UNRRA, this film also inspired the founding of UNICEF, a UN agency specifically designed to look after children's bodies, minds, and spirits through educational, medical, and nutrition programs.[44] In Canada, public support for UN child welfare ventures and other aims were channelled through the UNA, a club founded in 1946 and dedicated to celebrating and funding the UN.

The UNA: A Respectable Peacemaker

As an alternative to the presumed radicalism of peace organizations such as WILPF and later VOW, the UNA offered a more respectable path to global peace and security. As many parts of the world returned to a state of peace in 1945, hope was pinned on the UN as the foremost peacemaker, on one hand promising to intervene and avert war, and on the other, spreading a spirit of internationalism, economic development, social justice, and human rights. As the Canadian UN delegation in New York and Geneva worked to shape the world Canada wanted, Canadian branches of the UNA did the same on the home front by promoting internationalism, the belief that nations should co-operate politically and economically, as a key part of nationalism. They hoped Canadians would see themselves not only as citizens of their own nation, but as citizens of the world, taking an interest and responsibility in international affairs. UNA members pledged their support of these aims by developing programs to educate their fellow Canadians about the UN's goals and Canada's role in implementing them. As the Cold War progressed, the UNA supplemented its boosterism with constructive criticism, lobbying the Canadian government to propose structural and policy reforms that would make the UN a more effective world leader. This was not purely an altruistic venture; given the worry of a coming war fought with nuclear weapons, the UNA argued that Canadians had a vested interest in supporting the UN: it would make their nation and world safer. According to the UNA's first president, the postwar world was no time for apathy, isolationism, or defeatist talk: "The battle for peace has reached a critical stage ... This is surely the time for all who believe in international co-operation to speak out, insisting that a new world-conflict is madness that need not happen."[45]

Within a year of its founding, the Canadian UNA had grown to nineteen branches in seven provinces with over 2,000 paid members, many of whom had previously belonged to the LON's Society.[46] Branch activities were initially devoted to introducing the new world body to the public by hosting mass meetings with big-name speakers such Lester B. Pearson explaining Canada's position in the Korean War and Eleanor Roosevelt promoting the United Nations Education Science and Culture Organization.[47] The UNA also produced radio broadcasts about UN achievements, distributed free UN posters and literature, screened UN films, and raised money for UN agencies. Beginning in the mid-1950s, the UNA also promoted Canada's growing multiculturalism, spurred by postwar immigration, by hosting food, clothing, and music festivals and holding interdenominational religious services. These celebrations were meant to imply that, if Canada's diverse population could get along, so could the world. UNA programming was funded by membership fees ($2 for individuals, $10 for groups), donations, and an annual grant of $10,000 from the Department of External Affairs.

Initially the UNA was not very different from the real UN in terms of its male-dominated leadership. In the late 1940s the association's national executive was made up of what the UNA referred to as "opinion leaders ... [those] who could have direct influence on many other people."[48] This meant the executive was filled by men in leadership positions: businessmen, members of Parliament, journalists, professionals, clergymen, and former armed-forces officers. Few women were considered to be opinion leaders in this era. One exception was Cora Taylor Watt Casselman, a former teacher from Kingston, who had been active all her life in women's organizations and had also been a member of the LON's Society. When her politician husband died, she ran and won his seat in Edmonton West and served in Parliament as an MP between 1941 and 1945, becoming the first female Speaker in the House of Commons and the only female in Canada's first delegation to the UN. After the war, Casselman did not seek re-election and returned to Edmonton, where she worked as the Executive Director of the YWCA and joined the UNA, becoming one of its most dedicated patrons and influential members. By the mid-1950s the gendered makeup of the UNA gradually began to include more women leaders. This can be attributed to two specific reasons, one of them being women's consistent dominance in membership. The second reason was that more and more women were drawn to the UNA because of the association's new child-welfare-focused agenda.

Women had always laboured behind the scenes of the UNA to organize the educational campaigns and special events. As individual members and as representatives of women's associations, they joined the UNA in large numbers because it was a respectable outlet through which they could champion matters connected to peace, internationalism, and child welfare, which, as discussed in earlier chapters, mattered greatly to many women in the immediate postwar and Cold War years. In Edmonton, one of the most active UNA branches, membership was divided between 49 percent women, 41 percent men, and 10 percent organizations in 1949. By 1962 women members made up 57 percent of the membership, while men had dropped to 26 percent. In 1971, 57 percent of Edmonton members came from the new "family" category, followed by 31 percent women members and 12 percent men.[49] At the national level, the UNA had 479 women's groups (301 secular and 178 faith-based) as members in 1965, compared to participation from only 49 men's groups and 44 mixed-gender organizations.[50] These groups sent representatives from their organizations to attend UNA meetings and report back, recommending initiatives they should support. Group membership came from all the major women's organizations, including the NCWC and IODE, which were also very active in civil defence work. These groups did not consider it hypocritical to have one subcommittee preparing for war while another one worked for world peace.

The NCWC was a great supporter of the UN and the UNA, as it was of emergency preparedness programs. In 1949 the Edmonton Local Council of Women, a branch already working with the Edmonton UNA, urged the NCWC to "work with and for the United Nations," but added that it was not enough to pledge their support, they needed to work alongside the international organization and "make big plans, which have the power to move men's souls," stating this type of action would "recapture the zeal of the foresighted women who founded the National Council of Women of Canada 55 years ago."[51] Although "big plans" was an exaggeration, in 1950 the NCWC passed a resolution urging all local councils to plan three-to-five-minute spots in their monthly programs on a topic related to the UN.[52] A year later, Mrs. G. F. K. Kuhring, chair of the UN committee, proudly presented her report on how local councils incorporated support for the UN in 1951. Her examples included Halifax's fifteen radio broadcasts on the UN's work with refugees, Fredericton's competition for school children to design scrapbooks dedicated to a UN agency, and Brockville's series of UN library lectures. To Kuhring, this was proof that "women want, above everything else, a peaceful world, and they are beginning to recognize two facts; that to be lasting, peace must be worldwide; that peace does not come automatically after a world war."[53] Her comments came a month before the Korean War broke out, when there was a sense that the world was about to explode again. She warned the NCWC of the pressing need to continue this good work, reminding them that "these are dangerous days through which we are living. One crisis follows closely on the heels of another. One false step, a serious mistake in judgement, might precipitate a third world war at any moment."[54] Kuhring also claimed that their work played a critical role in helping Canada manage its foreign affairs. "By helping to inform public opinion," she stated, "we shall assist the Government in the difficult decisions it is called upon to make."[55] In this manner, the NCWC contextualized their efforts as making women voters knowledgeable about internationalism and Canada's foreign affairs.

The NCWC also frequently used the UN to frame their association's resolutions on national and international issues. For example, when lobbying the Canadian government, they found it was helpful to point out the differences between Canadian law and the sometimes more progressive UN policies. This occurred in 1949 when the Ontario Provincial Council of Women appealed to the federal government to end its discriminatory immigration policies toward China by arguing that Canada's quota and head tax were in direct opposition to the UN Charter.[56] During the Korean War, the NCWC sent the federal government their approval of the UN's Convention on the Prevention and Punishment of the Crime of Genocide and expressed hope that Canada would endorse the proposed Convention, a matter they found greatly important considering the Korean crisis.[57] They also used the UN to advocate for women's rights internationally. Generally the NCWC was pleased with the UN's progress in this area, noting "before 1945 in only 40 of the 80 sovereign states had women the vote. Since then, 75 countries have acceded to giving women political rights as well as in the educational, economic, and civil etc. fields."[58] But the NCWC also wanted the UN to do more to improve the status of women, such as when the British Columbia Provincial Council of Women petitioned Canadian representatives in the UN "in the name of 'National Womanhood'" (and in the name of thwarting communism) to allow Russian women married to nationals of other countries to be able to leave Russia, if they wished to be reunited with their foreign husbands.[59] In these ways, the UN became a useful tool to support the NCWC's indirect and direct efforts toward peace and gender equity. It raised the NCWC's stature if their resolutions reflected not only the humble efforts of Canadian women seeking change but the resolve of a respectable organization consisting of the world's leading intellectuals, diplomats, and service workers entrusted to guide and protect humanity's best interests.

In addition to stimulating interest in the UN within women's organizations, the UNA formed internal study groups to analyze specific problems and offer solutions. Although they firmly believed the UN was critical to achieving world peace, like WILPF and VOW, they did not see the UN in its current form as omnipotent. Each year UNA members proposed resolutions outlining policies they supported or wanted changed. These were voted on at the annual meetings and those which passed were forwarded to the Department of External Affairs. In 1948, long before Pearson's work in the Suez solidified the idea, the UNA advocated for a permanent peacekeeping force.[60] In the mid-1950s resolutions came forward that repeatedly asked the UN to be a leader in nuclear disarmament and place a ban on nuclear weapons testing.[61] One of the most controversial issues faced by the UNA was what to do with mainland China. While the organization did not condone Chinese policies, it believed shunning the communist state (and the world's largest importer of Canadian grain) would just add to the Cold War chaos.[62] In 1960, after years of internal debate among the membership and many failed resolutions, the UNA came out in favour of Canada and the UN recognizing the People's Republic of China, nine years before the UN did.

While the UNA were never as radical in their demands as WILPF or VOW, they openly debated the same controversial issues other peace groups were condemned for promoting, and in all three of these examples, the UNA approved reforms long before the Canadian government or the UN did. As a state-sanctioned body, the UNA was the only public forum to discuss matters of peace and security without being tainted with accusations of communist infiltration and suffering Red Scare harassment in the 1950s. This respectability also came from the organization's membership—a collection of leading and ordinary citizens, the majority of whom were women, whose gender and class ensured that their status and patriotism were rarely in question.[63] Even though the UNA at times criticized Canadian foreign policy and UN decisions, and advocated for controversial topics like disarmament, its faith in the UN as the solution meant that it was not ultimately challenging the Cold War consensus. Nor was the behaviour of UNA members threatening; there were no marches or protests—rather, they insisted problems could and should be worked out through debate and education. Embracing the UN became the most respectable way to advocate for peace during the early Cold War.

This respectability gave the UNA—unlike other peace groups—formal access to children and youth. In the 1950s and 1960s, the UNA had contacts in school boards, home and school associations, and parent-teacher federations across Canada, as well as in popular youth groups such as the Girl Guides and Boy Scouts. Through these connections the UNA distributed UN-focused social studies and history guides and ran UN clubs and pen pal programs that regularly became part of the academic and after-school curricula. One UNA branch even held an annual Miss UN pageant in the 1960s to increase and recognize the participation of young women in their association.[64] For many Canadian youth, the UN represented hope. Lorraine Oak, Miss UN 1967, who was a youth volunteer for UNICEF, recalls how she

> was acutely aware at a young age of the Bay of Pigs and world peace or we blow up, and of course we had the air raid practices and the sirens went off and we all went home, presumably to be annihilated. It was a time where serious kids were very aware about the dangers of the Cold War ... I had absolute faith. I truly believed in the United Nations and that would be our salvation.[65]

The UNA contextualized its education and service work with youth as a character-building exercise for Canadian children. As the future leaders of tomorrow, youth were seen to be critical players in achieving the UN dream, and the UNA's work ensured that children of the baby-boom generation were familiar with and generally supportive of the UN.[66]

The focus on children and youth meant that in the 1950s and 1960s the UNA considered teachers to be critical "opinion leaders," which opened more leadership positions to women. Bertha Lawrence, an unmarried high-school teacher who had immigrated to Alberta from England as a child, held many positions within the UNA locally and nationally, including that of Edmonton's representative to the UN High Commission on Refugees. In 1955 Lawrence co-authored a new edition of the Grade 10 social studies textbook *Canada in the Modern World*, used in classrooms across Alberta between 1955 and 1966. In the post-1945 section, Lawrence devoted a lot of space to UN affairs. In this text she called the Cold War "the greatest problem confronting the world in its search for peace" and agreed that the UN "it spite of all its shortcomings ... was a meeting place where common aims could be formulated and common policies worked out by nations that were sincerely desirous of improving world conditions."[67] Lawrence credits her experience of returning to England to serve with the British Auxiliary Territorial Service in the

Second World War as instrumental in shaping her desire for peace. To Lawrence, the UN seemed the only sane road to peace.

The UNA's most tangible success was seen in its work with youth. Reaching adults was much more difficult, and there was a constant fear that the UNA was only preaching to the converted. This is best illustrated by the organization's relatively small paid membership, which even in the organization's most active period (1945–1965) hovered between 2,000 and 7,000. Membership was highest in Toronto and English Montreal and was solid across the West, but there were few members in French Canada or in the Maritimes. Compared with other countries' UNAs, Canada's was viewed as not living up to its potential. In 1959 the UNA in Britain had a membership of 65,000; if support had been proportionally the same in Canada, the Canadian UNA should have had at least 22,000 members.[68] Theories abounded as to why more Canadians did not join: the cost, poor recruitment strategies, apathy, confidence in the government to manage foreign affairs, lack of awareness, and so on. Membership was an issue addressed at every annual meeting, branches constantly asked members to recruit among their friends and colleagues, and the National Director went on speaking tours across the country to drum up support. Still, none of these strategies got the UNA close to its 10,000 membership target. Not only did the low numbers suggest a failure to reach their goals, but with membership fees accounting for most of all the branches' and approximately a third of the national office's revenue, the scope of what the group could realistically accomplish was hampered.

Most likely the disappointing membership numbers had to do with Canadians' inconsistent opinion about the UN throughout the early Cold War years. In 1950 *Maclean's* rated the organization's first five years by stating, "It has been fashionable, in public, to take for granted that UN is worth while [*sic*]. It is even more fashionable, in private, to sneer at UN as an empty futile debating society." At the same time, the editorial concluded that while UN interventions in Kashmir, Palestine, and Indonesia were ultimately unsuccessful, they were effective, and events in Korea proved the UN was the "only machinery through which a threatened or invaded country could appeal for help and properly get it."[69] Canadian support for the UN wavered during and after the Korean War, when it was unclear what had been achieved by sending and losing Canadian troops. Three years of fighting in Korea had ended in a stalemate, and the lack of power the UN had to intervene in civil conflicts in Greece and Hungary and the outbreaks of violence between the United States and China on the Taiwanese straits proved the organization's limitations. Events like these caused Canadians to no longer consider the UN to be the beacon of hope for world peace. The UN's popularity rose in 1956 when Pearson's peacekeeping mission in the Suez brought Canada worldwide recognition. Pearson's approved recommendation for the creation of a UN peacekeeping force to monitor the ceasefire and withdrawal of the French, British, and Israeli forces from Egypt managed not only to cool the conflict over the Suez Canal but was a solution that kept the fragile British Commonwealth intact and re-stabilized the split Western Alliance. Although historians agree this was an example of Pearson's remarkable diplomatic skills, rather than something inherently Canadian, it is generally considered the moment when "Canada stood at the zenith of its prestige in the international community ... as an internationalist middle power, a mediator and a peacemaker."[70] Pearson's triumph was used as an example of the UN's legitimacy and Canada's leadership potential within the world organization, proving there were alternatives to militarism. Nevertheless, the financial crisis that followed the new and widespread need for peacekeepers brought uncertainty about the UN's ability to survive. Regardless of the funding crisis, even Pearson's version of peacekeeping could do nothing to temper the Cold War arms race. As original UNA members died and retired, Wilson Woodside, the UNA's national president in 1963, noted that younger Canadians were joining more radical peace organizations such as VOW, the Campaign for Nuclear Disarmament, or the World Federalists.[71] Despite a lack of faith in the UN's security plans and dwindling UNA memberships, however, Canadians continued to generously donate to UN programs, most notably UNICEF.

UNICEF: Children Helping Children

Established in 1946, UNICEF represented the start of the UN's attentiveness to international child rights and child welfare, a commitment later cemented in the production of the UN Declaration on the Rights of the Child in 1959. This document expanded upon the LON's earlier recognition of international governance and responsibility for children's well-being written by Eglantyne Jebb, the founder of the British relief organization Save the Children. The 1959 declaration opens with the same preamble as that of the LON, stating that "mankind owes to the child the best that it has to give" and justifies this by explaining "the child, because of his physical and mental immaturity, needs special safeguards and care."[72] UNICEF was founded with these principles in mind, and its immediate focus was delivering care to young refugees across war-torn Europe and Asia. UNICEF, like UNRRA, was expected to fold after the immediate concern for children affected by the Second World War was met; however, the huge scope of the problem, combined with a seemingly never-ending line of new wars and non-war-related development issues, forced the UN to reconsider their plan.

When debating the permanency of UNICEF in 1950, Canada, the agency's third largest contributor (behind the United States and Australia), initially withdrew its support.[73] The Canadian representatives explained that their decision was caused by the UN's impractical goal of saving all children and their reluctance to continue paying for the mistakes of irresponsible developing nations. This reaction illustrates the cost–benefit thinking behind the Canadian government's approach to foreign aid. It did not give money purely out of a sense of morality; it wanted clear results from its benevolence, ones that reflected Canadian interests.[74] The Canadian government was convinced to stick with UNICEF for three reasons. One was the persuasive argument from the American UN delegation about the necessity of specializing in children's needs rather than dividing UNICEF's responsibilities among other agencies. Secondly, the government was well aware of the Canadian public's unwavering support for UNICEF.[75] In a letter to the External Affairs Committee, the UNA's national secretary Kathleen Bowlby urged Canada to remain one of UNICEF key funders because

> we Canadians can well afford all the assistance we are giving to the less favoured countries. Indeed, if we want to work toward a peaceful world, we cannot afford to ignore the needs that confront us. UNICEF has already built strong bonds of friendship. We trust that Canada will continue to play her part in the entirely commendable endeavour.[76]

Finally, despite the Canadian representatives' concern about efficient spending, it was hard to deny the needs of suffering children and still consider Canada to be a benevolent nation. Therefore in 1952 the Canadian government confirmed it would continue to make an annual contribution of $500,000 to UNICEF, bringing its total contribution to date to $8 million, funds that by then had been distributed to 60 million children in more than seventy countries and territories.[77] Added to the government's annual contribution was $21 million raised for UNICEF between 1955 and 1975 through private donations by Canadians.[78] UNICEF's non-governmental support in Canada was coordinated by a committee within the UNA. The committee eventually became even larger than the UNA itself, with thousands of volunteers and with subcommittees in every province, run mainly by women. The enthusiastic service shown by UNICEF volunteers reflected women's special interest in a project dedicated to aiding children, as well as the tendency for the UNA to direct interested female volunteers to UNICEF.[79]

UNICEF's popularity among Canadians can be traced to two factors: an interest in helping improve the lives of children and UNICEF's low-cost and easy donation procedures. Unlike other foreign relief agencies, UNICEF's entire focus was on children, whose innocence and vulnerability made them the least controversial beneficiaries of aid. As seen in Freud and Burlingham's work, as well as in the ideologies present in civil defence and the peace movement, children's physical and psychological care in wartime required special attention. Not only did this appeal to the maternalistic energy of women's Cold War activism, it appealed to populations on both sides of the Iron Curtain. Making young people UNICEF's special mission allowed the new agency to avoid being a site of UN power struggles during the Cold War. This was helped by ensuring that funds were sent and received by nations on both sides of the Soviet and American alliances. Although the annual report for Canada's UNICEF Committee in 1961–62 mentioned a rumour circulating in the United States that most UNICEF money went to communist nations because most UNICEF volunteers were socialists, for the most part UNICEF avoided Red Scare controversy.[80] Ultimately, UNICEF came to be considered, in the words of Bowlby, the "United Nations organ for which everyone has the highest praise and which has a universal appeal. One of the world body's most cherished agencies."[81]

The organization's popularity can also be explained by how easy it made donating. It ran affordable and soon to be exceedingly familiar campaigns that only asked for a few dollars or even pennies. UNICEF's first national fundraising campaign involved the sale of greeting cards during the 1952 Christmas season. The Canadian UNA ordered 100,000 cards that depicted children greeting different kinds of animals used to transport UNICEF supplies around the world: an elephant in India, a water buffalo in Southeast Asia, a reindeer in Finland, a camel in the Middle East, and a donkey in Latin America. These cards were sold by volunteers, described by the Winnipeg UNA as "thirty women and some husbands."[82] The volunteers were advised to warn purchasers that "Because the United Nations represents all races and creeds the cards do not use special Christmas symbols. Appropriately, each carries season's greetings in the five official UN languages, English, French, Spanish, Russian and Chinese."[83] In the first year, Canadians bought 33,000 more cards than were originally ordered, raising $7,500 and making the country's per capita sales figure higher than that of any other participating nation. A press release for the UNA claimed the card sales were a coast-to-coast effort: "Anyone looking over the list of shipments would feel that there could hardly be a single community in Canada that was missed."[84] The cards became an annual fall project that by 1975 had raised over $11 million.

UNICEF's second fundraising project, Trick-or-Treat for UNICEF, became the agency's most successful fundraiser and was responsible for raising almost half of the $21 million earned between 1955 and 1975. The program's success can be attributed to recruiting a relatively untapped group of volunteers and supporters, children, whose participation opened new avenues and labour for fundraising. UNICEF was not the first organization to use children to collect money to send overseas; this had long been a mainstay of Sunday-school projects and children's clubs. For example, the French Catholic St. Enfance Association in Quebec had been asking students to save their pennies to redeem and educate the children in "unfaithful" countries since 1843. Between 1930 and 1950 their alms went towards "buying" the souls of Chinese children, a project that raised almost $2 million before it was abandoned when all foreign missionaries had to leave China after the Communist takeover.[85] UNICEF's Trick-or-Treat scheme saw thousands—and later, hundreds of thousands—of children go door to door on Halloween asking for small donations to save children around the world. The idea was born in 1950 when a Sunday-school class in Philadelphia decided to ask for coins instead of candy and raised $17 for UNICEF. In 1955 Canadian children joined the clamour for coins in addition to or in lieu of candy, raising $15,000 in their first year.[86] Four years later, 229,600 Canadian children were enrolled in the program.

There were organizational and ideological concerns to overcome before the Trick-or-Treat program became an entrenched feature of Canadian children's Halloween routine. Some parents questioned the suitability of turning a pagan or silly celebration into a charitable event, while others thought Halloween should be a lighthearted holiday. The adult workload appeared to be another roadblock. In preparation for making this an annual event, UNA members met with school boards, parent-teacher associations, youth groups, women's clubs, churches, and service groups, hoping to mobilize their support in launching this campaign every October. Although the collection took place on only one night per year, adult volunteers were needed to distribute UN literature in advance and educate the participating children and potential donors on the UNICEF cause throughout the autumn. Then on November 1 adults were needed to count, organize, and forward the collected coins to the local UNA. Since schools were the logical starting point, there were concerns over the increased labour bestowed upon teachers. The baby boom had put pressures on the school system, where the focus was on building new schools and hiring new staff, not on new extracurricular activities.[87] Initially schools were reluctant to commit, which left parents, women's clubs, and teenagers to pioneer the program with support from UNA branches. In many communities women's groups took the lead, making the milk-carton containers (in the years before the standard orange boxes became the norm) and holding roll-the-penny parties for the children after they came back trick or treating.[88] One Ottawa mother, Mrs. Phillion, attempted to run the campaign on her own when she had her four children collect coins one Halloween. Afterwards she wrote to the *Ottawa Citizen* explaining that the schools needed to take the project on because without large-scale awareness, Phillion found it difficult to raise much money in her neighbourhood.[89] In other locales, service-minded teens organized the collection with a little help from their moms and dads. High-school student Lorraine Oak recalls how she initiated the Halloween campaign in her Edmonton school district singlehandedly in the early 1960s:

> I contacted the UN association and they provided me with lots of little cardboard containers and my dear father ran around the schools with me where I went and gave talks about UNICEF and Brownie packs and whatever. I would then go and collect the little containers and count the money and turn it in to the UN association for UNICEF. I became very interested in the work of UNICEF … I was always particularly moved by children in need and this was certainly a major organization that was focusing on children.[90]

It is possible that schools eventually came on board because they saw the value of supervising an effort that was producing global-citizen-minded students like Oak. Therefore the program could be seen as part of the social studies, health, history, or economics curriculum, rather than extra work.

Eventually UNICEF persuasively sold the campaign to schools and parents as a character-building exercise for Canadian children. One promotional flyer described the Halloween program as "a sharing project designed to benefit children everywhere, both at home and abroad."[91] Just as the UNICEF money went to help develop the minds and bodies of children in places like France, Egypt, and Malaysia, UNICEF was seen as developing the hearts of Canadian children by teaching them the value of money, charity, compassion, and gratitude for their own circumstances. From the "seeds of destiny" perspective, it was equally important to create the right kind of child in Canada and abroad; this would help preserve democracy. This message was viewed as empowering for many of the young participants. Being consider mini-UN ambassadors gave a different spin to the oft-heard message of "do unto others." This time the so-called "others" were children just like themselves, an idea that was highly appealing and relatable to children. Oak explains she was drawn to participate in UNICEF because, "I remember [the UN] appealing to children to help other children … we sort of expect adults to do everything and there are children in need. So we as children should be doing something. And I really felt that as a child, I felt that children should be doing something."[92] UNICEF insisted that children could make a difference; they did not have to wait to be adults to influence the world. To emphasis this, UNICEF showed how even the loose change collected by one child could help change someone's life. Posters sent out to participants listed how just one penny could buy five large glasses of milk or enough vaccine to protect a child from tuberculosis, a nickel could buy enough penicillin to cure one child of yaws, and a quarter could buy enough DDT to protect two children for one year against malaria.[93] This aura of empowerment was illustrated in one UNICEF cartoon that showed two children dressed in costumes. The boy said, "SO far I've got three apples!" The girl, perhaps reflecting a gendered interest in UNICEF, looked into her UNICEF box, replied, "SO far I've saved three children."[94] When UNICEF won the Nobel Peace Prize in 1965, a newsletter recounted how one North American boy reportedly ran home to tell his mother that he won the Nobel because, since he had trick-or-treated for UNICEF, he was part of UNICEF.[95]

UNICEF attempted to mobilize everywhere in Canada, but their planning manual noted the difficulties this entailed. Children in rural areas and small towns were the first to get involved because it was easier to organize fewer people. It was more difficult to coordinate widespread support in urban centres where the prevalence of apartment buildings and dense neighbourhoods often made Halloween parties sponsored by schools or community centres the more popular and safer option than trick-or-treating.[96] This was the committee's reasoning behind regional variations in average participation and donations. For example, while children in Ontario and Quebec always brought in the most money, Prince Edward Island consistently had the highest per capita participation across the country.[97] Occasionally, Canada's climate also played a factor in geographic participation. Very often winter had arrived by late October, which made trick-or-treating times rushed for children bundled into snowsuits over their costumes—or even impossible.

In 1971 parts of Manitoba were hit by a major blizzard, an event that the national office expected would derail the province's UNICEF contributions. Surprisingly Manitoba managed to raise $9,500 that year, an increase of 78 percent from the previous year, proof that UNICEF had become entrenched in Canadians' hearts as a duty not to be overlooked for lack of clear skies.[98]

By the late 1960s, UNICEF had even spread to northern Canada, where inclement weather was a minor inconvenience compared to the problems of regional underdevelopment and a small population. In 1965, eight schools in the Northwest Territories participated in UNICEF's Halloween program for the first time. Kate Aitken, one of UNICEF's national chairs, explicitly stated the background of the children in one Inuvik school in her annual report, proudly noting how "ten Eskimo, five white, and two Indian children" had collectively raised two dollars for UNICEF.[99] This type of anecdote celebrates cross-cultural co-operation, a hallmark of internationalism. More importantly, it implied that all of Canada's peoples, even those presumed to be less fortunate, cared about UNICEF. This habit was not UNICEF's alone; other foreign relief agencies frequently used examples of the less affluent within Canada as propaganda to reinforce the diversity and inherent nobility of their donors. Still, among UNICEF's youngest fundraisers, confusion about where and whom their pennies were helping grew out of localized assumptions about need. For example, a group of students at one Edmonton elementary school assumed the Indian boy their class was sponsoring came from a local reserve instead of the country of India.[100] These children were not the only confused Canadians. Even the beloved UNICEF was plagued with debates over whether Canadians should spend their aid dollars at home, amongst their own underprivileged populations.

To combat these common critiques or confusions, the foreign relief agencies offered explanations about why their programs focused on assisting foreign children rather than those at home. They did not deny that "our Indians" needed attention; instead, they emphasized the extreme circumstances found in nations such as war-torn Korea or refugee-overwhelmed Hong Kong, where populations had been uprooted by war and where economic or political circumstances made governments and other local institutions unable to care for their own populations.[101] Canada, they pointed out, had federal and provincial agencies dedicated to helping the Aboriginal population, plus a growing welfare state that provided a safety net for all Canadian children's basic needs, through, for example, family allowance, widow's pensions, free schooling, and medicare. In a brochure explaining why it did not provide for children it referred to as "Indian" and "Eskimo," one foster parent plan agency explained that running a comparable relief program would be unaffordable at home in Canada, where the dollar could only go so far. In 1972 it cost $17 a month to sponsor a child in South Vietnam, but to do the same for a Canadian child would cost much more, and presumably this charitable act would be too expensive for the average Canadian donor.[102] It was never mentioned that helping "our Indians" was not as politically expedient or emotionally dramatic as assisting children whose fate was tied to Cold War conflict.[103]

While donations came in from all sectors of society, the women who sat on the Canadian UNICEF committee leaned toward the elite. Many of the chairs and executive were well known and established in their communities—some were even nationally known, such as radio personality Kate Aitken and Senator Muriel Fergusson. The committee also included VOW Presidents Helen Tucker and Muriel Duckworth and at least one woman with a connection to civil defence. Margaret Konantz was a mother of three children married to a Winnipeg businessman. She was active with the Junior League and the Red Cross, and she volunteered with the Women's Voluntary Services in England during the Second World War. After her children were grown and her husband died, Konantz devoted more time to service work. In 1956 she was invited to London to work with the Women's Voluntary Service, which at the time was deeply involved in Cold War emergency preparedness. When she returned to Winnipeg she decided against helping organize a civil defence program; instead, she joined the UNA, explaining, "I chose an organization working for peace, rather than preparing for war."[104] Through the Winnipeg and National UNAs, Konantz became involved with UNICEF, chairing its National Committee between 1959 and 1965. As chair, she personally subsidized trips to Asia, the Middle East, and Africa, where she viewed UNICEF projects in progress in seventeen countries.

In Canada Konantz embarked on a national speaking tour to schools, women's clubs, and public meetings, hoping to enlighten Canadians about UNICEF's accomplishments and consequently raise more funds for the organization. Her speeches contained stories about the children she encountered and her strong desire to rescue them from their unfortunate situations. One story that frequently appeared in her talks was her observation of a little boy in Calcutta sitting in an alley. She described how the boy's eyes haunted her. He was too tired to even move them when she spoke to him. She did not have her camera with her but she "thought maybe if I could get a picture of this child, I would have proof how great this need was to help 600,000,000 in this world that lack adequate food, clothing, shelter and protection from disease."[105] Her example was similar to imagery found in UNRRA's film *Seeds of Destiny*, where the silent sad faces of a few spoke for millions, and the children's appearance, demeanour, and homelessness contrasted sharply with her audience's idea of the lives of most Canadian children. Through her travels and passion for UNICEF, Konantz concluded that internationalism was not something Canadians could choose, but a reality that came from living in the modern world. In her speeches, like the one to the Junior League excerpted below, Konantz stressed the responsibilities that came with internationalism and warned how ignoring them would not only hurt children, like the little Indian boy in the alley, but also threaten Canada's security and commitment to freedom:

> Our world today is very small. Whether we like it or not, we can look over the fences of our international neighbours all too easily, and some of the things we see are not pleasant ... We of the West believe that slums should not be tolerated. We know that poverty, hunger, poor living conditions breed unrest, discontent, trouble, even rebellion. Surely in this constricting world of ours we cannot sit idly by and not try to do something about making basic improvements in health, education, production of food, and trade where it is needed most.

Konantz's speech concluded with an invitation to join an international organization, insisting that only through international understanding would peace occur.[106] Not happy with merely inspiring other individuals to carrying the torch for peace, at age sixty-four Konantz entered national politics, successfully running as the Liberal member for Winnipeg South.

Konantz explained her decision to enter formal politics this way: "I thought about it a great deal and realized that many of the problems we face can be solved only on the national and international level. It seemed a logical and almost inevitable step for me to run for office."[107] Konantz was also following in the footsteps of her mother, Edith Rogers, who had been the first female member of the Manitoba legislature. After losing the 1962 election, Konantz won in 1963 and became the first female Member of Parliament for Manitoba. This leap was one also attempted by fellow peace activists Thérèse Casgrain (CCF/NDP Quebec 1953, 1957, 1958) and Kay Macpherson (Independent/NDP Ontario 1972, 1974) and civil defence matron Hazel Braithwaite (NDP Alberta 1965)—all of whom ran unsuccessfully, though Casgrain was appointed to the Senate in 1970. In Parliament Konantz continued to champion international relief and development, arguing that this was the right thing to do, as well as being central to Canada's foreign policy and defence policy. As an MP, Konantz remained active with the UNA and UNICEF, becoming one of Canada's representatives to the UN in 1963. In 1965 she was selected to represent Canada in Oslo when UNICEF received the Nobel Peace Prize.[108] After meeting with Konantz in 1963, Prime Minister Lester Pearson promised to increase the Canadian government's annual contribution to UNICEF to $1 million, explaining that one of the factors in his decision was the "the nation-wide support for the work of UNICEF as demonstrated in Halloween collections and the greeting cards sales."[109]

The impetus for starting UNICEF and the concerns that drove women such as Konantz were the fractured childhoods depicted in the book *War and Children* and the film *Seeds of Destiny*, stories of individual suffering caused by persistent global insecurity, which if left untreated could cause future turmoil. Rescuing these bodies from war, hunger, sickness, and dire straits was considered a humane act for Canada, one that reflected its renewed commitment to internationalism and would bring the world closer to peace. Out of all the possible options, including civil defence and peace activism, the UN appeared to be the most popular and respectable vehicle to achieve these goals. Setting asides its successes and failures from a diplomatic perspective, most Canadians valued the UN's welfare activities in assisting postwar refugees and its continued efforts to improve the lives of children affected by war and poverty. They expressed their support most tangibly through volunteer hours and donations. The UN's supposed neutrality shielded it from Red Scare paranoia, which allowed the organization to speak openly about desires for peace when other peace groups could not. Additionally, it was hoped that the organization's sizeable resources and worldwide admiration gave it the best chance to accomplish monumental tasks.

The UN was also a space that welcomed women into its fold at most levels, as UNRRA employees Brown and McGeachy, UN representative Konantz, UNA executive members Casselman and Lawrence, and young girls like UNICEF youth coordinator Oak could attest. There were also the thousands of women who, as parents, teachers, social workers, and club members, worked behind the scenes to facilitate the food drives, speaker series, class projects, and coin counting. From the mid-1940s through to the early 1960s, the UN was the critical vehicle through which women could address their concerns about peace and security; however, many women did so in conjunction with civil defence, disarmament, or other foreign relief activities. This collaboration could be viewed as a form of covering all bases, but it more likely existed because each area of activity catered to a shared interest in protecting and caring for children. If the tangible support for civil defence and disarmament could be measured in first aid courses, fallout shelters, baby teeth, and test ban treaties, UN supporters could point to dollar signs. The enormous success in fundraising was proof of the optimism and devotion of so many Canadians—men, women, and children—regarding the UN. Foster parent plan programs, administered by religious and secular charities, were another form of Cold War activism that put great hope in monetary contributions making a difference in the lives of children, but they did so in a much more intimate and overtly politicized way than any UN program. Furthermore, foster parent plan relationships, often referred to as "adoptions," placed Canadians, particularly women, in the role of surrogate parents, providing long-distance love and care for their foreign sons or daughters, specifically those living in nations allied with Canada or nations where political or economic influence was desired.

CHAPTER FIVE

Long-Distance Mothers
Foster Parent Plan Programs

"Dear my loving mother …"[1] These are the words that open twelve-year-old Chin Ho's 1968 letter to his Canadian foster mother, Rita Black. Charlottetown resident Black sponsored the Korean boy through the Canadian foreign relief agency, the Unitarian Service Committee (USC). Chin Ho was Black's second sponsorship of a Korean child, having previously sponsored a little girl. Chin Ho continued his letter by asking Black, "How are you getting along nowadays? With your warm loving I am quite well and all things are going all right with me recently." In the same letter, he described the recent visit of USC founder, Dr. Lotta Hitschmanova, whom he referred to as "grandmother," to the disabled children's home outside of Seoul where he lived. "We greeted her shaking your Canadian flag," Chin Ho explained, and included with his letter a picture taken with Hitschmanova and a wish that one day he could also take a photo with Black. He concluded by writing, "I am waiting for your letter. God bless you richly. Good-bye, From your son in Korea."[2] Within six years of Black's sponsorship, Chin Ho was released from the Children's Home after being successfully treated for paralysis caused by polio and went to live with relatives. After Chin Ho's sponsorship ended, Black was matched with her third and final foster child, Biyu, a five-year-old Chinese refugee girl living in Hong Kong.

Foster parent plan programs were a unique method of philanthropy whereby orphaned or needy children living outside of Canada, whose mothers and/or fathers could not provide for them, became linked to a donor

Lotta Hitschmanova and USC foster child in South Korea, 1954. Courtesy of
USC Canada.

living in a Western nation who would send them a monthly sum of money.
Facilitated by non-governmental agencies, the donations were used to pay
for an orphan's care in an institution or assist a parent or relative in paying
rent and buying food, school supplies, clothes, and any medical necessities.
Donors were matched with a specific child; they received a photo, biography,
and measurements of the child (so they could send clothing) and were expected
to exchange letters processed through a translator. These were not legally
binding adoptions or similar to domestic foster parent guardianships, but
rather a charitable obligation, one where the money was only one part of
the sponsorship. "Money is important," Foster Parents Plan International
(FPPI) chairwoman Edna Blue acknowledged, "but love and attention are
even more important."[3] Therefore Black's financial support of Chin Ho was
not the only reason that the boy got better: her emotional role as his long-
distance mother was viewed as critical to his recovery. The idea of providing
substitute parents, even those oceans away, was one response to Freud and
Burlingham's theories about the importance of ensuring war-affected children had caring adults in their lives in order to minimize the developmental
impact of war. In Canada this idea was becoming increasing popular for

local child welfare solutions, too. As noted by Veronica Strong-Boag, "The Cold War celebration of domesticity as the solution to personal and national problems" meant the decline of state-run or privately run institutions caring for displaced children and the search for family-like settings in the form of group homes, foster parenting, and adoption.[4]

Foster parent plans gave Canadian women the opportunity to export their mothering as a means to improve the life of one specially selected boy or girl whose health and safety had been the casualty of war. At the same time, this small act was thought to mend global tensions by spreading love, money, and Canadian values. These goals parallel women's interests and commitments to maternalism, nationalism, and internationalism found in the other forms of activism presented in this study. Although the delivery of care differed from civil defence, the women who participated in foster parent plans as donors or employees were similarly recruited for their expertise as caregivers to perform paid and unpaid labour in the health and welfare fields. Moreover, just like their counterparts in the disarmament movement and in UN-based activism, participation in foster parent plans reinforced women's dual obligations as Canadians and global citizens. Conversely, unlike the internationalist message presented in WILPF, VOW, or UN programming, which emphasized collectivity and interdependence among all nations, the foster parent programs' geographic focus and political context were mired in Cold War agendas.

Although Europe remained a hot spot for aid, for the first time, the majority of Canada's international relief was being directed toward unfamiliar groups of people, those outside Western Europe and even the Commonwealth, who lived in regions where most Canadians had few personal ties or previous economic investments. Historian Robert Bothwell argues that it was not until World War II that Canadians interacted with Asia directly: "Culturally, Canadians, like Americans, faced East, not West, to Europe, not Asia."[5] Although India and China had always been of interest to missionaries, Asia's strategic position in the Cold War made the entire continent a major target for foreign relief. With North Korea under Soviet control, China's turn to communism in 1949 caused the Western allies to fear that this revolutionary spirit would spread throughout the continent, particularly in the recently decolonized nations of Southeast Asia. In 1954 U.S. President Truman rolled out his Domino Theory, which predicted that, if the newly independent Vietnam also fell to communism, the rest of the region would soon follow. Most Canadians were keen to save Asia from communism and became intimate with the civil conflicts in China, Korea, and Vietnam;

the crowded refugee situation in Hong Kong; and the development and decolonization of India.[6]

Prime Minister St. Laurent considered international aid to be one of three strategies (along with military defence and ridding Canada of communist supporters) that Canada should use to win the Cold War. Under St. Laurent's administration, Canada extended its non-UN-related foreign aid from Europe to Asia in 1950, starting with an annual commitment of $850,000 to aid the development of the decolonized British Commonwealth nations of Asia—particularly India—in a program called the Colombo Plan.[7] In a speech to the Canadian Club, St. Laurent specifically encouraged economic investment and relief in Asia, where

> hundreds of millions of people have become increasingly aware of their poverty even as they were obtaining their independence ... We must try to demonstrate that in the Western world we possess the real solution to the problem and that it is from us and not from Soviet imperialism that economic and social progress are to be expected.[8]

It was hoped Canada would form strong relationships with the Asian countries they were aiding and, in return, create stable nations whose political, economic, and cultural practices reflected Canada's own values. The new destination for Canadian relief efforts meant that the "foreignness" of the recipients could not be ignored. This can be seen in the correspondence between foster parents and foster children, where even the warmest gestures could be tainted by racist and imperialist understandings. These racialized assumptions also contributed to Canadian foreign relief offering a new form of child welfare support in Asia—family planning. In addition to foster parent plan programs, Hong Kong and later India and Vietnam were the site of USC and FPPI's first overseas family planning initiatives.

Whether the destination was Europe or Asia, the secularization of foreign aid did not diminish the "missionary" nature of these transactions. During the Cold War, the type of desired conversion was primarily political rather than religious. As with UN child welfare programs, it was believed that, by investing in impoverished or orphaned children, Canada could calm future dissent while collecting allies and spreading Canadian interests abroad. Under these conditions, foster children were not just needy children: they were ticking bombs that needed to be defused in order to tip the Cold War balance in Canada's favour. As the film *Seeds of Destiny* presented in stark terms, the threat of a new war lay not only in weapons but in the stomachs, minds, and hearts of the children living in the have-not or war-torn nations. It was imperative that these children grow up healthy and happy—otherwise they might be tempted to support communism or engage in other forms of revolt that could trigger global insecurity. Hitschmanova laid out these variables to foster parents when she indicated that sponsored children "represent the hope for a better tomorrow."[9] In this case, "tomorrow" referred to the individual futures of the foster children and the fate of the nations in which they lived. It was also meant to represent a long-term investment in Canada's own well-being, since, in Hitschmanova's words, assisting foreign children "is not only our humanitarian duty, but it is also a very wise move for the future to help your own Canadian children ten or fifteen years from now."[10] Such statements appealed to donors' dual identities and motivations as loving parents and representatives of the West in the Cold War struggle. Therefore sponsors were never just portrayed as caring adults, but were always identified as Canadians whose acts of charity demonstrated the benefits of capitalism and the generosity of democratic states, while concurrently acting as an insurance policy for their own national interests.

At the same time, the sponsoring agencies vigorously denied that their programs had any political dimensions and insisted foster parent plans were purely humanitarian gestures arising from a sense of love or charity. As postwar research on displaced children (examined in chapter 4) demonstrated, children were in real need and Canadians felt real compassion toward their circumstances. USC went out of its way to emphasis the children's innocence, declaring in one of their films about children in war-torn Greece and South Korea, "But for an accident of geography, these children might be our own. They have made no war, taken no part in politics, created no atomic weapons. They have no hatred in their minds. Should they not have a place in our hearts?"[11] The children may have been innocent, but buried within the humanitarian nature of this form of foreign relief were motives that were clearly inspired by the Cold War. Unlike UN-sponsored foreign aid, Canada's foster parent plan programs only assisted children living in nations where there had been a victory or an ongoing battle against communism. Therefore aid was given to children in post-civil-war Greece, where the communists had been defeated, but not to those in communist-controlled Hungary. Even though children in all parts of Korea were affected by the war, only children in the South became foster children to Canadian donors. To be fair, it is likely that the Canadian government would have prevented any Canadian agency from setting up a program in a communist-controlled country, and even if they had not, the Red Scare would have kept donors away. As shown by China's deportation of Western aid workers, communist regimes did not welcome aid from outside the Soviet or Chinese blocs. Still, USC or FPPI never publically expressed frustration about not being able to help children living outside of their reach. Furthermore, with the exception of Biafra aid, very few Canadian foreign aid agencies organized programs to assist children battling drought, debt, and civil conflict in non-aligned Latin American and African countries until the 1970s and 1980s. Sending aid to the enemy or to non-strategic regions was simply not a priority, which speaks to the often silent politics present in foster parent plan programming. Occasionally this message was overt, such as when sponsoring a foster child was described as giving "each of us a chance to fight a little cold war of our own."[12] These were the very words FPPI used to recruit Prime Minister Diefenbaker's wife, Olive, as a foster mother. As described in chapter 3, Mrs. Diefenbaker felt it was inappropriate to join the potentially controversial VOW, but she thought the right message would be sent if she became the foster mother to Huizhong, a Chinese girl living in Hong Kong who was described as a refugee from communism. Although the wording was not always as explicit as that of the note sent to Mrs. Diefenbaker, FPPI nevertheless clearly implied that Canadians could help win the Cold War one heart at a time.

Foster parent plan programs illustrate the tensions that were inherent in Cold War child welfare projects when the affected children were presented as both real and symbolic. These tensions will be explored by examining the recruitment and role of women supporters, the letters between Canadian foster mothers and their children, and the outcomes of the aid in three sites of Cold War conflict: Greece, South Korea, and Hong Kong. The collected evidence suggests the constructed relationship between foster mother and child could be one of great affection; however, it could also be awkward and disappointing due to cross-cultural misunderstandings, the broader Cold War politics triggering this form of relief, and the sometimes conflicting expectations of the foster child, the foster parent, and the sponsoring agencies. As a result, foster parent programs should be considered an intimate form of Cold War imperialism, one in which thousands of Canadian women participated with great enthusiasm, both as foster parents and as welfare workers supervising the overseas distribution of aid to orphanages and families.

A Feminized Front of Donors, Dollars, and Diapers

Several secular and faith based charities active in Canada ran foster parent plan schemes in the first three decades of the Cold War. Two of the most popular programs were FPPI, an American agency operating in Canada, and USC, a Canadian organization. FPPI was established during the 1930s to help child refugees fleeing the Spanish Civil War. By 1944 FPPI had 1,228 foster children from four European countries sponsored at the cost of approximately $10 a month, a figure that by 1975 had risen to 56,520 children from ten countries, including several Cold War hot spots, at the new cost of $17 a month.[13] FPPI's head office was in New York City, and a secondary office was opened in Montreal in 1949 to handle the rising number of Canadian donors. Initially the office was not much more than a board of directors and a post office box set up for tax reasons. Yet by 1968 it was noted that one in four foster parents were Canadian, so a national director and staff were hired to manage Canadian donations.[14] FPPI had a permanent office in each of the countries they worked in; each was run by an American or Canadian Director who worked with a team of local social workers. FPPI localized their affairs so as to be able to closely supervise the distribution of sponsorship money to orphanages and families.

USC was founded in 1945 by Hitschmanova, whose own experience as a young woman fleeing Nazi-occupied Czechoslovakia inspired her to return the help she received as a refugee in France. Hitschmanova was not a physician but referred to herself as a doctor because of her PhD in journalism. Upon her immigration to Canada in 1946, she launched a national fundraising drive to collect supplies and cash to send to Europe to help with the enormous refugee situation. Soon after it began, Hitschmanova's venture developed into a permanent organization with a head office in Ottawa and branches across the country. USC continued to provide emergency relief and also began a foster parent program similar to FPPI's, except USC only catered to children in orphanages, while FPPI assisted impoverished children living at home, too. Despite the Unitarian moniker, USC was a non-denominational group— the name was chosen in honour of the Unitarian association that cared for Hitschmanova as refugee in France—and had no connection to the Unitarian Church or the American service organization of the same name.

Compared to FPPI, USC was a one-woman show. Although both agencies had a small staff, a board of directors, and hundreds of volunteers, the name USC was inseparable with the image of its founder. Unlike FPPI, no USC staff lived in the field. Instead Hitschmanova travelled several months each year visiting her organization's overseas projects and spending time with the children under USC care. Hitschmanova never married or had children of her own, but she took great pride in being known as "Godmother from Canada," "Mother of a Thousand Children," and "World Orphans Mother,"

Lotta Hitschmanova in her distinctive uniform with a Vancouver
schoolgirl during the "Milk for India" campaign in the 1940s.
Courtesy of USC Canada.

the maternal nicknames given to her by the recipients of her aid.[15] When
she returned home to Canada, she would hit the road again, travelling across
the country sharing stories about what she had seen abroad and asking for
help.[16] In these appeals, her personal refugee experience was used to sell the
need for relief, as well as to demonstrate what could be accomplished when
one was safe and comfortable in a country like Canada. Her distinctive
high-pitched and heavily accented voice was familiar to Canadians who
listened to her frequent radio appeals; the foreignness of her voice and origins
was mitigated by her patriotism for Canada.[17] Although she was not a Cold
War migrant, her recent exit from Czechoslovakia positioned her as being
on the "right" side of the Cold War. Hitschmanova frequently spoke of how
happy and proud she was to be in Canada, sentiments symbolized by the
maple leaf pin she always wore on her lapel.[18]

Hitschmanova's image was just as distinctive and memorable as her
voice. She was never seen in public without her personally designed wool
uniform, which resembled that of a military nurse. She explained the reason
behind her uniform had nothing to do with militarism and everything to
do with being practical: "the kind of life I lead would be unnecessarily
complicated if I wore the customary woman's attire, consisting of frilly

dresses, hats and elegant shoes. How could I possibly travel thousands of miles, especially overseas, but also in Canada, if I had to change clothes several times a day?"[19] The uniform also reflected the vow of poverty she strove to uphold in her personal and professional life. She maintained it was her moral responsibility to stretch her donors' dollars and was appalled when on one occasion UNRRA officials took her out for a fancy dinner, stating, "I would have liked a piece of dry bread and nothing else."[20] Hitschmanova's pious attitude as reflected in her dress and personality, a relic of her own experiences as a refugee, could have turned off potential donors who did not wish to be made to feel guilty about how good life was in postwar Canada by a holier-than-thou outsider. In fact, Hitschmanova's nationalist and internationalist rhetoric only seemed to make Canadians more generous. In 1946, USC's first year of operation, the organization raised money and goods worth $225,000. By 1960 this figure had almost tripled to $757,000, tripling again by 1974 to over $2.2 million.[21]

Although the USC often appeared to be a one-woman operation, it depended on volunteers staffing branches across the country. Based on the personal information contained in letters to USC, Hitschmanova was able to identify her support as coming mainly from "women ranging in age from barely 20 to well over 80 and 85. They come from many backgrounds and belong to every denomination. A goodly number remember hardship at home or during the war."[22] As a result, Hitschmanova told recipients that their gifts came in the name of Canada and in the name of Canadian mothers. This was more than just hyperbole. A sample of donors between 1954 and 1975 showed that the highest number of sponsorships were in the name of married women (27 percent), followed by women's organizations (15 percent), couples (14 percent—where it was most often the women who handled the correspondence with their foster child), women whose marital status was single or unknown (14 percent), men whose marital status was single or unknown (11 percent), married men (8 percent), schools and church groups (6 percent), businesses or groups of co-workers (4 percent), and men's organizations (1 percent).[23] FPPI had a similarly gendered donor base. One 1971 survey of existing foster parents by an external marketing company found that 62 percent were female.[24] Despite this evidence, one male member of the USC board of directors disputed the notion that USC was a women's organization and asked *Maclean's* to withdraw this claim from an article profiling the organization. His concern implies he might have felt the connotations of calling the USC a woman's organization were limiting, in that it could suggest a frivolous nature, one that might only draw female supporters.

He might also have been concerned that the label called to mind bridge clubs or sewing circles and have feared USC's work would not be taken seriously. It is also possible that he personally did not like the idea of working for a group skewed to women. Whatever the reason, his response implies that the maternalistic rhetoric might have closed as many doors as it opened if women's legitimacy as political actors was considered something that should be hidden.[25]

There was enough demand for both FPPI and USC, along with several agencies with similar foster parent schemes, to operate in Canada without stepping on each other's toes, even if they targeted the same group of donors. Donors came from a variety of backgrounds; however, there appears to a typical foster parent. She was a married female who had an income large enough that it allowed her to keep up with a monthly donation. She was of European origin and most likely lived in English Canada. This information was gauged by a sampling of the last names, language, and origin of the letters sent to USC.[26] The occupations of foster parents included students, workers, professionals, and retired senior citizens. It appears that, for every Marie Labelle, a single woman from a small town in Quebec who could not afford the full cost of a sponsorship, but wanted to send in $1 to $2 a month for "un petit protégé," there were wealthy donors such as the married couple from Bridgewater, Nova Scotia, who could afford to send their foster son extra gifts, such as a watch and camera on his birthday.[27] Labelle appears to be one of the few foster parents from French Canada. Although several foster parents resided in Quebec, only two of the letters in the USC sample were written in French, which seems to indicate that most sponsors within and outside of Quebec were Anglophones. The lack of Francophone representation appears to stem from there being little French or bilingual promotional material. Even though the FPPI's head office was located in Montreal, the organization deemed it unaffordable to translate their publicity material into French until the late 1970s.[28] Additionally, despite the focus on Asia, it does not appear that many Asian Canadians donated to USC and FPPI. Rather than conclude these two groups of Canadians were not interested in participating, it is quite possible similar types of donations were made through ethnic or church organizations.

The first Cold War relief mobilization for both FPPI and USC was in post-civil-war Greece. During the Second World War the Greeks had found themselves fighting on two fronts, a collaborative effort against German occupation and internal tension between right-wing and left-wing political factions. In 1946 this sparring evolved into a three-year civil war between the right-wing government backed by Britain and the United States and a coalition of socialists and communists supported by the newly formed communist governments in Yugoslavia and Albania. Communities and families still rebuilding from the Second World War were once again thrown into turmoil as battles raged around the countryside. Some 700,000 civilians living in the north fled south to government-secured areas, and the overall health of the population plummeted to below the levels seen in World War II. As before, children became the unfortunate victims of war and a large part of the refugee crisis. Amid the fighting, the UN investigated charges that the leftist guerrilla forces had taken more than 23,000 children to neighbouring socialist countries, reportedly for their safety and re-education. In response, the government relocated 18,000 children, taking them from their families and placing them in children's villages in regions under its control.[29] When the fighting concluded in 1949 with the communist forces defeated, the repatriation of the removed children from each side began. It was estimated that 270,000 children had lost at least one parent and another 36,000 were missing both parents. Most refugee children required some form of medical treatment. Days after the peace treaty was signed, a FPPI representative working with the Greek Ministry of Coordination, Finance, and Social Welfare reported the aftermath of the conflict in the simplest of terms: "Children are dying here in hundreds from exposure and privation. Beg you make people understand and help. Thousands without shelter tragically orphaned without food or clothing. Please ship warm clothing immediately. Delay means death."[30]

Immediately FPPI expanded their foster parent program to include Greece, and they started their 1949 campaign with a profile of Yolanda. At age twelve, Yolanda was already a veteran of two wars; orphaned during the Second World War, she later lost an eye when hit by a mortar shell during the civil conflict and needed an operation so she could be fitted with a glass eye. Her story and photograph were featured in advertisements entitled "I want a blue eye!" The goal of this campaign was to pull at the heartstrings and make the recipient of Canadian help seem closer by giving her a name and face. The enthusiastic response to Yolanda's ad demonstrates the popularity of this form of appeal. FPPI received an outpouring of support from Canadian women wishing to offer Yolanda what her advertisement requested, that is, "the loving care that so rightly belongs to childhood."[31] A Holocaust survivor living in Canada sent in five dollars, explaining that she was moved to help Yolanda because she had lost two blue-eyed children in the Second World War.[32] Another woman explained how her own five-year-old daughter sold her tricycle to send the money to help the Greek girl with the hurt eye.[33] From this perspective, the sponsorships appear to be driven by empathy; however, Yolanda's campaign also hinted at the global insecurity found within Cold War politics. Potential donors were openly advised of the broader goals of the foster parent plan program, such as the notion that "by aiding these children you are working for the greatest aim of all—peace."[34] But FPPI went even further and specified the type of peace desired. Subsequent FPPI advertisements featured Yolanda, now with the Anglicized name of Annie, expressing her thanks to FPPI and her Canadian donors for helping her get well and allowing her to pursue her dream of becoming a nurse or hairdresser.[35] FPPI strove to show that its children were happy and grateful, subtly inferring that, if they were ever forced to choose sides in a Cold War battle, they would remember the generosity of their North American "mothers."

Yolanda, an FPPI foster child from Greece, pictured prior to her sponsorship. Courtesy of PLAN Canada and the Foster Parents Plan International fonds, Special Collections, University of Rhode Island.

Yolanda, renamed Annie, as a teen after her eye surgery. Courtesy of PLAN Canada and the Foster Parents Plan International fonds, Special Collections, University of Rhode Island.

The events taking place in Greece—described by the press as the first front of the Cold War—were front-page news in Canada, yet aid workers worried that the dominant image of Greece for most Canadians was ancient ruins and sandy islands. There was a need to update this picture in order to build a specialized relief effort. Hitschmanova, who had been the first Canadian to enter rural Greece and meet with villagers after the cessation of fighting, asked Canadians to imagine a similar situation happening at home:

> Suddenly, within a few weeks, ten percent of our Canadian population, namely one million two hundred thousand people, would be uprooted by some enemy and would be pouring into one certain security area, let us say around Montreal or Toronto. What would happen? ... All normal life would suddenly cease to exist ... This is exactly what happened in Greece.[36]

She went on to list the various problems caused by the fighting and displacement, including a lack of food, clothing, electricity, water, coal, school supplies, blankets, pot and pans, and medicine. Interestingly, the scenario Hitschmanova described, an imagined attack on Canada, the displaced population, and the end of life as it was known, was similar to ones used by both civil defence planners and ban-the-bomb groups. Canadians had only to look abroad to existing non-nuclear conflicts for a reminder of what would be lost in a war. The tactic seemed to work. Canadians responded by signing up to be foster parents and by becoming long-distance mothers through other means—by sending baby clothes, diapers, and food. This aid could be seen not only as relief, but also as a reward for the victors defeating the communists. The Greeks were seen as valiant, worthy, and ideologically deserving of Canadian help. Had the communists won, it is doubtful that any Western agency would have offered the same support. Within a year, USC had collected 22,235 pounds of relief items valued at $158,000 along with $48,000 in cash donations.[37]

The fundraising for Greece reveals the special gendered message of the appeal and the important role played by women's organizations. One issue that Hitschmanova frequently mentioned in her speeches was how few resources Greek mothers had to raise their children, calling on Canadian mothers to fill the gap. "Help us ... to save our children!" she claimed the Greek mothers pleaded, and she described how they were forced to dress their babies in rags, newspapers, and potato sacks, and how the children she saw were covered in sores from the lack of soap.[38] These descriptions undoubtedly shocked many Canadian mothers, who launched a specialized campaign for Greece in Western Canada called the March of Diapers, evoking the popular North American polio campaign, the March of Dimes. Coordinated through five women's organizations, volunteers vowed to collect 12,000 diapers for USC. As demonstrated in previous chapters, women's organizations were effective networks to publicize a cause and recruit participants. They were suited to this action because at their disposal was a body of women dedicated to service and skilled in directing local and national campaigns. "Diapers from mothers and dollars from dads" was one way this project was advertised.[39] This slogan was a simple way to sell an idea by making a popular assumption about the gender divide within philanthropy; women would reach for their sewing baskets, while men would reach for their wallets. USC records show a less neatly split donor profile, with married and single women, mothers, and childless women sending in most of the cash and in-kind donations, and men relegated to packing crates for shipment overseas.

The gender division was accurate in terms of who was reaching for their sewing baskets, however. It was women who did the sewing, and during times of crisis this type of homecraft was revered for being more than a domestic skill. As had also been the case during the two World Wars, overseas relief during the Cold War involved vast amounts of knitting and sewing. Lucille Marr's study of Mennonite women's relief sewing circles in the 1950s and 1960s reveals that the demand for their work gained the women more respect among the men in their community. Both the church and their relief body, the Mennonite Central Committee (MCC), were forced to recognize the sewers' economic value and expertise when the women established their own autonomous enterprise in the 1940s and began to send their goods through the Red Cross instead of the MCC. To woo them back, the church had to provide them with more financial resources and recognition for their efforts. This shift in power allowed the Mennonite seamstresses better control over their work, and they were seen as more than just auxiliary to the men's projects.[40] Not all men were opposed to being involved in this "feminine enterprise." One example in the USC records describes a ninety-three-year-old man who discovered that he could unravel the wool of worn pullovers as his contribution, passing the recovered yarn to his eighty-five-year-old neighbour for her to knit baby shirts.[41] Even if men wanted to help, it was unlikely they would know how to sew or knit. The same was becoming true for the younger female volunteers. USC observed in 1965 how few of its volunteers "still possess[ed] the art of sewing and knitting and quilting and making new things out of old" and reflected that the next generation of women might not have the same handiwork skills needed in relief circles.[42]

Together with the help of the women's organizations, USC collected "eighteen miles" (if strung end to end) of diapers, along with other homemade and store-bought items. These were organized into layettes containing four diapers, two nightgowns, two shirts, two vests (one cotton, one knit), one towel, one cake of laundry soap, and four large safety pins, to be distributed for each baby. To some donors, this small package of goods did not seem adequate; Hitschmanova remarked how

> across Canada women asked me over and over again how a mother overseas can possibly manage with the scanty contents of a basic layette. I tried to explain that even these few items are a godsend, lovingly contributed by sympathetic mothers half around the world. The plight of refugees living in the Middle East, in isolated Greek Mountain villages or in a Korean slum has to be seen, to realize that even newspapers and shreds are often a great luxury.[43]

This comment shows that the USC attempted to educate their donors about the wide variations in standards of living between Canada and elsewhere, comparing basic needs with luxuries. Given Hitschmanova's personal frugality, this statement was also a critique of the increasingly consumer-driven and materialistic culture found among the middle class in baby-boom Canada. Her words also imply some arrogance—that the less fortunate should be grateful for anything Canadians send.

Managing Racialized Foster Families

Although Greece remained the most popular destination for NGO aid sent to Europe in the 1950s and 1960s, it was South Korea that became the overall priority after 1953 and the most popular location for foster parent sponsorships. Like Greece, Korea spent the Second World War and the immediate postwar years recovering from occupation by a foreign power: first the Japanese, then in 1945 the Soviets and Americans, who divided the country into two separate nations. Both North and South insisted there should be only one Korea, and in the summer of 1950 Soviet-occupied North Korea made the first move for reunification, crossing the border and moving into the American-occupied South. By September, the Northern forces controlled most of the country. Seeking to stop Korea's fall to communism, the United States asked the UN to intervene. The Security Council (missing its Soviet delegate due to the USSR's boycott over the UN's failure to recognize communist China) voted to send military assistance to the South. Meanwhile the North received support from the Russians and the Chinese. Canada did not rush to volunteer, but when asked to join the UN forces the Canadian government reluctantly remobilized almost 27,000 servicemen and women. Bothwell characterizes Canada's participation as not streaming from "any intrinsic concern for Korea and Koreans, but because of an interest in the UN, first, and in relations with the United States, second."[44]

Due to Canada's involvement in the conflict, Canadians had more familiarity with the Korean War than they did with the Greek situation. Personal observations by Canadian journalists and servicemen illuminated the suffering of Koreans, specifically the non-communist South Koreans. In an article for *Maclean's*, Pierre Berton called Seoul "the saddest city in the world."[45] He described the city's social breakdown, caused in part by Seoul's governance having changed back and forth between the North and the South four times in 1951. The images Berton presented paralleled those in *Seeds of Destiny*: desolate adults and children reduced to shells of humanity, surviving by being refugees, foragers, beggars, prostitutes, and child labourers. The widow of a soldier who had served in Korea wrote a letter to a columnist at the *Winnipeg Tribune* on Remembrance Day conveying a similar picture. She asked Canadians "as we mourn our dead, let us not forget the living, those innocent little victims of man's senseless tyranny, who my husband described as 'The unwanted waifs of warfare.'"[46] Her letter was followed with information on how to contribute to the USC Korean relief effort. The more Canadians knew, or thought they knew, about Korea, the less work foreign aid organizations had to do in raising awareness about the consequences of the war. Canadians also donated generously because there was fear that the conflict could spiral into something bigger. Unlike the fairly self-contained situation in Greece, the multinational forces on both sides of the Korean conflict generated fears of the civil conflict spreading outward and progressing into a third world war, which in turn could escalate into a nuclear confrontation. This was the same fear that prompted some Canadians to turn to civil defence, and others to protest the war. However the futility of the military effort in Korea signalled that it was "impossible to fight communism with guns alone."[47] Perhaps foreign aid could accomplish what three years of war had failed to do.

The war ended in 1953 with almost no territory changing hands. Despite the return to the status quo, both North and South Korea were in shambles. Six million civilians had been killed during the war or died from war-related causes. Families were separated by migration, military duty, and death, while hunger and malnutrition were common afflictions. It was estimated that 33 percent of housing, 43 percent of industries, and 80 percent of hospitals had been destroyed. There were 5 million refugees in Seoul, including 830,000 civilians from North Korea. The state and the local churches provided special assistance for the affected children, those orphaned from the war or abandoned afterwards, many of whom were labelled "mixed-race" children, the offspring of relationships between foreign soldiers and Korean women. Orphanages, not normally a feature of Korean child welfare, became the predominant form of care for displaced or orphaned children. In 1945 South Korea had thirty-eight orphanages holding 3,000 children; by 1955 there were 534 orphanages with 54,927 children, and by 1965 there were 565 with 69,487 children.[48] Significant levels of international money poured in to help these children, making Korea the biggest aid mobilization project since the Second World War. Alongside support from non-government agencies, the Canadian government gave $8 million to the United Nations Korea Reconstruction Agency (UNKRA). Once the war ended, USC and FPPI moved into Seoul to assist with the displaced children. Working with UNKRA and UNICEF, USC started three programs, which provided milk for 25,000 school children, a thousand quilts, and a collection of school books and pencils.[49]

From the mid-1950s through to the mid-1960s, South Korea was the most popular site for foster parent sponsorship, followed by Hong Kong, South Vietnam, and India.[50] For the first time, the majority of sponsorships were of non-white, non-European children. Scholars have shown for centuries that North Americans have had very specific impressions of the peoples and cultures of Asia; for the most part, these were based on reports from explorers, missionaries, novelists, and artists, who generally portrayed the region and its inhabitants as anywhere from exotic to barbaric and, most always, "lesser than" those of the West. Drawing on Edward Said's theories of orientalism, literary scholar Christina Klein argues that the Cold War and post-colonialism prompted intellectuals to developed a more evolved orientalism that included a reciprocal relationship between East and West, at least among the non-communist Asian countries.[51] Still, as historian John Price points out, "racializing the 'Oriental other' ... was fundamental to [Canada's] state formation, to the creation of notions of 'whiteness' in Canada, and to the construction of Anglo-Saxonism in international affairs as articulated by Canadian officials such as Lester Pearson."[52] These ideologies helped inform the distance measured between foster mother and foster children, gauged not only by geography, economic circumstance, and exposure to war, but also by culture, ethnicity, and language. While Canadian foster parents embraced their new charges with enthusiasm, their correspondence with their foster children in Korea and other Asian countries reveals a great deal of uncertainty, naïveté, and, at times, racism.

Letters exchanged between foster parents and foster children reveal the politicized and racialized nature of this intimate form of aid. Children were expected to write frequently to their foster parents, telling them about their daily lives and ideally sharing examples of how their sponsorship had improved their circumstances. In return, the parents were encouraged to write back and introduce themselves. It seems the frequency of this communication was a concern for both sides. Some of the children's letters mentioned they wished to hear more from their Canadian parents and when they did not, they grew despondent, fearing they had done something wrong. Parents also grew worried when they believed their child did not write enough; some took it as a sign that the child was perhaps unwell or maybe not grateful enough for their support. The agencies tried to calm these worries by explaining that the mail delivery to and from war zones or even postwar cities was problematic.[53]

The letters offer some access to children's thoughts and experiences with the foster plan program, but given USC's and FPPI's guidelines about what could and could not be discussed, presumed censorship, and the role of adult translators, we need to carefully read between the lines to seek out children's voices and agency. USC had strict rules in place forbidding foster children to discuss politics or communicate directly with their sponsors. USC explained these rules were in place because they were a "non-political" organization and it was important to protect the foster parents from being exploited.[54] While many of the letters followed an approved script that resembled a mere exchange of routine pleasantries, there were examples of candid exchanges that wandered into problematic territory. So when ten-year-old Anil from India discussed his feelings about Bangladesh's independence after viewing a film, his Vancouver-based foster parents, the Nelsons, grew concerned he might be a radical and wrote to USC complaining of his behaviour. Hitschmanova agreed they had a right to be "distressed" and promised to investigate the matter when she visited India on her upcoming world tour.[55] It is unknown whether Anil was chastised for this act, but it does show that he felt it was important to share his opinions with his foster parents, and the Nelsons continued to sponsor him for three more years. Another foster mother, Laura King, was upset when her former foster daughter, twenty-year-old Sang Hee from Korea, who suffered from cerebral palsy, wrote directly to her, asking for money because her husband, also a former USC ward, was unemployed and she was struggling to raise two sons. In response King complained to USC for allowing this dialogue to exist, preferring that her former foster daughter remain modest about her prospects.[56] Given their history together, presumably Sang Hee saw her former foster mother as a legitimate person to assist her family. Her last letter to King apologizes for asking for money, but also clearly reiterates her desperate situation: "Mother. Have you received my letter I sent before? I am sorry for having sent such a letter to you. However, I was in a very difficult situation then and it was necessary for me to begin any kind of work to help the destitute family situation."[57] Sometimes the opposite occurred and the tone of a child's letters was so happy that it hid the reality of their lives. One woman remarked that her Vietnamese foster daughter never mentioned the war during their fourteen-year sponsorship. She recalled being surprised when FPPI was forced to leave Saigon in 1975 because "we got used to it after a while, we almost forgot the war was going on."[58]

One critical goal of foster parent programs was to turn unhappy and unhealthy children into happy and healthy adults who would build stable societies. Therefore it is not surprising that while foster mothers were encouraged to tell the children about their lives in Canada, they were cautioned against offering to sponsor their child for immigration, to legally adopt them, or even to invite them to visit Canada. The organizations enforced these guidelines for several reasons. Any one of these plans would have been difficult to arrange legally, particularly during the 1950s and 1960s, when Canadian immigration rules did not allow unaccompanied minors to immigrate for the purposes of adoption and migration from Asia was heavily restricted. Even if a visa could have been arranged, parents were cautioned not to invite their child for a visit, because, it was said, the temporary exposure to a different standard in living would be a great shock to the child. Unlike real families, a distance was always meant to exist between donor and recipient so as to make the inherent differences in the lives of foster parent and child invisible and silent. Even if foster parent plans were meant to draw people living around the world closer together, it also emphasized a geographic divide between the haves and the have-nots. Communicating solely through words and photos prevented any discomfort that may have come from face-to-face interactions that would have emphasized the lack of equality between parents living in relative comfort and children with few opportunities. Unlike the World University Service of Canada, a sponsorship program that raised money to bring overseas students to study in Canada, foster parent plans were never designed to give foreign children access to a middle-class Canadian lifestyle.

The correspondence between foster mother Libby Austin from Kamloops, B.C., her teenage foster daughter Ho Sook living in South Korea, whom she had sponsored for fifteen years, and Hitschmanova reveals how awkward the topic of visits could be for all involved. In the fall of 1972 Austin wrote to Hitschmanova asking about how to make arrangements for Ho Sook to come for a holiday in Canada. Hitschmanova responded coldly to the idea, with the following explanation:

I hope you will understand if I sound a word of warning against such a step. The difference between our own high standard of living and the comparatively still very low one in Korea is so great that it would mean to your foster daughter to take her into an earthly paradise for a few days or weeks and then to be returned to conditions which will be very, very hard to accept again. Whenever I am asked for advice by our USC Foster Parents, I always strongly counsel against such a step because it can be disastrous. It is in the interest of your foster daughter to give her every possible opportunity to develop within her Korean tradition and opportunities, but not to lift her from her familiar surroundings for a little while.[59]

Hitschmanova's response can be read in multiple ways. Certainly her warning appears to be sensible advice from someone who had personal experience with the USC foster children and presumably knew that such a trip would stir up possible guilt, confusion, resentment, and jealousy, emotions that the program tried so hard to avoid. Undoubtedly life in a Seoul orphanage was far less pleasant than day-to-day existence in a Canadian suburb; however, Hitschmanova's exaggerated language implies that the differences between Canada and South Korea were nearly impossible to overcome. The use of the term "earthly paradise" suggests a heaven-and-hell comparison between Canada and Korea. Presumably, as a refugee herself, Hitschmanova was trying to reflect reality rather than xenophobia in her choice of words. Yet her divisive characterization, as well as prophesying the visit would be "disastrous," implies that Ho Sook herself was as backward and ruined as her nation. Ironically, this discounts two decades of international relief and local development as having made little or no difference to Koreans, while simultaneously supporting the desperate need for continued financial aid. Austin's response to the heavy-handed warning stated, "We didn't realize there was *such* a difference in the standards of living. I'm afraid we are now in confusion over which course to take. She [Ho Sook] has often expressed a wish to visit in her letters over the years and we invited her without thinking."[60]

But perhaps Austin and Hitschmanova should have given Ho Sook more credit, since she seemed perfectly aware of the differences between Canada and South Korea. Rather than frightened, she appears excited about visiting a new place. In a letter sent during the ongoing debate about the visit, Ho Sook acknowledges the Austin family's higher standard of living:

> Dear Mother, Father and family, how are you? I was very pleased with your letter, coloured card and lovely Christmas card. Thanks to your such loving care, I am well. I was glad to hear that you had changed some parts of your house for the better. I wish I'd be able to visit the beautiful and convenient house someday.[61]

Meanwhile Austin writes back to her foster daughter explaining the visit must be postponed, and, perhaps as someone used to being disappointed,

Ho Sook claims to understand.[62] She also moves on, leaving USC's care when she drops out of school to become a nanny for a local dentist. Austin writes to Hitschmanova, saddened by the turn of events, since without a USC translator, she will not be able to stay in touch. At this point Austin suggests going to visit Ho Sook in South Korea, an idea she also shared with her foster daughter in their final correspondence.[63] In her response, Ho Sook presents a much sunnier picture than Hitschmanova of her nation's present-day situation and her own resiliency:

> How nice it would be if you could meet me! Our country has developed much and you can have a really nice trip here. I got a side job, and it was too hard to continue school. I am going to work hard and devote myself to the work. It is a great joy for me to hear from you and write to you. I try to write to you often this year. Can you imagine how much I become mature and lady-like? I try to be beautiful and good woman always, thinking of your great love.[64]

This is the last letter on file from Ho Sook. Whether these were truly her own thoughts or not, she presents a confident, proud, and grateful image, something of the type the USC would share in an annual report. It is unknown what happened to Ho Sook after she left USC, though it is known that Austin decided not to visit Korea and moved on to sponsor two new foster children, another in South Korea and one in India. Not only does Austin and Ho Sook's correspondence represent a strong, even loving, connection, it shows the inability to truly know and understand each other as institutional policies, cultural perceptions, and distance prevented the foster mother–daughter relationship from being taken to the next level. It also emphasizes the temporary nature of these constructed relationships.

Visits between sponsor and child were also deemed problematic because it was antithetical to the foster parent programs' intent to remove the children from their home country. USC and FPPI were concerned about the children adjusting to new worlds, but also about the instability that would come from removing part of a generation from a developing country such as South Korea. With so much emphasis on the children being the future, the programs were reluctant to remove such a future from the country, even if they knew the children would benefit from a different standard of living in Canada. As Brown, the Canadian FPPI director in Saigon, stated, "We try very hard not to infringe on their cultural patterns, and try to help them become citizens of their own countries. We don't want to Westernise them. The whole idea is ensure the child keeps the family together, rather than become detached from it."[65] This made FPPI an agency ahead of its time in terms of respecting indigenous practices and recognizing the importance of keeping the biological family together. Brown believed it was enough for the children to benefit from the long-distance fostering; there was no need to turn these into real parent–child relationships. As a result, Brown became a vocal critic of international adoption programs for providing an alternative solution, a subject that will be explored in chapter 7.

Despite the miles between foster children and their sponsors, in some cases the foster child appeared to become part of the Canadian family, like a clucked-over distant relative. Sometimes the relationships between parents and child became quite intense. This is not surprising given the length of the sponsorships; on average they lasted approximately five years, though at least 10 percent of USC cases lasted between eleven and eighteen years.[66] After sponsoring Ho Sook for fifteen years, Austin decided to make a provision for her foster daughter in her will.[67] This was an unusual decision, but one that was mentioned in a handful of the other archived letters. Foster parents were also naturally upset when something unexpected happened to the child, whether it was good or bad. Rather than being pleased, one college student demanded her donation back when her foster child was reunited with her birth mother after a long separation. The young woman clearly had no understanding of the challenges of life in a postwar region, since she exclaimed, "I had another friend who told me after three years of sponsorship, her [foster] child died. I did not believe that this could happen."[68]

Since the programs were built on the dream of these children improving themselves and becoming the leaders of a new generation, the programs tried their best to ensure the children had all the resources they needed to become independent. Children generally left the program if they were reunited with a family member, no longer needed specialized medical treatment, or came of age. It was not uncommon for the agencies to ask donors for one last gift in the form of tuition for a training program or contribution to a dowry once the foster child reached adulthood. Most children went on to work in a trade or get married. Few children took or passed their university entrance exams. In the case of those with disabilities, those young adults often stayed in the institutions they grew up in, performing housekeeping work for room and board. Disappointment from foster parents was quite profound when an individual child's future did not appear to be as bright as they had hoped or were promised. Such was the case of Candice Carnegie, who wrote to USC expressing her annoyance when two of her three Korean foster children quit the post-secondary training she had helped pay for, an act she attributed not to the fickleness of youth, but rather claimed was proof "that the Oriental mind is unfathomable to a westerner and that their customs and values are entirely opposite to ours."[69] Despite this, Carnegie continued to sponsor a younger polio-stricken child whom she thought was still worthy of her attention. While the programs might have saved the children from destitution, there was no proof that foreign aid in any form helped turn children into Marie Curies and Albert Einsteins, the claim made in the UN film *Seeds of Destiny*.

From Foster Families to Family Planning

While foster parent plan programs aimed to give a future to children born into poverty and war, FPPI and USC directed a portion of their funds to curtailing the numbers of children born into such situations. In the 1960s both agencies began to fund their own or support local family planning initiatives as a secondary means to improve child welfare. This task was undertaken with the realization that foster parent plan schemes and general relief campaigns could not solve the underlying problems facing impoverished children and their families. Therefore ensuring fewer children were born into poverty or war would help women, families, and welfare services better manage the available resources to care for existing children. Ruth Compton Brouwer calls family planning "one of the hundreds of development strategies" Western states and voluntary aid agencies engaged in during the mid-1960s in aiding Asian nations.[70] Using birth control as a form of child welfare sparked considerable controversy and forced sponsoring agencies and donors to give considerable thought to the ethics of promoting family planning. This project was also seen to have a specific Cold War agenda. Linda Gordon argues that some Western relief workers saw birth control as a means of countering the "population powder keg" in developing nations and another way to diffuse Cold War tensions and assert Western control on these regions.[71] For the USC, Hong Kong became the test case for seeing whether it was possible to convince donors that there was no inherent contradiction between sponsoring foster children and simultaneously advocating family planning.

Like Greece and South Korea, Hong Kong was a highly politicized site of Cold War foreign relief, as it was the locale where Canadians could help the "good" Chinese—that is, those who had escaped communism. Prior to the Communist revolution, FPPI had been working in mainland China for four years arranging a small number of sponsorships for Chinese children in conjunction with Madame Sun Yat-sen's Child Welfare Institute. FPPI maintained that it planned to stay on in China after 1949; however, it abandoned work within a few months of the revolution, claiming its relief supplies were being interfered with by Mao Zedong's new government. Additionally, FPPI stated that half of the already-arranged foster parent plan sponsorships collapsed in 1950, suggesting that North Americans did not care to sponsor children who had become communist almost overnight.[72] Even if it had decided to stay, FPPI would not have been welcome for long. With the outbreak of the Korean War, China expelled its Western aid workers and condemned Westerners' relief work as an example of imperialistic interference.[73] Meanwhile the People's Republic of China continued to receive external relief from fellow communist countries, while capitalist countries threw their support behind the Republic of China acting from Taiwan.

In the late 1950s, FPPI, USC, and a handful of other Canadian charities started working with the hundreds of thousands of refugees from mainland China living in shanty towns in the British colony of Hong Kong. The influx of refugees, beginning in the 1930s and continuing for years after the revolution, meant that between 1939 and 1960, the population of Hong Kong more than doubled from 1.5 million to over 3 million, and the density grew to 5,000 people per square kilometre overall, with 25,000 people per square kilometre in metropolitan areas. (For perspective, there were only 20 people per square kilometre in Canada's most densely populated province, Prince Edward Island.)[74] In the declining years of the British Empire, Hong Kong remained a key colony and Britain's only significant presence in Asia. Britain fought to maintain its grip on Hong Kong despite pressure from China that the island belonged to them.[75] The British connection meant that Canadians had a somewhat closer relationship with Hong Kong than it did with other East Asian countries. Along with India, Hong Kong's status within the British Empire allowed it to bypass to some degree the ban on Asian immigration to Canada that was in place until 1967. A small number of British residents from Hong Kong were allowed into Canada each year. Refugees with relatives in Canada could apply to be sponsored for immigration under this special quota.[76]

The dramatic population increase in Hong Kong led to sanitation problems, unemployment, and lack of basic resources from housing to food to shoes. Canadian foreign relief agencies saw plenty they could do to improve living standards and child welfare. In addition to setting up foster parent plan sponsorships, FPPI and USC raised funds to build much-needed institutions to serve the growing population—housing projects, hospitals, nurseries, and schools. The influx of refugees tapered off in the early 1960s, but the population continued to increase due to high birth rates. This contributed to more children being placed temporarily or permanently in orphanages. Exact statistics are not known; however, one relief worker from Canada's United Church mission estimated that babies were being abandoned in Hong Kong at the rate of one per day.[77] Identifying Hong Kong's main problem as overpopulation forced USC to commit to a family planning policy.

Initially most of the controversy about Canadians advocating for family planning overseas had to do with what that option meant to Canadians, not the recipients of the aid. Angus McLaren and Arlene Tigar McLaren claim that lowering the birth rate was the biggest social change to occur in the twentieth century in Canada. In the postwar period, and even after the Criminal Code was amended in 1969 to allow for the legal sale of contraceptives, the public and private struggle to control fertility remained an extremely sensitive issue for Canadians, triggering debates about women's rights, religious beliefs, eugenics, abortion, and Canada's vitality.[78] Even though USC recognized the merits of family planning, it was initially wary to link its name to the cause for fear of alienating support for its more traditional relief efforts. For example, in the 1950s when the USC branch in Toronto recommended supporting Dr. Marion Hall, a Methodist missionary running a family planning clinic in India, Hitschmanova asked the branches for feedback before she made her decision. Understandably, given the Catholic base of its population, the USC branch in Montreal was against supporting the clinic, but even USC supporters in Vancouver felt the idea was too risky to get involved with.[79] By the mid-1960s the influence of the counterculture and second-wave feminism's more liberal ideas about sexuality and women's rights helped shift Canadian attitudes towards birth control; plus, the birth control pill had been approved for sale in 1960. The more liberal attitudes toward family planning at home coincided with growing concerns about global overpopulation, and USC was willing to take the risk to implement family planning as a practical solution for addressing Hong Kong's poor maternal and child health.

In 1965 USC gave a grant to the Family Planning Association (FPA) of Hong Kong, a program that provided family planning advice and distributed free or below-market-cost birth control devices. Prior to 1965, the FPA's work had been largely media based, providing pamphlets and films explaining the services available at their maternal health clinics. The FPA concluded that "personal influence exerted by field-workers making home visits"[80] was the most effective tool to educate women about family planning, so they used USC money to implement more face-to-face interactions between social workers or nurses and married women living in resettlement and low-cost housing estates, tenement houses, and shanty towns or receiving postpartum care in three benevolent hospitals. To encourage women to consider using birth control, USC also utilized food incentives, such as offering a forty-four-pound barley bonus to women who visited an FPA clinic. In conjunction with family planning as a solution for child welfare, USC also viewed it as a way to improve women's lives. In the 1970s the USC expanded its program to include a gender-equity "no sex preference" campaign, aimed to counteract the belief that boy children were preferable over girls.[81] Along with rapid industrialization, the FPA's educational programs and its provision of inexpensive and convenient forms of contraception have been cited as major factors in the 6 percent decline in Hong Kong's fertility rate between 1965 and 1971.[82] USC followed up its efforts in Hong Kong with a similar program in India in 1967. Concurrently, FPPI implemented a policy whereby it would sponsor birth control distribution if family planning initiatives were already a part of the national policy of the countries in which it was involved.[83]

Despite the agencies' concern that encouraging family planning would stifle donations, the opposite occurred. USC noted that, for every donor who left because family planning was against his or her religious or moral beliefs, more donors signed up—including a new type of zealous donor whose head danced with visions of eugenic solutions. These Canadians insisted that family planning was the key to solving the problems of overpopulation and poverty in developing nations. Some went as far as to suggest that sterilization and castration were preferable to other forms of relief, options that were later implemented in a state-sponsored program in India.[84] This opinion is demonstrated most viciously in one anonymous letter sent to USC that questioned the right of people in developing nations to have children at all: "Why should we support all the breeding of the world? If they can't feed their own people, then they have no business breeding them like animals."[85] Although the tone was different, this ugly attitude did share something with the grander, self-serving goals and cost–benefit realities found in foster parent plan programs. Just as such letter writers thought aid should go only to deserving people, those they believed would use their aid responsibly, agencies such as USC and FPPI also made choices as to the people they thought deserved Canada's help. In the 1950s and 1960s these decisions were based on Cold War–created borders. Countries whose fate was seen to be tied to Canada's security were helped instead of every country suffering from war or poverty.

After two decades' worth of child welfare projects, ranging from diaper drives to foster parent plan sponsorships to family planning education, how did the agencies, donors, and recipients measure the success of their interventions? One only needs to scan the annual reports of USC and FPPI to see the significant numbers of foster parents and children involved in the program: 17,000 children sponsored by FPPI in Greece between 1949 and 1975; a high of 2,490 Canadian FPPI foster parents in 1968; over $13 million in cash raised by USC between 1946 and 1975, with almost triple that number in non-cash donations.[86] By the mid to late 1970s, USC and FPPI had closed their programs in South Korea, Hong Kong, and Greece because those nations' economies and internal welfare services were deemed stable enough to subsist on their own, and it was thought that the children most affected by the immediate wartime violence and postwar disruption had grown into adults. It is also significant to note that each of these nations remained close allies of Canada. From the Canadian perspective, foster parent plans were a great success in helping individual children and in building peace and stability in the world. This work also appeared to satisfy a number of personal interests of the active women involved. For Hitschmanova, her work with the USC repaid the debt she felt to those who had helped her when she was a refugee. For the thousands of foster mothers, "virtually" raising children like Chin Hoo, Yolanda, and Ho Sook from afar, presumably this relationship fulfilled their desire to share their love and good fortune with an underprivileged child.

What is less certain is exactly how this outpouring of money, resources, and indeed "love" from Canada affected the children themselves during their sponsorships and afterwards. Did it improve their quality of life during childhood and adulthood? The surviving fragmented correspondence is the only insight we have into the lives of the foster children, and this correspondence was mediated through strict guidelines about what could and could not be said. We can only speculate that some of the children were comforted or at the very least intrigued by the idea of a concerned adult in their lives, even if that adult lived in a country the child would never see. But when miscommunications occurred or the promised letters, gifts, and visits did not materialize or the sponsorships were suddenly cancelled, presumably confusion and ill will may have been the result. Another concern was whether or not the money actually made it to the children. Due to the chaotic postwar contexts in which aid was being distributed, it is possible that sponsorship money went missing or was used for bribes. Claude Sanger, Hitschmanova's biographer, mentions in passing that South Korean children's homes used by USC and other agencies acquired a dubious reputation abroad in later years due to rumours about unscrupulous local directors stealing sponsorship money.[87] In all probability, when the money went where it was intended to go, the financial portion of the sponsorships made some difference in the children's impoverished lives by providing them with funds for medical treatment, schooling, food, and clothes.

According to Marianne Brown, a McGill-trained social worker who worked in an orphanage in Pusan, South Korea, in the late 1950s, there was an unfortunate side effect to foster parent plan sponsorships.[88] Although FPPI sponsored children who lived with their parents and families, the majority of foster plan programs (such as USC and Brown's employer, Save the Children) only assisted children who were without legal guardians and lived in orphanages. Many of these children were orphans, but others, Brown noted, had been specifically abandoned by parents who believed the children would have a better standard of living and opportunities for education if they lived in an orphanage served by an international foster parent plan. In Brown's one-year stint in Pusan, the sponsorship numbers doubled to 800, partly because of an influx of children whose parents left them in Save the Children's care so they could benefit from the sponsorships.[89] Beyond Brown's recollections, there is no documentation recording how widespread this practice was in South Korea or elsewhere. Presumably the situation was not unique to Pusan. Local social workers in South Korea and South Vietnam are on record noting the phenomenon of deliberate abandonment occurring in orphanages that began to arrange for international adoptions, an issue that will be discussed in chapter 7. But if the flood of foreign dollars triggered this response, clearly the purposeful breaking up of families went against the mandate of the foster parent plan system. In Brown's estimation the sponsorship programs accomplished "nothing" because they bred family breakdowns and dependency on charity.[90]

The foster parent plan programs in Greece, South Korea, and Hong Kong represent an era of international child welfare projects when money and attention followed Cold War bullets and consensus. The USC and FPPI projects were based on three assumptions: that the aid they offered was a good thing for all parties involved, that their work was non-political, and that aid should be directed to specific geographic regions worthy of Canada's support. The escalation of the war in Vietnam in the mid-1960s, coupled with increasing media reports about the war's effects on civilians and the subsequent critique about Canada's complicity in the conflict, shattered these previous assumptions and triggered a new set of responses from activist women.

CHAPTER SIX

A Change in Direction
Starving, Knitting, and Caring for Vietnam

One October morning in 1968 Claire Culhane began a ten-day hunger strike and demonstration on Parliament Hill to protest what she considered to be the Canadian government's hypocritical position on the war in Vietnam. Culhane, a fifty-year-old mother of two grown daughters, took this action after conventional lobbying techniques failed to get Parliament to address her scathing report about her experiences managing a Canadian-funded medical clinic in South Vietnam. Culhane, who had a background in health administration, had been inspired to work in Vietnam after reading a *Weekend Magazine* article about a Canadian medical team providing health care for Vietnamese civilians living in Quang Ngai province, a region heavily affected by the war. The magazine's cover featured a photo of Quebec nurse Louise Piché holding a Vietnamese baby and behind her a long line of Vietnamese children waiting for immunization, ostensibly representing the endless need for assistance.[1] Having been interested in what she called "the international character of the struggle for human rights" since she was a teenage girl horrified by the Spanish Civil War, Culhane felt she could be of use in Vietnam despite her misgivings about the war.[2] Most likely ignorant of her past membership in the Communist Party, the Department of External Aid hired Culhane to be the administrator of their new anti-tuberculosis clinic. Culhane stayed in Quang Ngai for only eight months before returning to Canada in a state of shock, appalled not at the desperate situation of the Vietnamese people—that was to be expected—but at what she considered a betrayal by the Canadian government.

In Quang Ngai, Culhane claimed to have witnessed the "sham of our medical aid program in South Vietnam," what she believed to be a "front for intelligence activities" conducted by the Central Intelligence Agency. It was her opinion that the clinic's "main purpose [was] to serve the military needs of the U.S. in Vietnam, and *not* the needs of the Vietnamese people."[3] Culhane insisted the humanitarian project was being undermined by political motivations that, among other things, instructed the staff to provide patient information to American military personnel and prevented them from treating suspected Viet Cong patients. Once she was back in Canada, Culhane was debriefed by Maurice Strong, head of the Department of External Aid, with whom she detailed her belief that it was worthless for Canadians to offer support to the Vietnamese in the face of the larger corruptions. She offered Strong this analogy:

> If an Armada of 100 planes were to suddenly bomb Albert Street [in Ottawa], where we were sitting, and the last two planes, bearing Red Cross markings, were to swoop down to patch up survivors, would *we* appreciate such attention? Why should the Vietnamese people be expected to be grateful for that kind of "aid"?[4]

Although Strong listened to her, Culhane got the impression that he did not truly understand the politics involved, so she later sent a sixteen-page report about her experiences in Quang Ngai to every member of Parliament. When this failed to get the government's attention, she held a ten-day vigil and fast on Parliament Hill, an event endorsed by VOW, asking the government to investigate the compromised neutrality of their aid program and cancel Canada's defence contracts with the United States. Her protest was widely covered by the media, who were struck by a woman of Culhane's age taking such a radical action; they nicknamed her the "Fasting Grandmother."[5]

In the last hour of her fast, Culhane was invited to meet with Prime Minister Trudeau. According to Culhane's memories of the event, Trudeau never had any plans to take her seriously, since as soon as she began to speak about her wishes for Canada to declare an unconditional halt to the bombing in Vietnam, Trudeau's secretary appeared to escort him to a dinner engagement.[6] When the press asked Trudeau and Mitchell Sharp, Secretary of State for External Affairs, to comment on Culhane's stand, they dismissed her concerns, calling her only a "casual observer" of affairs in Vietnam.[7]

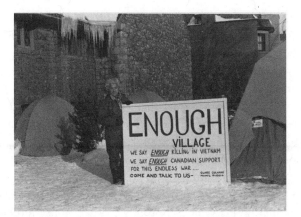

Claire Culhane poses by demonstration tent during fast, Ottawa, 24 December 1969 to 12 January 1970. Courtesy of The William Ready Division of Archives and Research Collections, McMaster University Library.

Undeterred, Culhane refused to let the government or the national conscience off the hook, so she spent the next five years speaking and writing about her experience in Vietnam for anti-war organizations, including VOW. She continued to mount other public demonstrations in Ottawa, including a second fast in 1970, and she once chained herself to a seat in the viewing gallery of the House of Commons.[8] Although her activism did not change the government's policy toward Vietnam, the image of a radical granny starving herself for peace was helpful in broadening the image of the anti-war movement; it was not just for rowdy American youth, but something women and Canadians of all ages should care about. Activism such as Culhane's helped make the war "a wearisome, depressing issue," and in the last years of the conflict more and more Canadians expressed distaste for the war and the United States' involvement in the conflict.[9]

Beginning in 1955, Vietnam had become an arena and prize in a Cold War battle of wills, in which Canada was a minor—but nevertheless significant—player. The divided nation's twenty-year war for independence was fought between the northern-based communist Democratic Republic of Vietnam, supported by its allies in the Soviet Union and China, and the American-fronted Republic of Vietnam in the south. Canada did not participate militarily, though some citizens joined the American armed forces. The Canadian government had been actively involved in Vietnam since 1954 as a member of the UN's International Commission for Supervision and Control (ICSC). Along with India and Poland, Canada was to (1) monitor the ceasefire after the First Indochina War (1946–54) between France and Vietnam, (2) organize free elections, and (3) work toward a truce between the southern and northern governments, with the ultimate goal being to build peace throughout Indochina. When this failed, Canada remained part of the commission until 1973, acting as a supposedly neutral observer. Political scientist Douglas Ross argues that Canada was motivated to join the ICSC in order to reduce the threat of a nuclear war in Vietnam, but the nation's policies for accomplishing this goal were complicated by Canada's close relationship with the United States, which intervened in the region to stop Vietnam's fall to communism and protect its trade with Southeast Asia. Ross claims this led Canada to provide an inconsistent foreign policy toward Vietnam, oscillating between compromise, concessions, and criticism as diplomats were torn between being an American ally and doing what they thought was best for Vietnam and global security.[10]

From the mid-1960s through to the end of the war in 1975, Vietnam became the focal point for Canadian women's peace activism and foreign relief efforts. The conflict drew the attention of women in WILPF and VOW who had previously been active in the disarmament movement and whose activism was reignited by a new phrase of Cold War politics. The war also mobilized a new wave of politicized women infuriated at Canada's failure to play peacekeeper, who demanded their government hold some responsibility for the people in Vietnam. Much like Greece, South Korea, and Hong Kong, Vietnam represented a site of great suffering from an ongoing, lengthy war and a refugee crisis, both of which had created a flood of displaced families and unaccompanied children living in orphanages and on the streets. Peace groups collaborated with Canadian relief organizations and UN agencies to send money, food, and other resources to Vietnam. One of the more popular campaigns was VOW's Knitting for Vietnam project, which saw Canadian women and girls knitting baby clothes in dark-coloured wool so as to camouflage children from danger in combat zones. Meanwhile, USC and FPPI set up foster parent plan programs and general relief campaigns for Vietnam, the first of their child welfare programs to be delivered amid an ongoing war.

As with the previous forms of activism presented in this study, this mobilization was framed as a maternalistic and internationalist venture. Growing awareness about the impact of war on children—this time not Canadian children, nor even children in a familiar or allied country—triggered women's mobilization for change and their responsibility to do the right thing for the people of North and South Vietnam. Evidence displaying the war's terrible toll on children and youth, from Vietnamese war orphans to the young American soldiers dying overseas, was not only a powerful force in mobilizing women, it served to deconstruct decades of Cold War dogma that emphasized the superiority of the West and the evils of communism. This mainstream shakeup of the Cold War consensus prompted Canadians to reassess the United States' actions and their own nation's complicity in the conflict. It also forced the women to re-evaluate the strengths and limitations of their own activism. In particular, for many activists and aid workers, the war in Vietnam shattered the illusion that any type of foreign aid could be considered non-political. Upon returning from Vietnam, Culhane concluded, "If I went to Vietnam as a humanitarian, I returned with the renewed conviction that a true humanitarian must also be a political being."[11] This revelation led some of the involved women to loudly champion the importance of assisting women and children living on both sides of war, while activists reconsidered whether their political and charitable efforts only made the war more palatable.

VOW Shifts from Ban the Bomb to Stop the War

Since its early disarmament crusade, VOW had been what historian Frances Early called the "lightening rod for women's discontent with Cold War politics."[12] With the Test Ban Treaty and more cordial relations between Soviets and Americans cooling the arms race, VOW redirected their energies toward ending the war in Vietnam. Vietnam began to appear on VOW's agenda as early as 1963, when VOW sought to verify stories coming from international contacts who characterized the fighting and living conditions as "brutal," claims it discovered "were soon documented as being only too true."[13] By the 1964 Gulf of Tonkin resolution, when President Johnson escalated the American military intervention in Vietnam, VOW had made Vietnam its number one priority.[14] In its attempts to end the war or at the very least get the Americans to withdraw, VOW took a threefold approach to their activism: bring attention to the suffering of the Vietnamese, question Canada's role in the war, and use their country's neutrality to help Vietnamese civilians and American draft dodgers.

Much like the nuclear threat, the anti–Vietnam War campaign was positioned in VOW's rhetoric as a critical child welfare crisis and a test of Canada's moral principles. The organization primarily recruited supporters to their cause by showing the war's effects on women and children. They did this not only because maternalism was VOW's typical framework, but because evidence showed that these two population groups were most affected by the reported bombings, violence, and destruction of farmland and homes. VOW gathered first-hand graphic stories of this suffering from the Vietnam Women's Union (VWU), a socialist women's organization started by the Vietnamese Community Party in 1930. In 1968 VOW president Kay Macpherson travelled to Hanoi on a two-week trip as a guest of VWU, where she acted as a "would-be diplomat" in meetings with Soviet and American women, along with Vietnamese women workers, students, soldiers, and politicians.[15] Macpherson returned to Canada particularly moved by the plight of peasant women in North Vietnam and the North-controlled or "liberated" areas of South Vietnam; she had been told that these women lived with their children in underground tunnels as protection from bombs, emerging only under the cover of darkness to cook, plough their fields, and attend school.[16] Upon her return, Macpherson shared these stories in VOW newsletters and speaking engagements, where she presented the North Vietnamese women as mothers whose parenting was being made almost impossible by the American bombing campaigns. She asked Canadian women to help end the war by joining protests and raising money to send to war victims.[17] Although many VOW members were moved by Macpherson's experience in Hanoi, not all Canadian women trusted her source of information. In one letter to a Saskatchewan newspaper, the writer critiqued Macpherson for naively believing everything the North Vietnamese told her, since they were "most anxious to present to the world an impression which [will] cast them in a favourable light."[18]

If some Canadians were wary of reports coming from foreign women living under communism, VOW found a more reputable anti-war ally in Dr. Benjamin Spock, a familiar voice and welcomed authority on children. His *The Common Sense Book of Baby and Child Care*, first published in 1946, was considered by many mothers to be the child care bible for baby-boom parents. The pediatrician and author had joined the peace cause in the late 1950s and was one of the founders of the American disarmament organization Committee for a Sane Nuclear Policy. Spock later became an outspoken activist against the Vietnam War, and in 1968 he and three other male activists were convicted of conspiracy to counsel, aid, and abet resistance to the draft, a verdict later overturned.[19] The support of a male authority figure and medical professional further legitimized VOW's maternalistic crusade by making its concerns appear scientific as well as emotional. Like many VOW members, Spock believed that if you cared for children, you cared about peace. VOW quoted Spock in their documents, using his familiar name to encourage women's involvement.[20] In December 1970, VOW invited

Spock to Ottawa, where he spoke to high-school and university students and parents about the war. Although his speech focused on resisting American imperialism, he also made comparisons to Canada's own internal turmoil during the recent October Crisis and called for the removal of the War Measures Act and any law "that is not absolutely necessary to prevent violence."[21] Coincidently, publicity for Spock's Ottawa visit coincided with newspaper coverage of the trial of Lt. William Calley, the American soldier arrested for the alleged murder of Vietnamese women and children in the 1968 event known as the My Lai Massacre.[22] Revelations about what happened in My Lai led VOW to support the Democratic Republic of Vietnam's Committee for the Protection of Mothers and Children, which asked all mothers around the world to "strongly condemn the U.S. Administration's deliberate attempts to massacre mothers who generate life, and children who are the precious offspring of our nation."[23]

VOW also collected statistics and stories about the experiences of Vietnamese women and children from Canadian ICSC officials, UN sources, and the Canadian media, most of whom supported the VWU's and Spock's accounts. According to Hugh Campbell, an ICSC member from 1961 to 1963, 160,000 Vietnamese civilians died from war-related causes in 1963, bringing the total number of civilian deaths to 415,000 since 1961. A UN study had put the population of Vietnam at almost 48 percent under the age of sixteen, so VOW estimated that approximately 50 percent of Campbell's reported casualties had to be children, and in some rural regions that figure went up to 70 percent.[24] Additionally, by 1968 there were an estimated 1.5 million refugees living in 850 refugee camps. By 1973, South Vietnam's population was thought to include 9 million children. Out of that population, it was estimated that 1 out of every 10 children—or 880,000—had lost one or both of their parents.[25] Writing ten years after the war's end, Ross conservatively placed the total number of Vietnamese casualties, including civilians and soldiers, at over 1 million, with almost another million wounded.[26]

These statistics were vividly illustrated in the late 1960s and early 1970s by the Canadian media's coverage of the war, which frequently put the spotlight on the tragic fate of Vietnamese women and children living on the front lines. The Vietnam War lived up to its moniker as the "television war," a new phenomenon that prompted American President Nixon to complain how the "relentless and literal" reporting of the conflict via the nightly news focused on the "terrible human suffering and sacrifice of war."[27] The transmitted images of body bags, blood, and burning villages confused, demoralized, and disturbed Americans and incited thousands to protest their government's involvement in the crisis. A different version of this phenomenon occurred in Canada, where the war was less personal but nonetheless haunting and provocative. As seen in the following examples from the *Star Weekly* and *Maclean's*, by the late 1960s many media outlets in Canada presented the war in decidedly anti-war tones that paralleled VOW's position. In 1967 the *Toronto Star*'s weekend supplement ran an article that featured several photographs of wounded Vietnamese children, including a small girl on the cover with a burned face and only one eye.[28] Not only did the magazine devote several pages to this story, the next issue included a follow-up article entitled "Canada Awakens to the Agony of Viet Nam's Maimed Children," which recounted the visceral reaction of readers, most of them women, who were devastated by the photos and inspired to do something. "When I saw those photographs I broke down and cried right in the drugstore," stated Elizabeth Voight, a thirty-five-year-old mother of four from Cornwall.[29] One Toronto mother, Barbara Huag, was similarly affected by the photos and could easily imagine herself in the same position as a Vietnamese woman. "I keep looking at my children and thinking of the mothers in Viet Nam," Huag told the magazine. "This morning I was feeding my baby—she's seven months old—and she was so hungry I thought, 'Suppose I have no milk to give her.'"[30] In 1968 *Maclean's* created a special issue dedicated to Vietnam that left little room for readers' own interpretations. The cover featured a young woman dressed in the traditional *ao dai*, holding a baby. The caption next to the photo read, "If she is not dead yet—she may be soon. And we will have helped kill her baby. Our war."[31] Both publications capitalized upon the compelling symbolism of children as war's innocent victims. *Maclean's* and *Star Weekly* presented Vietnamese children as having uncertain futures, conveyed by their physical wounds, unhappy faces, and broken families. This was an effective conduit to send a powerful message: the cost of war is too high. The secondary message was that Canadians needed to play a role in guaranteeing these children had a future. It worked for Voight and Huag, who turned their tears into action and were inspired to organize local fundraisers and charity walks to support Vietnamese women and children; in the words of Voight, "Someone has to do something, because those fuddy-duddies in Ottawa are doing nothing."[32] On a larger scale, VOW was similarly inspired to ensure Canadians took responsibility for the lives of Vietnamese children.

Spurred on by the mounting evidence of the war's terrible consequences for women and children, VOW demanded the Canadian government take a stronger stand in Vietnam. Between 1965 and 1976, the organization asked that the House of Commons, at a minimum, hold debates on Vietnam. VOW remained confident that, if the matter were ever fully addressed, the Canadian government and people would see Vietnam in terms of human rights and "accept the full implications of their claims to be a peace-keeping nation, and express openly their disapproval of U.S. actions in Vietnam."[33] Although the Canadian government did indeed express concerns about the war in Vietnam, any formally expressed disapproval was mitigated by a lack of outright condemnation caused by Canada's allegiance to and dependence on the United States. Pearson, whose tenure as Prime Minister coincided with the American escalation of the war, supported the Americans' long-term goals for Vietnam but not their methods. "On one hand," historian Andrew Preston observed, "Canada indeed supported America's policy of sponsoring and maintaining a non-communist South Vietnam, condemned the communist North Vietnamese for instigating and perpetuating an aggressive war, and feared the effects of falling dominoes, at least those of a psychological nature."[34] This sentiment was offset by Pearson believing that the United States' military escalation was "a threat to world peace" and essentially "futile."[35] In 1964 Pearson urged Johnson to withdraw American troops from Vietnam and seek peace through diplomatic channels; however, there was not much force behind this suggestion. As Preston points out, Canada never presented an alternative diplomatic solution, and even if it had, he remains doubtful that Canada had the clout to convince its more powerful ally to negotiate rather than fight.[36] Nor would Canada dare to vehemently insist on this action for fear of causing a rift with their most critical economic and defence partner. So although Canada urged an American withdrawal, the government never came out directly against the war, and instead preferred to allow what historian Robert Bothwell describes as "its anti-war inclination to be understood rather than explicitly stated."[37] This was not good enough for VOW or the growing tide of other Canadian anti-war groups. "By keeping quiet," one interested woman claimed, "Ottawa is agreeing with the war, agreeing with the U.S."[38]

The Vietnam issue continued to linger as a prickly issue throughout Trudeau's reign as prime minister. In 1969 VOW's president, Muriel Duckworth, along with past presidents Macpherson and Thérèse Casgrain and physicist Ursula Franklin, presented Trudeau with a proposal for Canada to take a non-aligned course of action—not only in Vietnam, but everywhere—so as to project a "credible voice" in foreign affairs. Along these lines, VOW also encouraged Canada to pull out of NATO and NORAD. Speaking for Trudeau, Sharp met with VOW and, similar to the way he dismissed Culhane during her hunger strike, claimed to be "not impressed" with their ideas, especially since they did not present an "alternative maintenance of peace."[39] When interviewed about the meeting with Sharp, Duckworth claimed not to have been surprised at his pessimistic reaction, but she felt VOW had to say something because "we believe we speak for a substantial body of opinion in Canada."[40] Much like their demand for the government to unambiguously resist nuclear weapons and promote disarmament, VOW's calls for a clear policy change went unanswered by the government. It should be noted that, under Trudeau's leadership, Canada did allow draft resisters to immigrate, a symbolic act that "allowed the Canadian government to demonstrate its independence from the United States and its opposition to the war."[41]

In addition to looking for policy changes in the Department of External Affairs, VOW lobbied Canadian industry to stop what VOW viewed as profiting from the sale of chemical weapons, including napalm, being used in Vietnam and along the borders of Laos and Cambodia. Napalm's horrific effects on humans were most vividly portrayed to Canadians in June 1972 when the infamous photograph of children coming under fire from the incendiary weapon during an accidental air strike was featured in newspapers around the world. In the centre of the photo is Kim Phuc, a nine-year-old girl running naked down the street and crying "nong qua, nong qua" (which translates to "too hot, too hot"), her clothes, skin, and hair burned by 800–1200°C napalm.[42] Phuc survived the attack and became an international symbol of all that was wrong with the Vietnam War. (In 1992, almost twenty years after her photograph came to symbolize the war's brutality, Phuc defected to Canada, where one of her first phone calls was to VOW member Nancy Pocock.)[43] Even before Phuc's scars made headlines, VOW asked members to boycott household products made by Dow Chemical, a manufacturer of napalm who also made Saran Wrap and Handi-Wrap. VOW joined forces with a California peace group that urged women to write to the Detroit-based company, which sold its napalm for $3.5 million to the American Air Force. The letters explained that homemakers refused to buy their products because it was "hard to wrap food in these wrappers without giving a thought to the peasants wrapped in the flames of DOW's incendiary jelly."[44] Following the napalm boycott, VOW turned its attention to home-grown laboratories suspected of researching biological and chemical weapons for the Canadian government, including one such facility in Suffield, Alberta, located near a Canadian Forces Base. In 1969, VOW executives toured the Suffield facilities, where they met with the research director, who explained their research had no offensive purposes; however, suspicion lingered, since he was unable to comment on 85 percent of the facility's work because it was classified. Duckworth and Franklin subsequently presented a brief to the Canadian Senate's Special Committee on Science Policy outlining their concerns over the Suffield research station, and they urged the Canadian government to discontinue any research on biological or chemical weapons.[45]

While VOW tried to uncover military-industrial connections within research, Culhane pointed to a more obvious conflict of interest, the 1956 Defence Production Sharing Agreement between the United States and Canada. As part of this agreement, Canada supplied $2.47 billion worth of military goods produced by American-owned firms operating in Canada, Canadian crown corporations, or Canadian-owned corporations between 1965 and 1973. The majority of these goods ended up in Vietnam, including military equipment, vehicles, uniforms, weapons, ammunition, grenades, napalm, TNT, and Agent Orange.[46] During her hunger strike, Culhane asked the government to account for the profits made by creating killing machines to be used in a war Canada claimed to have no involvement in or responsibility for. Minister of Manpower Jean Marchand responded to Culhane's accusations by explaining that to end the agreement would mean unemployment for the 150,000 Canadian employees working in firms producing defence material, something that he predicted would bring down the government. Culhane challenged Marchand's figures as being closer to 7,500 and suggested that work could be redirected to domestic contracts or civilian production. Franklin countered Marchand's points by claiming it was absurd to speak in a dichotomy that forced a choice between "no jobs" and "war jobs." Meanwhile Culhane presented a more cutting metaphor, suggesting that history will compare the so called "Good Canadian" who produced "timing devices for the bombs which are destroying lives in Indochina" to the "Good German" who constructed "furnaces which incinerated Jewish victims."[47] NDP leader Tommy Douglas may have concurred with Culhane's harsh settlement, since in 1975 he referred to the sale of these arms as Canada's "blood money."[48]

Although VOW presented evidence to show that Canada was never non-aligned, the organization took advantage of its country's official neutrality to offer hospitality to American draft dodgers and Vietnamese visitors. Historian David Churchill estimates that between 30,000 and 100,000 draft resisters and deserters came to Canada between 1965 and 1975, with 40,000 probably being the most accurate figure.[49] VOW did not have an explicit program to reach out to these men and their families; however, it supported the efforts of the mixed-gender peace group the Committee against the War in Vietnam (CAWV), to which many of their members belonged. Through

CAWV, Canadians opened their homes to the American men fleeing conscription or enlistment and helped them find work and achieve citizenship. VOW member and chair of the Ottawa branch of CAWV Goldie Josephy recalled that young men about to be drafted would frequently appear on her doorstep unannounced. She estimated that at times she worked eighteen to twenty hours a day "helping the kids" and notes that her household "got some pretty crummy guys" and "some wonderful guys." She took them all in because, as she said, "I unrepentively [*sic*] feel that any young man is better off in one piece than in a plastic bag."[50] By calling the young men "kids" and referring to the possibility of their imminent deaths, Josephy's mothering of these draft dodgers strikes a powerful comparison between the young soldiers fighting and dying in Vietnam (on both sides of the conflict, though Canadians only regularly singled out the American combatants) and the children suffering in Vietnam. Both groups of young people represented a generation whose nationality gave them no choice but to participate in the war, whose age and status handed them an uncertain future, and whose bodies became intentional targets and collateral damage.

VOW members also opened their homes to women visiting Canada from North Vietnam, South Vietnam, and Laos in 1969 and again in 1971. Since the North Vietnamese women were considered enemies, they were barred from entering the United States, and VOW was pleased to act as a neutral and sympathetic host for their anti-war presentations. These visits culminated in conferences attended by American and Canadian women and offered opportunities for the visitors to share their war experiences in person, raise money for their cause, and fuel the anti-war movement in North America. More broadly, the goal was to "bring together women of different groupings" to learn from each other about the devastating impact of war, certainly in terms of the loss of life, but also because war was "the prime cause for their own oppression."[51] Ideally these visits were meant to strengthen the bonds of international sisterhood and facilitate ways in which to build momentum among women's shared desires for peace and justice; however, things did not always go as planned. The 1971 visit illuminates a number of practical and ideological issues that challenged putting this vision of internationalism into practice. According to VOW's records, the different groups of women who participated in 1971 arrived with competing agendas, none of which were entirely met at the conference.

Six women from Southeast Asia visited Canada in 1971, all of whom were highly critical of American involvement in Vietnam. Representing the Democratic Republic of Vietnam were Vo Thi The, a professor of literature

VOW's Vietnamese guests meet Toronto school children, 13 Apr. 1971. Courtesy of Lil Greene fonds, Library and Archives Canada and Voice of Women.

from the University of Hanoi who had been part of the 1969 visit to Canada, and Nguyen Thi Xiem, vice-president of the Hanoi chapter of VWU. The delegation also included Minh Hien, a teacher, and Dinh Thi Houng, a housewife, who were members of VWU living in South Vietnam. Two Laotian women working as primary-school teachers, Khampheng Boupha and Khemphet Pholsena, also attended the conference to call attention to the war having spread to their country. The women were accompanied by three male interpreters. The delegation visited Winnipeg and Montreal and was part of two large multi-day conferences in Vancouver and Toronto, which were attended by over 1,000 people, including members of VOW, WILPF, and other Canadian women's groups; American women belonging to the equivalent of VOW, Women Strike for Peace; and American women active in the other social justice causes from feminism to civil rights. There were also a handful of attendees identified as Vietnam veterans and GI wives. What drew the participants together was a shared interest in ending the war in Vietnam; nevertheless, the meetings were also a convergence of broader political goals related to a general spirit of anti-imperialism and women's liberation. Among the North American representatives, tensions arose when it became clear that there was no one shared vision on how to achieve these goals, or even on how to run the conference.

From the beginning VOW was worried that their vision and organization of the event had been compromised, or at least co-opted, by the American guests who did not truly wish to include a Canadian perspective or respect Canadian values. As Macpherson recalls, "Canadian women and sensitive ex-Americans became *very* conscious of 'American Imperialism,' not only the usual kind but 'of the left.' Our visitors from below the border tended not to remember that Canada was—still—a separate country, and our hospitality and patience were often tested."[52] Meanwhile some of the American guests complained that Canadians simply did not *get it*; in their opinion this was best demonstrated by the minimal security measures VOW had put in place, which involved some police protection. Fearful that they had been infiltrated by the RCMP, security of the participants and their overseas guests was a concern for all involved and resulted in disruptions as meetings were cancelled and the Indochinese women shuffled from one location to another.[53] The Americans insisted on taking over security and refused to let the Canadians help because "VOW just doesn't know what security is."[54] It was the strong opinion of several American guests that Canadians were naive because they had "never lived in a ghetto with the fear of FBI undercover agents who provoke something, or right wing nuts who will do something. That is why there is this type of security."[55] Meanwhile some Canadian women were appalled to discover that a few of the American peace activists came armed in order to be able to protect themselves in case riots broke out.[56] These tensions went beyond a Canadian–American divide and represented the disconnect between militant and moderate activists.

Reflecting on their experiences after the visits, participants noted how true collaboration was made impossible by divisions drawn along national, racial, political, and sexual orientation lines. One Canadian attendee, Mary Bolton, commented on the lack of sisterhood present, noting that

> the thing which disturbed me most at the Conference was the attitude of distrust and alienation among women. Prior to the Conference, labels like "feminists," "radical lesbians," and "anti-imperialist women" ... were thrown around a lot, creating divisions before a woman even began to arrive. Women became categories, not people.[57]

Women with more revolutionary agendas, including those in the Black Panthers, complained that the conference included too many "women who work entirely within the 'system'" which, depending on the perspective, could mean middle-class women and white women in general or specifically

VOW.[58] Meanwhile, lesbian women felt left out because not enough attention was being placed on the fact that "war is a male institution" and "only when women turn away from men entirely, withdraw their psychological and physical dependence on men, will male supremacy end, [and] thereby male defined issues and institutions."[59] More generally, there was disappointment that the visits had drawn only those already committed to the cause, which reminded VOW president Macpherson that "the apathy, in general, is great and the support minimal."[60]

Given these difference of opinions, it is not surprising there was little agreement on what the 1971 conference achieved. The women from Vietnam and Laos came to Canada hoping to raise American support to end the war, yet they left with little tangible action planned and few financial resources. Ten thousand dollars had been raised to pay for the trip, most of which went to cover the cost of travel between Canada and Vietnam. It was Macpherson's opinion that too many North American women gave impractical handmade gifts to the visitors instead of cash. The crafts, Macpherson states, were "put together with great care and devotion" but were "inappropriate in ways not imagined by the donors," and the gifts "had to be abandoned by the Indochinese" due to having no room in their luggage to take them home. Macpherson worried that the expense and time dedicated to the project were not overly effective if all the Vietnamese women gained from the visits was "an impression of friendliness and support from Canada and the United States out of proportion to the actual state of affairs."[61] Some women spoke more positively about the conference being an important moment in consciousness-raising for the North American delegates. Canadian Judy Gill reflected on her experience attending the conference in Toronto:

> I listened to our Indochinese sisters' accounts of their individual striving to survive and realized that for them, reality was a day to day struggle in hell. And I understood from many Third World and poor white sisters in Canada and U.S. the harshness of their struggle which had begun at birth. The horrors of war, of poverty, of racism were not new to me, yet I was struck by the contrast between the physical realities that are a part of their daily lives and those that are a part of mine. I experienced a new awareness of the safety and security of my own circumstances.[62]

As a mother, a middle-class Canadian, and a member of a local women's liberation group, Gill felt personally fulfilled by this visit. The post-conference reflections from Gill and those less enamoured with the experience show that the visits incited much-needed reflection on the strengths and weaknesses of the women's anti-war movement in North America. The visits were also good opportunities for VOW to call attention to the suffering experienced by women and children in Vietnam, which anchored its involvement in the cause and generated publicity for its relief projects and other aid work by FPPI and USC.

Foreign Aid: For the South and the North

The same sad images of bombed bodies and broken families that had driven VOW's anti-war campaign propelled an outpouring of money and supplies to help civilians stay alive until the war was over. Before VOW entered the fray, FPPI was one of the first voluntary agencies to work in South Vietnam, arriving in 1957 to establish a foster parent program and offer civilian relief in Saigon. Safety concerns did not stop the program from expanding to provinces surrounding the capital, though at times services and mail were delayed because of the war. In order to confront the toll the war had taken on children's bodies, FPPI made medical treatment a priority for its Vietnamese foster children. It hired doctors to make house calls to all the children enrolled in the program and treat them for malnutrition, sickness, and war injuries. It identified access to footwear as being an inexpensive means to improve health. According to FPPI, most Vietnamese children living in rural areas went barefoot due to the hot weather and the cost of shoes. Western physicians considered shoes to be just as important as medicine in preventing the spread of infection from cuts, insect and snake bites, parasites, and leprosy. So FPPI ran a shoe drive that collected 40,000 pairs of second-hand sandals and sneakers from Canadian and American donors. As the number of shoes donated vastly exceeded the number of Vietnamese foster children, the extra shoes were given to teachers to distribute to children not enrolled in FPPI sponsorships.[63] FPPI also worked to improve sanitation in refugee camps and orphanages and developed a program to increase the training of local social workers.

In the early 1960s FPPI became very aware of the American face of its organization. That had been a benefit in South Korea and Hong Kong, but the rising anti-American sentiment in South Vietnam caused by the United States' increased military and diplomatic presence, coupled with its support for the unpopular regime of President Diem, caused FPPI to fear that the organization's origins could thwart its work. This was one reason it replaced its American director in Saigon with Canadian Elizabeth Brown in 1962.

While FPPI was impressed with Brown's previous UNRRA experience in the Middle East and Europe, it also believed that what it called her "non-political" nature, in terms of both her citizenship and her personality, would be an asset.[64] It was hoped that having a representative from a supposedly neutral nation would allow the program to run smoothly. In addition, her knowledge of French would help her communicate with the staff until she learned Vietnamese. However, while Brown's citizenship was considered a benefit, her sex was a concern. Previously, FPPI's female directors had only been placed in Europe; all the ones working in Asia were men. Because Asia as a continent was presumed to be different and dangerous, Gloria Matthews, FPPI's international director, was concerned that it would not be safe for a single woman to be the director, especially in a country where there was an ongoing war. But the male FPPI director in the Philippines thought the right type of woman would do fine in Vietnam. In a letter to Brown, he explained,

Elizabeth Brown at her desk at the Foster Parents Plan office in Saigon. Courtesy of PLAN Canada and Foster Parents Plan International fonds, Special Collections, University of Rhode Island.

"Gloria asked me once more if I thought a woman would be right for Viet Nam, and I had replied that if you were prepared to take the risks—which I knew you would be—I didn't see why you wouldn't do very well there."[65]

Brown's letters to family and friends were full of candid observations about her accomplishments and challenges in Saigon. She believed FPPI was making a difference; sometimes a foster child's sponsorship could double a family's income. Brown admits it was difficult at first to interact with Vietnamese people because she found the culture and war situation quite different from her experience in the Middle East. Despite this, she stated, "The work is a joy to me. I have experience enough to know that I'm lucky to come this distance and [find] in day to day existence such pleasure. There's a lot to do, but there's the challenge of new possibilities within the program that make it fun."[66] Just like her employer, she considered herself and FPPI unconnected to the American government's interference in the region. "Plan's work is completely outside of politics," she wrote in a letter to her brother, explaining she could say this because she rarely interacted with American officials. Furthermore, she wrote,

> with a program for almost 5,000 families whose problems are largely health, housing and poverty, and with a staff of 35 Vietnamese to help them, we keep busy enough that we call only occasionally on the government or on the various American hierarchies, and we keep well out of the way of the developing war machine.[67]

To Brown, FPPI's humanitarian mission was innocent and welcome in Vietnam. Yet it became harder for Brown to find solace in her theoretically non-political mission by the time of the Tet Offensive. From January to June of 1968, Saigon and other regions came under heavy attack by the Viet Cong, the communist guerrilla force operating out of the South. Brown sent letters to Canada and the FPPI office informing them of her safety but admitted she could hear and see explosions from her house. She recalls being undecided whether to stay or flee to Hong Kong. In the end she decided to stay, hoping the Viet Cong would not see FPPI as a target for attack, because

> we are not military experts, nor do we presume to know about these things. We do know that the VC have said all military installations and American offices are targets for the next round ... Since Plan has been here eleven years there is nothing the VC do not know about us. They know we are non-political, [and] have no religious affiliation.[68]

Brown hoped her humanitarian effort (and citizenship) would offer her personal protection. At the same time, she recognized that the FPPI local staff and the sponsored children might become targets because of their association with an American agency, so she closed the FPPI offices for the duration of the offensive.

Brown left Vietnam in 1969 at age sixty-seven to start FPPI's first program in Australia. She was replaced by Marion Guild, formerly a supervisor at the Children's Aid Society in Winnipeg. Coming in the aftermath of the Tet Offensive and during a generally more aggressive stage of the war, Guild's perception of Vietnam was different than Brown's. She felt unsafe almost as soon as she arrived, a perception she linked to an escalated crime rate caused by the growing presence of refugees and the war's toll on Saigon's economy. Her fear was heightened by the rising threat of attack as the Viet Cong pressed closer to the capital city. The increasing insecurity of Saigon affected the foster parents program. In a letter to her American supervisor, Guild remarked that, among FPPI's foster children who lived at home, many of their parents were saving their child's monthly allowance from their North American foster parents to buy small gold objects to use as portable security. At first Guild thought this was inappropriate; why not use the funds to buy food and medicine now? After talking to Mrs. Tri, a Vietnamese social worker, Guild conceded the gold financing was a smart thing to do in case a family had to flee.[69] Unlike Brown, Guild thought the time had come that her nation's neutrality or the good work of FPPI could no longer protect her. She was quite shaken when her American assistant's wife was robbed and raped, and she resigned soon after, claiming discomfort in walking or driving alone due to the increased "anti-foreign feeling."[70] The next director hired was a man, who remained in place until 1975 when the war ended and all foreign programs, clearly political in the eyes of the communists, were told to leave. Brown's and Guild's directorships reveal the personal risks they took when delivering aid in a war zone. Their experiences also show that despite their organization's claims otherwise, FPPI's very presence in Saigon, as opposed to Hanoi, and its reinforcement of imperialistic ties between West and East were impossible to separate from the larger global politics percolating in Vietnam.

Fear of being part of the problem, rather than the solution, almost kept USC out of Vietnam altogether. Hitschmanova had been reluctant to start a program in Vietnam while the war was still on and only decided to investigate the possibility because donors and the Canadian government had begun in the late 1960s to press USC to get involved. At the same time, it was getting harder and harder to sell USC relief projects for South Korea because donors considered that country's problems to be "old hat."[71] Additionally, the Canadian International Development Agency (CIDA) was looking to fund Canadian voluntary agencies working in Vietnam and offered USC a $20,000 grant to start a project. In response to these demands, Hitschmanova traveled to Saigon in 1967 to explore the possibility of USC involvement in Vietnam, and potentially in Laos and Cambodia as well. She met with Brown, representatives from the South Vietnamese government, UNICEF, and other social welfare agencies to discuss what USC could do. While in Saigon, Hitschmanova had expected to find the situation similar to what she had seen when she visited South Korea in 1952, so she was surprised to find Vietnam very different. These differences, she argued, would make it almost impossible to work in the war-torn nation; there were no defined battle lines, and because of the war there would be no logistical support from the Vietnamese or the UN for the delivery of aid—only "endless red tape."[72] Moreover, she claimed not to understand Canada's policy toward Vietnam.

Seeking advice about whether USC should work in Saigon, Hitschmanova turned to Culhane as a fellow Canadian holding insight into managing relief efforts in Vietnam. Presumably, before she had been to Vietnam, Culhane would have viewed a USC project as an expression of love in the face of evil and international solidarity in times of great divide. However, due to her troubling experiences in Quang Ngai, Culhane remained firm that nothing should or could be done in Vietnam until the war was over. She argued that it was ridiculous to be helping Vietnamese children if they were only going to be bombed again the next day. In her eyes, to be healing the country amid the chaos of an unjust war was almost an acknowledgement that the war was acceptable. As she had with Canada's so-called blood money (profits made by supplying armaments and military equipment to the war), Culhane compared any USC relief effort as equivalent to going into Hitler's Germany and setting up a relief project outside the gates of Auschwitz.[73] Although she valued Culhane's opinion, Hitschmanova decided she could not turn her back on the suffering in front of her, not even for the greater good. For her it was better that some people would be alive to enjoy the peace. When asked if it was the right time for Canadians to send relief to Vietnam, even with the war's end not in sight, Hitschmanova said yes: "I believe the time is ripe because our investment is in human beings who desperately need our help *now*." She went on to explain, "The unhappiness of Vietnam haunts me day and night. It ought to be in the heart of everyone who is sensitive to the shocking injustice of war. Surely we cannot do enough for its brave people."[74] Hitschmanova considered the region too unstable to start a foster parent plan program, but she thought it was possible to do something smaller on a controllable scale. The USC used the CIDA money to build and staff rehabilitation centres that cared for blind children and children with polio.[75]

While FPPI and USC concentrated their efforts in and around Saigon, WILPF and VOW developed and assisted with foreign aid projects designed to help women and children in North Vietnam. This pointed decision brought aid to a population that was thought to need it the most and that had previously been neglected by Western donors. WILPF's and VOW's donations were channelled through the Canadian Aid for Vietnam Civilians (CAVC), an organization created by anti-war protesters in Vancouver in 1966 and sponsored by a group of well-known left-leaning men, including René Lévesque, Tommy Douglas, Rabbi Abraham Feinberg, and Pierre Berton. The same year, a Montreal-based organization called Quebec Medical Aid for Vietnam (QMAV) was created with former VOW president Casgrain as its president. CAVC made clear to all donors that 90 percent of its assistance was destined for North Vietnam and the National Front for the Liberation of South Vietnam, also known as the Viet Cong; parcels were sent to Hanoi via Vladivostok in the Soviet Union, with only 10 percent of the money and goods going to civilians in Saigon. In the early 1970s funds and relief goods were also sent to neighbouring Laos and Cambodia.

Sheila Young, a widow and long time WILPF member, was head of the CAVC children's committee and coordinated the collection of goods and clothing appropriate for infants and children living in jungles or underground shelters. Having gone through the Red Scare of the 1950s as a WILPF representative, Young noted that the controversial destination for the CAVC goods brought her familiar but worthwhile notoriety. "I've been called Communist and worse, but I don't care," she told *The Globe and Mail* in 1968.[76] After consulting with women's organizations in North Vietnam, Young requested donations of a particular sort: new or used women's shawls, blankets, children's pants and shirts, and no dresses. Everything needed to be in dark navy, green, black, or grey and made of warm, lightweight material. This was not because the people in the North were seen to be drab and unfashionable; rather, the dark colours would camouflage civilians from searchlights. Young explained bluntly to donors that any clothing not following the rules would be rejected because bright colours would attract American bombers. She used the opportunity to create a picture of North Vietnam as being in the depths of despair: "We must bear in mind that

Ontario VOW member Lil Greene with darkly coloured knit goods for Vietnamese children. Courtesy of the Lil Greene fonds, Library and Archives Canada and the Voice of Women.

many of the children of Vietnam are living under conditions utterly unlike any other children in the world." Young explained, "To these Vietnamese little ones the sun and sky do not signify warmth and beauty, but rather danger and death."[77] The dark colours became a poignant touchstone for the knitters who would comment on how heartbreaking it was to be making baby clothes in such dark colours. As one mother of five said when turning in her drably coloured vests, "it really brings the tragedy of war home."[78]

Young's knitting requests were taken up by over 15,000 Canadian women who were described as coming from "all walks of life and from as many different backgrounds," including "Church women, trade union auxiliary women, senior citizens and high school girls."[79] More than a quarter of the items donated were collected by Lil Greene, a VOW member and supporter

A Kindergarten class in the mountains, 100 miles from Hanoi, is the recipient of goods from VOW's Knitting for Vietnam project, c. 1971. Courtesy of the Lil Greene fonds, Library and Archives Canada and the Voice of Women.

of the Communist Party, whose three daughters joined her in knitting and helped her coordinate knitting circles across the country. Although Greene's politics drew her into the cause, Young's vivid portrayal of Vietnamese children hiding in the dark transcended complex geopolitics and interested many women and women's organizations that were not leftist or even very political in orientation. For example, the Brownies and Girl Guides—bastions of God, Queen, and Country—sent in hundreds of knitted items made for people in North Vietnam.[80] In 1967 a Brownie troop from Scarborough, Ontario, knitted several blankets, and the following year a group of twenty-four Brownies from nearby Etobicoke presented VOW with a quilt.[81]

Presumably some of the young Canadian knitters and other youth volunteers found kinship with the unknown Vietnamese children they were assisting or were frightened when they imagined themselves in the same situation. Zoya Stevenson, a Toronto teen, participated in the CAVC knitting campaign because she could relate to the Vietnamese children affected by the war. "The napalm bombing of innocent women and children (like myself) shocked me," she recalled, elaborating that "the fact that these acts of terror were sanctioned by citizens of my own country, frightened me terribly."[82] Just as adult members of VOW saw their anti–Vietnam War activism as an opportunity for consciousness-raising, youth participants discussed how CAVC challenged their world views. For Stevenson this occurred during tag day fundraising events for CAVC. These afternoon activities began at Greene's house with a youth discussion group for six to eight teens, coordinated by Dave Ferry. Together the youths discussed controversial matters related to the war and, in Stevenson's words, "learned how to express themselves."[83] Afterwards the teens would pair up and go to malls, where they would ask shoppers to donate to CAVC in return for paper tags they could wear as buttons publicizing their donations. "The afternoons weren't exactly fun, but they were engaging," Stevenson explained, noting that the tag days

> helped me to overcome my own terrible sense of helplessness about what I felt was a terrible injustice being perpetrated against a whole people and their country. The money we raised would support the shipment of goods from the knitting project to Vietnam and surely, I thought only good things happened when women were involved in the knitting project, just as it had been so in the Second World War.[84]

As in the Trick-or-Treat for UNICEF campaign, the symbolism of children helping children was an effective way to draw attention and funds to the cause. Also like the UNICEF project, this activism was viewed as an educational opportunity, meant to shape the internationalist characters of Canadian youth; however, in the CAVC's case, this involved the politicization of youth in a more radical direction, one which included a criticism of the Canadian government's foreign affairs.

Stevenson was not the only participant to use the knitting campaign as an occasion for reflection on the war's politics and the historic act of knitting. Many knitters reflected on how this knitting campaign differed from those of the past, when "grand Canadian women of an earlier era" sent care packages "for fighting men—to bring them some comfort in the agony and hurt of battle. Today Canadian women knit for little children; babies in their mother's arms."[85] One knitter in Saskatchewan expressed great joy that a project like this existed because it was a channel for her guilt and helplessness at the effects of total war:

> I was so glad to find there was a place where I could send some little bit of help; knowing that there are some people in this country that are getting some help to North Vietnamese people was such a relief to me ... [and] this medical help means a lot to me because I work as a nursing assistant, with

children yet! You can imagine what I think when I look at Canadian children and think of the kids in Vietnam.[86]

Despite the political overtones of much of the commentary, apolitical maternalism was also present in the knitter's reflections. One women described her knitting as "Millions of stitches carry[ing] our love," which implied that, with each click of the needles, the wool was interlaced with the invisible threads of mothers' love.[89] As with the foster parent plan letters, this love was seen to be as important a gesture as the gift of clothes.

Much as they had with the 1969 and 1971 conferences, VOW used the knitting project to highlight Canadian women's special internationalist role in creating a dialogue between American and Vietnamese women. Since it was illegal for Americans to give money to an enemy country, both CAVC and QMAV encouraged open-minded American citizens to use Canadian organizations as channels for sending goods and money to North Vietnam. Casgrain recounts in her memoirs the time she advertised QMAV at Expo 67 and an American woman with her son came up and pressed $2,000 cash into Casgrain's hand, promising more would be on the way.[87] VOW used one letter by an American mother as the central text of a poster recruiting support for the knitting project. In her "United States' Mother's Note," the anonymous woman acknowledged the cruel irony of her and other women "knitting camouflaged blankets to shelter the babies American men are dropping napalm on." Taking responsibility for her nation's role, the woman included an apology "to the mothers and children [in Vietnam] for all the barbaric crimes we have visited upon them." Fearing for her own family's safety, she concluded with the remark, "Since I have three draft-age sons, and the American post office is reported to act as an unconstitutional censor, I am not signing this note."[88] By calling attention to the poignancy of American mothers assisting their nation's enemy, VOW vividly illustrated its belief that women could rise above the politics driving the war because they prioritized life above all else.

The mobilization of women knitters was considered by many to be VOW's and CAVC's greatest achievement. Overall CAVC sent $200,000 in cash and 46 shipments of children's clothes, quilted blankets, health care supplies, and school equipment worth $275,000 to Vietnam.[90] In return the VWU sent "our sincere thanks to all Canadian mothers and other women who volunteered to make garments and bed covers for our children."[91] They explained that "the moral and material support constitutes a stimulus for our people now struggling every hour and every minute against an extremely brutal enemy, to wrest back independence and freedom, and defend the sacred right of life to our nation, and our children."[92] The VWU cheered when, after fifteen years of involvement, in January 1973 President Nixon announced the cessation of the United States' offensive against North Vietnam and the withdrawal of American forces from Indochina. Following this withdrawal, a ceasefire was declared between North and South Vietnam, with the hope that national elections would follow. (A few months later Canada withdrew from ICSC, citing its satisfaction with the peace process; it was replaced by Iran on the committee.) When the Americans withdrew from Vietnam at the end of 1973, the bombing campaigns largely ceased. The VWU celebrated their near victory with a new message to VOW. It asked them to "continue knitting ... but bright colours please—our people are so happy to wear colours again and be able to move freely about our own country without fear of being bombed."[93] The Laotian ambassador was also quoted as saying, "No colour would be too bright for our children now!"[94] According to these accounts, the knitting project was a successful relief and anti-war venture.

The idea that knitting, a seemingly innocuous domestic act, could generate such significant public awareness about the war, so many donations, and such righteous anger was another example of the powerful ways Canadian women's expressions of maternalism and internationalism combined to influence public opinion. Much like VOW's earlier collection of baby teeth, the knitting of black baby clothes created a visually powerful campaign steeped in maternal symbolism. In her analysis of VOW's Vietnam activism, Early argues that the knitting project served as more than a reminder of women's mothering; it drew attention in a disruptive manner to the corporality of both the knitters and the recipients. "Deliberately calling attention to their bodies," Early states, "has been an important strategy for women engaged in dissident citizenship."[95] Here VOW members and allies contested the political domain by calling attention to their own agency through the production of goods and the performance of activism. In doing so, they also called attention to the fragility of the children's bodies. Just as the piles of loose baby teeth, detached from children's mouths, being tested for strontium-90 was eye-catching in is disembodiment, seeing baby clothes presented in colours outside the pastel palette was inherently—and graphically—unsettling. Resembling miniature mourning garb, the empty shirts and dresses, sometimes strung across clotheslines in anti-war displays, emphasized the absence of bodies to fill them, a subtle reminder of the constant threat of death that was stalking these children.

Canadian women's anti-war and relief efforts in Vietnam represent both continuity and change. As with all the activism featured in this study, the

VOW members marching in Toronto against the war in Vietnam, April 1969. Note the clothesline of knitted baby clothes carried by two members. Courtesy of the Lil Greene fonds, Library and Archives Canada and the Voice of Women.

mobilization for Vietnam was framed by women who found children's vulnerability during times of war unacceptable. They responded in two ways: by providing resources to help the children and their families survive the war, and by lobbying governments to end the war. In both cases the women used their identities as mothers and grandmothers to bring attention, respectability, and sympathy to their cause. Yet members of WILPF and VOW and their fellow peace activists were not the only Canadians who found the war in Vietnam repugnant. By the late 1960s, many non-activist Canadians, influenced by the extent of the peace activism around them, the high death tolls of soldiers and civilians, years of bloody media accounts, and revelations about atrocities such as My Lai, began to consider the Vietnam War, if not wrong, then decidedly problematic. The Americans' eventual disengagement with Vietnam in 1973, viewed as a withdrawal, surrender, or defeat, further complicated the Cold War climate. Amid this chaos, even the staunchest Cold Warriors had trouble making the case that one could automatically align right and wrong or success and failure with opinions about capitalism and communism or an East–West divide.

While Canadians openly reassessed the meaning and consequences of Vietnam, the active women also achieved a heightened sense of awareness about their own activism. More so than any other cause, the war in Vietnam forced the women to question the motives, tactics, alliances, and outcomes of their activism. Although few women took as vehement a stand as Culhane, members of VOW, WILPF, USC, FPPI, CAVC, and QMAV openly questioned and confronted the political dimensions of their work and the consequences of their actions. If they had yet to make peace with their individual and organization's choices, they valued the importance of taking the time for self-reflection. This contemplation meant that, by the time international adoption was introduced as a welfare solution for the children of Vietnam, activists such as Brown, Culhane, and Pocock were well prepared to speak out about what they saw as right and wrong for Vietnam—and, in their opinion, adoption was the last thing Vietnam needed.

International adoption is the final child welfare initiative proposed by Canadian women examined in this study. Drawing inspiration from similar strains of maternalism and internationalism found in peace activism and foreign relief work, international adoption actually has more in common with the protectionist attitudes of the civil defence movement. Rather than work towards ending war or helping indigenous communities and families care for their own children, the women engaged in international adoption programs felt it was in the best interests of each displaced child or war orphan to remove them permanently from the dangerous sites of Cold War conflicts and have them seek shelter in the peace and security of Canada, in the arms of a Canadian family. International adoption was and remains the most controversial form of activism discussed in this study. On one side, there were women who argued persuasively against the removal of children from their communities and cultures. To them, whisking a child away to Canada was not a rescue but a theft of a country's most cherished resources, an act no different than the imperialistic politics that triggered the wars that orphaned the children in the first place. The adoption advocates responded to their critics by acknowledging that, under ideal circumstances, a child should not have to cross borders to find a family, and resources should be dedicated to encourage birth mothers to keep their babies or find adoptive homes within their own nations. In wartime, however, these were unafford-able luxuries. Just as Hitschmanova could not heed Culhane's warning that engaging in aid work in Vietnam legitimized the war, the women behind Canada's first foray into international adoption argued that this choice was a valid response until a country's infrastructure stabilized enough to provide the necessary local social services needed to care for orphaned, ill, or abandoned children in their home countries.

CHAPTER SEVEN

The Politics of Orphans
Origins of International Adoption and Operation Babylift

As a teenager in the 1950s, Sandra Simpson watched a newsreel about postwar South Korea. She was so moved by the plight of the Korean orphans featured in the film that she left the theatre in tears. "It was already in my mind but I guess it was then that I decided that someday I would do my bit," she recalled. "Someday."[1] Approximately ten years later, when she was a married mother of four living in a Montreal suburb, images of refugee children returned to haunt her. This time they were from Vietnam, and when they appeared nightly on her television, Simpson decided to help by adopting an orphan.[2] Eventually, she managed to untangle the bureaucratic red tape in Ottawa, Montreal, and Saigon and adopted a little girl, Mai Lien, in 1970. Simpson linked her teenage experience watching images of Korea with the ones she saw in Vietnam: "I went after her [Mai Lien] like you can't believe. There was no stopping me. It was like as if [after] all those years that child that had cried in that newsreel was in some way going to be residing in my home."[3] Simpson's interest in reaching out did not stop with Mai Lien. Over the next three decades, she personally adopted 28 children and helped hundreds of other Canadian families adopt from Asia.

Simpson was part of a small group of mothers who took leadership of Canada's first major wave of international adoptions because they believed a Canadian family was the best gift they could give a foreign child whose life and future had been disrupted by war, poverty, and civil unrest. Simpson and her cohorts argued that, until lasting peace treaties were signed, infrastructures stabilized, and hatred healed, adoptive families would be found outside of the children's nation of birth, in the bosom of Western affluence and peace. Motivated by a maternal internationalism caused by concern over the suffering of children affected by war and guilt over the West's responsibility for their fates, these women placed approximately 700 displaced children from Asian sites of Cold War conflict with Canadian families between 1968 and 1975. They did so by lobbying the government to change immigration and adoption laws, charging through war zones, and personally negotiating with foreign heads of state. The actions and identities of these maverick mothers pushed the boundaries of recommended Cold War homemaking by creating unusually large and interracial families, by leaving their husbands and children in order to work overseas, and by often taking action beyond what the government and host countries had authorized. According to representatives of the federal and provincial governments, at times, these women's radical behaviour and gendered motivations threatened the legitimacy of international adoption as a means of child saving. The adoption advocates also faced the wrath of some peace activists and foreign relief workers who believed international adoption was detrimental to the peace cause and to the countries relinquishing their children.

The transfer of children across borders for the purpose of adoption has always been a controversial issue for child welfare advocates, government officials, the families on both sides of the adoption equation, and the adoptees themselves. In their histories of adoption in North America, Veronica Strong-Boag, Barbara Melosh, and E. Wayne Carp have problematized the shifting social and political meanings embedded within interracial and international adoptions, questioning whether this post–World War II phenomenon was an embrace of global citizenship, child rights, and cross-cultural understanding or an example of the most intimate form of imperialism.[4] Rickie Sollinger's radical feminist analysis of international adoption leaves no room for pondering the ethics. She considers all kinds of adoption, but especially its transnational form, as the ultimate commoditization of children. Sollinger characterizes the exchange of babies, always from poor to rich countries (or marginalized mothers to privileged women), as a process that serves and protects the needs and wants of the "buyer," in this case the adoptive parent, not the child or the birth mother.[5] Meanwhile Laura Briggs historicizes the visual trope that spawns Sollinger's criticism. She claims Westerners' use of international adoption as a solution to help the foreign "waifs" they saw in photos and on television is dangerous because it takes attention away from the "structural explanations for poverty, famine and other disasters, including international, political, military, and economic causes," and reinforces the idea of wealthy Western nations needing to rescue developing nations.[6]

More recently, historian Karen Dubinsky has suggested that scholars need to move beyond the moralizing dichotomy found in the humanitarian rescue versus imperialist kidnap ideology. She proposes a finer lens to view transnational adoptions because they include the experiences of real children and real families, with culturally and historically specific responses to their adoptions—everything cannot be reduced to iconic symbols of power. Certainly, Dubinsky agrees, adoption is a means to study the ways in which "the sound of unhappy children provides common cultural ground ... [and] illustrates the symbolic and actual power of babies" to influence social meaning and foreign policy.[7] Yet she also asks scholars to acknowledge that "the intense emotional attachments between adults and children in our world are too complicated to fit into simple binaries."[8] Dubinsky's contextualization of international adoption as undoubtedly emotional and complicated for all involved, especially the adults and children breaking and forming families, is particularly helpful in understanding the motivations of the adoption advocates and their critics, and most importantly, the experiences of the adopted children.

Origins of International Adoption in Canada

Long before the transnational Cold War adoptions of the 1960s and 1970s, Canada had been seen as an ideological and physical sanctuary for orphaned, impoverished, and displaced British children.[9] For the most part, these earlier waves of child migrations, including the Irish Famine children, the British Home Children, and World War II evacuees, did not result in legal adoptions; instead the migrating children were placed temporarily within Canadian families as guests or labourers until they came of age or circumstances changed to allow them to return to their home country. In the meantime, the child migrants were expected to benefit from exposure to Canada's wholesome atmosphere, both environmentally and culturally, a welcome change from famine-stricken rural regions, overcrowded urban slums, or war zones. On the surface these experiences might seem to have little in common with the airlifts from Cold War Asia; however, they reveal a tradition whereby Canada and Canadian families were positioned as providing a better life for the migrating children than their birth parents and nation of origin. As well, many of these historic incidents dissolved into discourses about the vulnerability of unaccompanied children leaving one country to find a home and family in another nation.

A closer connection to the Cold War adoptions can be seen in the arrival of 1,100 Jewish refugee children and teenagers in Canada from across Europe between 1947 and 1952.[10] It was not until after the Second World War that child migration schemes were extended to non-British children. Throughout the war the Canadian Jewish Congress (CJC) had petitioned the government numerous times to allow Jewish children fleeing Nazi-occupied Europe the opportunity to come to Canada. In 1942 it received permission from Prime Minister King to bring 1,000 Jewish children from France. Unfortunately, the plan was aborted at the last minute, ostensibly because the ocean crossing was thought to be too dangerous and the Vichy government refused to grant exit visas. Still, the federal government did not push the cause, which was likely a sign of the "none is too many" ideology openly practised by the Canadian federal government in this era.[11] It was not until after the war when the full horrors of the Holocaust were revealed that King permitted the immigration of one-fourth of the surviving European Jewish youth. (A similar gesture was made to 1,000 Roman Catholic refugee children.) Despite the permission, the government expressed concern that the Jewish refugee children would be too damaged to adapt to life in Canada and feared astronomical welfare costs related to their care and assimilation into Canadian society. Consequently, as part of the agreement, the government would only provide the visas. Everything else, the placement, reception, and any public costs incurred by the children in the five years after their arrival would be arranged and paid for by the CJC.

This milestone migration raised several issues about the adaptability of adoptees and responsibility for their welfare that were still present twenty years later when the setting switched from Europe to Cold War Asia. The experience of the Jewish refugee children reveals the awkwardness that comes from attempting to heal the wounds of war by making families from strangers. Fifteen years after this migration *Maclean's* reported on the status of the "redeemed" Jewish children.[12] The magazine listed the personal, academic, and professional successes of the refugees turned Canadians, now doctors, dentists, artists, writers, skilled workers, and parents—all fine contributors to nation building. The article gave equal space to tragedies and failures, revealing that many of the children were too traumatized by their wartime experience to "span the gap between the European death camp and the Canadian home."[13] This stress, combined with adaptation to a new country, culture, and family, was sometimes too much for the child and their new guardians to work through together. In Winnipeg, for example, over half the children had more than one placement, while one in five had over four placements before they settled with a fitting host family. A few were admitted to mental hospitals, and at least two were known to have committed suicide. One *Maclean's* reader, Rosalie Shapiro from Montreal, challenged the success of this project; she felt it was Canada's past negligence that made its postwar actions too late for most of these children.[14] Overall, the refugee adoption scheme raised the question of who was responsible for these children's lives while they were in the war zone and once they came to Canada.

During and after the experience with the Jewish refugee children, the federal government was wary about setting precedents regarding Canada's obligation to the world's children, whether they came from the ancestral stock of privileged Canadians or those who were deemed "others." Not only was it a potentially expensive proposition, it also challenged ideas about nation, childhood, and family by making them fluid and adaptable concepts. This became even more apparent when the next group of children being saved from bombs were from Asia; they were neither blood kin nor from any of the major ethnic groups existing in Canada at the time. The government's reluctance to get involved in international adoptions from sites of Cold War conflict in South Korea, Hong Kong, and South Vietnam left the door open for private citizens groups, assisted by professional social workers, to continue the tradition set by the CJC—to bring vulnerable children to Canada.

The earlier migration schemes also reveal an unwillingness to invite the visiting foreign children to become a permanent part of the nuclear and Canadian family due to fears about their cultural, ethnic, and linguistic differences. This attitude began to shift after World War II, partly because of the reforms made to domestic adoption practices. In the postwar period, adoption as a solution to fertility problems had become less stigmatized domestically and became an increasingly popular practice for white middle-class couples wanting to start or expand their families.[15] According to traditional social work practices, prospective adoptive parents were usually matched with a child of the same ethnic background and religion and, if possible, a similar appearance. Due to a shortage of healthy white infants and more liberal ideas circulating about ethnicity, this practice was modified to allow for more diverse adoption matches in the 1950s and 1960s.[16] The Montreal Children's Service Centre (MCSC) was a North American leader in the innovative and experimental practice of interracial adoption, and it had moderate success in finding adoptive homes for black children and other minority and "mixed-race" Canadian children who had previously been marginalized in the adoption market.[17] The MCSC worked closely with the Open Door Society (ODS), a support and advocacy group founded in 1959 by the first white parents who participated in interracial adoptions. Together these two groups undertook a massive publicity campaign to educate the public about the need for and the normality of interracial adoptions.

As they implemented and celebrated these new practices, the MCSC began to receive inquiries about extending their services internationally to assist the children known to be orphaned, abandoned, or separated from their parents during World War II, and the thousands more affected by subsequent Cold War conflicts in Europe and Asia.[18] Many of these early requests featured a commitment to the maternal internationalism that would dominate the rhetoric of the adoption advocates a decade later. For example, in 1956 Kathy Lewis of Drummondville, Quebec, a married mother pregnant with her second child, wrote to the MCSC explaining that she wished to adopt a child from "the Eastern world" because her "deep interest and concern lies with the children in the over populated undernourished countries of the east, especially India and Korea."[19] Thelma Baker, a childless homemaker from Winnipeg who had been on a waiting list for years to adopt domestically, also wrote to the MCSC to ask how she could adopt one of "Europe's homeless kiddies," so she and her husband could "share our home, our life and our love with some unwanted waif."[20] These queries are typical of the common motivations expressed by Canadians wishing to pursue an overseas adoption in this era. The women presented themselves as having something to offer an underprivileged child—a country, a family, and love—and believed their actions would relieve some of the pressure on war-torn or impoverished nations.

At the time of Lewis's and Baker's requests, no Canadian child welfare agency had a system in place to process non-kin international adoptions. Furthermore, up until 1965, immigration regulations made it nearly impossible for unaccompanied minors to immigrate for the purposes of adoption to a Canadian who was not a relative. Additionally, due to the racialized hierarchy of Canada's immigration system, no refugees of any age were welcome from Asian countries outside of the British Commonwealth.[21] These immigration roadblocks did not stop adoption enquiries from prospective adoptive parents; in fact, as the Cold War grew hotter, the demand increased. During the 1950s, a handful of children from Western and Eastern Europe came to Canada for adoption, and these adoptions were process through the American branch of International Social Services (ISS), a transnational agency headquartered in Geneva that was dedicated to handling cross-border welfare issues requiring international co-operation, including child support, custody, deportation, desertion, immigration, paternity claims, repatriation, and adoption.[22] In the beginning, the American ISS branch did not mind handling the Canadian casework, but by 1955 Canada's increasing international presence, a sign of the country's growing global stature, placed a burden on the American caseworkers. More and more Canadians were travelling abroad for business, tourism, or diplomatic purposes. Moreover, in 1957 Canada had 140,700 military personnel living outside of Canada serving as NATO troops stationed in Germany, UN forces in the Middle East, and military personnel in Korea. With these postings came the "inevitable international marriages, illegitimacy, adoption of foreign children, [and] unstable family life."[23] Additionally, more than a million immigrants had arrived in Canada since World War II, almost all of whom had left behind relatives or had personal entanglements requiring social assistance. According to an ISS memo, these developments meant that "some social problems here or abroad will develop as a result" and therefore, "these projects should be paid by Canadian funds, as a service for Canadians by Canadians."[24]

In recommending to Canadians that they establish their own ISS branch, the American branch positioned its request as an opportunity for peace-making. Speaking to an audience of Canadian social workers, Susan Pettiss, an American ISS staff member, called the organization a worthwhile national investment, because alleviating

> individual problems that strike families separated by distance ... [can] minimize the possibility of these problems growing to proportions which will interfere with the relationships between countries and thereby cause a threat to world peace. It is perhaps by relieving the high tensions on an individual case-by-case basis that real progress can be made in this direction.[25]

This suggests that Pettiss saw the potential for an international incident to arise from a poorly handled transnational welfare case. She believed that having a mechanism to offer counselling, legal advice, and welfare assistance was a critical part of building and maintaining global peace and security. After having no luck in finding a voluntary agency to take over ISS duties in Canada, the federal government reluctantly agreed to devote half the time of a social worker from the Canadian Welfare Council (CWC), a government advisory body, to supervise the Canadian ISS casework.[26] A board chaired by Canadian UNICEF committee chair Mrs. Jean Tory was created to offer guidance, along with board members from several women's organizations, including La Fédération nationale des femmes canadiennes-françaises, the Canadian Teachers' Federation, the Catholic Women's League of Canada, the Federated Women's Institutes of Canada, the National Council of Jewish Women of Canada, the YWCA, and the Women's Auxiliary of the Anglican Church of Canada.[27] These representatives became the first organized international adoption advocates in Canada.

CWC-ISS already had one international adoption expert in their midst. Kenric Marshall, a board member representing Save the Children, had previously been the chairman of Child Placement Services in South Korea, an organization that matched American parents with Korean adoptees. Through this experience he had become "painfully aware of the sad lives such children endured" in countries such as South Korea and he stated that he was "ashamed as a Canadian that my country alone of those we appealed to responded negatively … Surely Canadians are capable of going to a little bit of trouble to overcome red tape in order to help solve one of the world's very real problems."[28] He believed CWC-ISS should consider challenging Canada's immigration laws in order to expand their scope from kin-adoptions because Canada had a humanitarian obligation to refugee and orphan children.[29] Marshall proposed that CWC-ISS should take advantage of the federal government's upcoming plans for the UN's 1959 World Refugee Year by inviting a small number of children from major refugee areas in Asia to come to Canada to be adopted. The CWC-ISS coalition applied to the Canadian Committee for World Refugee Year and received a $15,000 grant to facilitate adoptions between Hong Kong and Canada. Before it could begin the project, however, it needed to convince the Canadian government to amend the immigration laws.

Given the Cold War context, it is not surprising that the first immigration reforms related to international adoption were focused on Chinese children who were living in overcrowded orphanages in Hong Kong after having been orphaned or separated from their parents when families were fleeing the new Communist government in the People's Republic of China. The reasons behind this choice were both political and practical. According to Florence Boester, an ISS representative working in Hong Kong, Chinese orphans resided in "rather wretched conditions" where illness, particularly polio, flourished. In her opinion, "it was evident that the only chance of most for any kind of normal life lay in the possibility of their being adopted abroad."[30] While CWC-ISS acknowledged that the cultural differences inherent in international adoption would offer some challenges, it concluded that the situation in Hong Kong orphanages was "often a matter of life or death, which makes the question of integration to Western culture seem a minimal consequence."[31] As a member of the British Commonwealth, Hong Kong was a more familiar Asian locale than South Korea. It was also full of the "good" Chinese, those who had rejected or escaped communism. Public and private propaganda suggested that the sad fate of the orphans was the result of communism and therefore they were especially deserving of being saved. Rescuing these children proved Canada's humanitarianism and the West's superiority in matters related to child welfare, an attractive concept to ordinary Canadians as well as the Canadian government. This ideology was represented in one ISS pamphlet that featured the cover photograph of a tear-stained anonymous Chinese toddler dressed in patched clothes—the ultimate symbolic child. Below the photo was the slogan "Communism Failed Her ... Will We?"[32] In the spring of 1960, CWC-ISS sent a delegation to meet with Prime Minister Diefenbaker, and at first his answer to that question appeared to be yes. It took five years of lobbying for Diefenbaker to cede to CWC-ISS's requests to allow into Canada orphaned refugee minors from any country. After changes to immigration policy were made, Diefenbaker became more accommodating and encouraged the provinces to co-operate with CWC-ISS by performing home studies on the approximately 200 Canadian couples who had already requested a child from the "Far East." By 1965, 25 Chinese adoptees (and one Korean child) were placed with Canadian families of Chinese and European backgrounds in seven provinces.[33]

One of the first adoptive families was Dr. and Mrs. Chaing, a research chemist and his wife, a former high-school teacher from Montreal. The story of their adoption of Ching Ching, a two-and-a-half-year-old girl, and Loa Ka, a one-and-a-half-year-old boy, was featured in *Canadian Welfare* as an example of how easily foreign children adapted to life in Canada. A few days after the children arrived in Montreal from their native Hong Kong, a social worker from MCSC reported that "the children [renamed Lisa and Joel] could not be in a better home. They have settled in remarkably well."[34] Once she got them on an Eastern Standard Time sleep schedule, Mrs. Chaing was reported to be "thoroughly enjoying them and says the days seem all too short and that her husband is enjoying the children as much as she is."[35] This example made the children's adaption to their new country, family, names, and culture appear to be as easy as adjusting to jet lag, making the process seem unbelievably smooth once all the red tape was cut.

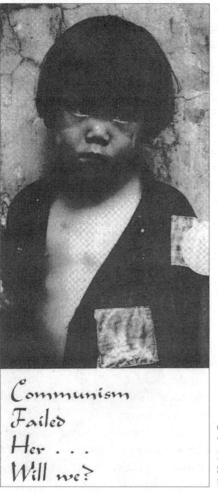

Communism
Failed
Her . . .
Will we?

Chinese refugee relief pamphlet,
Washington, c. 1960. Courtesy of
International Social Services fonds,
Social Welfare History Archives,
University of Minnesota.

Vietnam: Rescue and Rainbow Families

Over the next few years a small number of children trickled in for adoption
from Hong Kong and South Korea. As the war in Vietnam escalated in the
mid-1960s, public interest shifted to rescuing a new and very public pool of
displaced children. ISS claimed there were 10,000 homeless children in South
Vietnam housed in 63 registered orphanages in 1965.[36] By the end of the
American phase of the war in 1973, the orphan population and number of
orphanages had almost doubled. Traditionally, orphaned Vietnamese children

had been absorbed into extended families or families within the same village, but decades of war had made this form of child care difficult to arrange among impoverished and displaced families. The solution was the creation of orphanages funded by the Catholic Church, American military units, and foreign relief agencies.[37] The long-term presence of foreign militaries in South Vietnam meant that, as in Japan and South Korea, there was a growing population of children fathered by foreign soldiers. This was not a new demographic for Vietnam. Over a hundred years of French colonial rule had produced a sizable Eurasian population in Vietnam.[38] By the early 1970s, the number of Amerasian children was estimated to be between 15,000 and 25,000, most of whom lived with their mothers or extended families. ISS representatives in Saigon noted that most mothers were keeping their half-American children because they were as yet only infants but predicted that, as the children grew older, or if their fathers left the country or were killed, fear of stigmatization or lack of economic resources might lead to their abandonment.[39] This prediction was not realized in large numbers; by 1973 it was estimated that only 1,000 "mixed-race" children lived in orphanages.[40]

As discussed in the previous chapter, the plight of the Vietnamese children, including orphans, was well publicized in the Canadian media. The idea of adoption being the answer to their abandonment was first vigorously pursued by three Montreal housewives: Sandra Simpson, Naomi Bronstein, and Bonnie Cappuccino. These women—who were white, and either Christian or Jewish—lived in middle-class neighbourhoods in anglophone communities in and around the West Island area of Montreal. All three of them had young children of their own and wanted to add a Vietnamese orphan to their families. The Cappuccinos had already adopted internationally, a "mixed-race" girl, Machiko, from Japan and Annie Laurie from South Korea, while living in the United States. According to Cappuccino, she and her family had chosen to move to Canada after adopting Machiko when their congregation in Chicago informed her minister husband that they could stay as long as they did not adopt anymore "controversial"—that is, non-white, non-American—children.[41] They expected Canada would be more tolerant, and they were surprised to find their new home far behind the United States in establishing policies to adopt overseas. The three women became acquainted through their repeated inquiries to various government and voluntary agencies in Canada and Vietnam. They were frustrated that no one, not even the supposed experts in international adoption such as CWC-ISS, could tell them if it was possible for Canadians to adopt a child from Vietnam. Although ISS had a presence in Vietnam, it had never before made adoption placements during an ongoing war, and the organization was reluctant to start such a program. The war and the frequent regime changes in South Vietnam did not make it an attractive country in which to establish the necessary diplomatic ties and communications between child welfare agencies. Also, lessons learned from experiences in postwar South Korea had proven to ISS that reliance on international foster parent programs and international adoptions stunted the growth of local solutions and possibly contributed to the abandonment of children and the expansion of orphanages. To address its concerns, ISS had its local representatives, Phan Thi Ngoc Quoi, a social worker trained in the United States and England, and Mrs. Raphael, the wife of a British diplomat, research Vietnam's adoption traditions before it agreed to discuss processing adoptions.

Quoi and Raphael directed ISS's attention to Vietnam's legal and cultural practices that might discourage international adoption. Quoi reported that the country's adoption laws dated back to the sixteenth century and were primarily concerned with issues of kinship and inheritance. The law had been amended in 1959, 1964, and 1965 to clarify rules regarding the adoption of the wards of charitable institutions, primarily for the purposes of adoption to France and the United States. Adoptions would be approved if the child passed a physical and the adopters met the age and marriage requirements and had undergone a background check. Additionally, the child's legal guardian, in most cases the orphanage director, had to prove the child was abandoned.[42] Quoi's report noted the poor living conditions at most orphanages and was concerned that many children would not survive the wait to be adopted. Despite her similar acknowledgement, Raphael concluded,

> as in all countries at war, it is dangerous to presume any child is an orphan. The Vietnamese sense of family is very strong, and the tradition of the country, if anything, is against inter-country adoption. Therefore no child can be released for adoption unless it can be proved to be either an orphan, which is very rare, or an "abandoned child."[43]

Based on this research, ISS did not foresee international adoption as a service it would provide, except perhaps for Amerasian children with known American fathers. Instead ISS believed the priority should be placed on the reunification of children with their relatives.[44] This sentiment was echoed in the Leysin Principles, a set of recommendations prepared for the UN by child welfare experts on alternatives to international adoption in 1960.[45] CWC-ISS agreed with this plan and advised Canadians inquiring about adoption from Vietnam to consider adopting elsewhere or, instead, make a donation to one of the many Canadian relief agencies assisting children in Saigon.[46]

Not only did this answer not satisfy Simpson, Bronstein, and Cappuccino, it offended them. The media had led them to believe orphaned children were living in the streets, being subjected to abuse, and needed to be helped immediately. Not only were there nightly television reports and daily print stories, the National Film Board of Canada had released two compelling documentaries about the war's effects on children. Working with FPPI's Elizabeth Brown in the late 1960s, American-Australian filmmaker Mike Rubbo directed *The Sad Song of Yellow Skin* (1970) and *The Streets of Saigon* (1973), which documented the resilience and devastation of parentless street children who had witnessed the horrors of war. Sources such as these two films painted a bleak picture of the children's living conditions and stoked fears that, due to racism, the plight of half-white or half-black children fathered by American soldiers was particularly precarious. Margaret Valk, a senior case consultant with ISS, claimed that stories of mistreatment came directly from the "mixed-race" children themselves, who described being jeered at or stoned by children and adults while in public and being rejected or hidden or disguised by their mothers (by dying hair and eyelashes or keeping hair and the forehead covered).[47] It became generally agreed among American adoption workers that the fate of these children would be "at best, that of a second-class citizen and, at worst, that of a displaced or stateless person."[48] In response to these concerns, the three Canadian women decided to create their own agency called Families for Children (FFC) to further investigate the possibility of opening adoptions between Canada and South Vietnam. The women met in the basement of the Unitarian Church directed by Cappuccino's husband to share advice and moral support about the adoption process, and they initiated a letter-writing campaign to open the proper diplomatic channels. They were bolstered by the news that Lizette and Robert Sauvé, a well-connected francophone couple in Montreal—he was a judge and she was a journalist—had used their political connections to adopt the first Vietnamese child to come to Canada, a three-year-old boy, in 1968.[49]

While they waited to get their own approvals, the FFC women collected diapers, food, and medical supplies to send to orphanages in and around Saigon. After finding it difficult to ship such supplies privately, Bronstein persistently and successfully lobbied Prime Minister Trudeau to allow the

Canadian Air Force to include their relief packages on two humanitarian airlifts to South Vietnam on behalf of FFC.[50] Bronstein felt there was more she could do than pack boxes of donated goods. "I have to help," she recalled. "This is something that's inside of me." She acknowledged that there were needy children to help in Canada, "but people here are not dying of starvation. There are no three-year-olds [in Canada] that weigh six pounds, seven pounds."[51] In 1969, Bronstein left her children, including a newly adopted child from Montreal, in the care of her husband and travelled to Vietnam to volunteer in a Saigon orphanage.

In Saigon, Bronstein met Rosemary Taylor, an Australian high-school teacher, who had begun to arrange international adoptions to Europe and had recently opened her own orphanage. Taylor had also formed a partnership with an American woman, Wende Grant, and together they had founded a private international adoption agency, Friends for the Children of Vietnam (FCV). The agency was licensed by social services in Grant's home state of Colorado, where she had rallied a community of couples interested in adoption, much like FFC had done in Montreal. While volunteering in one of Taylor's orphanages, Bronstein arranged for FFC to be the Canadian partner of FCV. With Taylor's help, she was able to adopt into her own family Tam Lien and Tran, a little boy and girl, and brought several other children back for members of FFC. By 1971, the FFC founders had facilitated the adoption of thirteen Vietnamese children for several other Quebec families, including their own.[52] Meanwhile FFC opened a new orphanage in Phnom Penh, Cambodia, where they assisted children affected by the Vietnamese war's spillover and a burgeoning civil conflict.

News about FFC's work in Quebec spread across the country. In particular, a number of families in Ontario began to pursue adoptions from Vietnam. Much like the original group in Montreal, the prospective adoptive parents were concerned about the effects the war was having on children and felt they had loving homes to share. They also framed their interest in a number of contexts: spiritual, political, and humanitarian. One woman, Pauline Grey, originally from the United States, explained that her desire to adopt stemmed from a family history full of missionary work and service. She herself was a teacher at a Christian school, where she had met her husband. Furthermore, as an American, with relatives fighting in Vietnam, Grey felt a responsibility towards the orphans. She ended up adopting ten children, including one from Vietnam, and considered international adoption normal because, as she explained, "if God tells you to take care of your neighbours yourself, then your neighbours, anyone you see or hear ... [extends to] the whole world of course."[53] Meanwhile Hans and Roma Talboom, a couple from Guelph, had already been thinking about adoption before they thought about Vietnam specifically. In addition to their love of children, the Talbooms were inspired by the political consciousness-raising of the 1960s and 1970s. Hans notes that overpopulation was a big deal in the 1970s, recalling how "the thinking at the time was that everybody should just have two children and both of us wanted a bigger family ... so we had decided maybe years before that, that if we had two of our own, and wanted more, then we would look at someone less fortunate ... and increase our family size that way."[54] After giving birth to a son and daughter, Roma thought international adoption could work as a means to expand their family when she saw a program on television about Americans adopting from Vietnam. Roma recalls being very aware of the cost of the war because of the media and her interaction with American war resisters. "We knew some draft dodgers from the States," she explains. "I felt for them because I wouldn't want to join up."[55] With no Ontario international adoption services in place, the Talbooms worked with FFC to arrange an adoption from Vietnam. In 1974 they travelled to Montreal to meet their daughter, Thida (renamed Julie), adopted from Cambodia.

Much like the other Ontario families, Helke Ferrie, a housewife and mother of three living in Burlington, first became interested in adopting internationally when she read about the work of FFC. She relates her desire to help the children in Vietnam as stemming from her parents' experiences in World War II. Ferrie's German mother and father had opposed Hitler and ended up in a concentration camp, where her brother died during the war. She claims his death and the suffering she later saw growing up in India made her sensitive to the disposability of children's lives in wartime.[56] Ferrie explains that her philosophy was

> based on the conviction that every child has a right to a home of his own and that the family is the best possible setting in which a child may develop his potential. Barriers of race, nationality, religious background and special physical, mental and emotional needs are not recognized as valid if erected to prevent a child from having a family of his own.[57]

Despite this eloquent explanation, her first adoption request was denied because Quebec was the only province that had developed policies to allow Vietnamese adoptions. Appalled by the lengthy waiting times for home studies and other red tape she encountered in Ontario, Ferrie petitioned the provincial government to move things forward and, when that did not work, she went on a three-and-a-half-day hunger strike to alert the public to the province's stalling while children's lives were at stake. NDP Leader Stephen Lewis rallied support for Ferrie's cause in the Ontario legislature, accusing the government of denying foreign adoption for fear that the adoptees would be sickly and end up a burden on the provincial health and welfare system. The combined public and political pressure worked, and Ontario slowly began to accept adoptions from Vietnam.[58] While waiting for the paperwork to go through on adopting two school-age boys, Ferrie opened her own adoption agency, the Kuan Yin Foundation (KYF), named after the Buddhist goddess of mercy, to assist Ontario families.

The main responsibility of FFC and KYF was to ensure that all their prospective adoptive parents met the immigration and adoption requirements of the Canadian and Vietnamese governments. They also had their own procedural and moral guidelines for their clients to follow. Since it was the goal of both agencies to bring out children whom they identified as having the hardest time surviving in their home country, adopting handicapped and "mixed-race" children became the priority. So, while FFC tried to match as closely as possible requests for children of certain ages or gender, they refused to match on the basis of skin colour or other facets of appearance. FFC's number one rule was that every client had to be willing to take a half-black child. Bronstein recalled how FFC threw out requests from people who said they "were willing to take a child if it didn't have curly hair, dark skin, or thick lips … Sorry, we do not fulfill those orders. Families for Children works with families who will accept a child of any racial background, that's half-black, half-yellow, half-green. Whatever the child is."[59] Both agencies were also active in attempting to place children with health problems or disabilities.[60] FFC or KYF would not match such a child unless parents specifically requested one and proved they could handle the responsibilities of raising a child with special needs. For example, the Bronsteins adopted Sanh, a five-year-old boy diagnosed with thalassemia, a severe form of anaemia that required monthly blood transfusions and the removal of his spleen. Originally, a Swedish couple planned to adopt the child, but they pulled out of the adoption when they learned the boy would most likely die in his early teens. Bronstein and her husband arranged to adopt him instead and received special permission from the Department of Health and Welfare to bring such an ill child into Canada. Sanh lived with his Canadian family until he succumbed to his illness at age twenty-three in 1989.[61]

FFC and KYF continued to operate in Vietnam and Cambodia after the American withdrawal in 1973. They also expanded their adoption programs to Bangladesh, another nation experiencing great upheaval due to civil war. By 1975, these two groups had brought approximately 600 children to Canada. Amazingly, 58 of those children were adopted by the Ferrie, Simpson, Cappuccino, and Bronstein families. This generous and extreme act raised quite a few eyebrows and put pressure on the families' finances, marriages, and parent–child relationships. Ferrie's husband was a well-established doctor, while Simpson's and Bronstein's husbands were businessmen with salaries described as modest. Money was tighter for the Cappuccinos, whose only income came from Fred Cappuccino's ministry. The families made ends meet by purchasing used clothes and toys, buying food in bulk, and, in the case of the Simpsons, depending on the generosity of friends who rented them a twenty-two-room house for a below-market price.[62] The Cappuccinos eventually moved to a log cabin they built in Maxville, Ontario, where they could grow most of their own food.[63] For the adopting mothers, money never seemed to be a factor in the decision to add to their families. Bonnie Cappuccino recalled how it was the wives who usually called FFC to initiate an adoption, expressing their heartfelt desire to help the children, while their husbands fretted behind the scenes, worrying about paying the bills or saving for college. Cappuccino simply dismissed the men's financial concerns, saying, "These overseas babies, it's silly to talk about their education

"The Little Family That Grew and Grew," the Cappuccino family in 1990. Courtesy of *Chatelaine*.

when their lives are at stake."[64] She firmly argued that it was possible to make do, even in the case of the FFC founders' own enormous families.

The "rainbow families," the name given to large interracial adoptive families, pushed the boundaries of conventional homemaking, something that was not always appreciated by the communities in which they lived or the children themselves. Not only did many of the adopted children require physical and psychological therapy in Canada, they also had to deal with racism and prejudice from neighbours, schoolmates, and strangers. Once, the Simpsons' neighbours called the city to complain that they were running an illegal group home in a neighbourhood zoned only for residences. This mistake was understandable considering that, to most outsiders, the sizable multicultural brood of children did not resemble a "normal" Canadian family. The Talbooms' daughter Julie remembers having to explain to neighbourhood kids why she looked different than her sister Tina, her mother's biological daughter, who was only three months older. She confesses to having had some fun with the persistent questions; one time she explained to a younger boy on her street that "my sister is three months older than me and we are twins and my skin is darker because I was in my mother's womb for a lot longer."[65] The adopted Bronstein children recall being teased and spat on at school and called "dirty" because of their skin colour. One of Bronstein's biological daughters remembers how notorious her family was in their suburban neighbourhood. People would approach them and ask, "Which one of you guys are 'real'? As opposed to the fake ones ... people couldn't understand that we were just a family like anyone else."[66] In other cases, the rainbow families received admiration and support from the community. "I knew that ... our family was unique too because my father was a pastor, so he's already kind of the centre of attention," Thanh Campbell stated, adding, "And having an international adoptee made it even more so ... people were very encouraging to my parents. It was a great environment to grow up into, knowing that I was loved by my family, but people loved my family as well."[67] Campbell was not the only adoptee to reminisce about feeling welcomed, especially among those with strong connections to congregations who volunteered to help with meal planning and babysitting.

Another tension arose in families where the mothers also spent considerable time away from home looking after the orphans in Cambodia and Vietnam. The Bronstein children remember missing their mother as she rushed from one country to another helping other children and leaving her own behind. They were often annoyed when strangers told them how lucky they were to have a mother like Mother Teresa. "She's been driven all her life," one of Bronstein's grown children said of her mother. "She's always had something, a project, this or that ... if there was some child in need, she wouldn't hesitate to go."[68] Bronstein herself admitted that on low days she sometimes resented the responsibility she took on and the time she spent away from her own family, stating, "But then I think if I'm not here, these kids would be dead. And I just feel if I don't do it, there are not too many people doing it and it has to get done. I can't change the balance. But if even one or two children have a life that they couldn't before, and they grow up, then it's just worth it."[69] The travelling women juggled their workload by relying on babysitters, help from older children, and their husbands to make it work as best they could. The Bronsteins divorced in the 1990s, but not until after all their children had grown up. Ferrie's husband routinely accompanied her abroad to administer medical checkups for the orphans. Simpson's husband did the weekly grocery shopping; however, he drew the line at other household chores and child care responsibilities, explaining "the odd baby I've cuddled years ago but ... Sandra's the master of that."[70]

Caring for their own families was one challenge; another was seeking the approval and support of the federal and provincial governments for their work. From the start, the adoption advocates' most vocal critics were professional social workers employed in provincial child welfare departments. Many social workers were reluctant to applaud the work of FFC and KYF because, they argued, the heightened focus on the exotic tragedies of foreign orphans meant it would be harder to find homes for the Canadian children up for adoption, especially minority children.[71] However, the more troubling issue for social workers was that these private organizations were run by women with little to no professional welfare training. Social workers feared the private agencies' inexperience could lead to bad judgment, such as mis-identifying temporarily abandoned children as orphans or rushing through the selection of adoptive homes in order to get the children quickly out of a war zone. There was already a long-established rivalry in the United States between amateur philanthropists and professional social workers. Since the 1950s, adoption agencies established by Christian fundamentalist Harry Holt and author and adoptive mother Pearl Buck frequently butted heads with ISS and state welfare departments. Holt and Buck suggested that ISS unnecessarily layered the red tape and therefore delayed adoptions, possibly allowing children to die, while in turn ISS accused the private agencies of selecting homes poorly and gave examples of multiple adoption breakdowns.[72] Each party thought its decision—on the one hand, to trust maternal (or, in the case of Holt, paternal and evangelical) instincts, and on the other hand, to follow a professional code—was the superior one.

The rivalry between professional and amateur child welfare workers was somewhat replicated in Canada. As a result of this tension, representatives of the provincial and territorial child welfare departments met in 1973 to discuss international adoption and, in particular, the controversial role of private agencies. At this conference, Roland Plamondon, the child welfare representative for Quebec, claimed his province had no problem with the private agencies and fully supported the work of FFC. Meanwhile representatives from British Columbia and Ontario felt the private agencies were a threat to children's well-being and were especially wary of KYF, whose founder had a habit of radical behaviour and disregard for protocol.[73] Betty Graham, Ontario's director of child welfare, claimed that one time Ferrie's sloppy paperwork allowed children to arrive in Canada without the proper legal documentation from local authorities. She speculated it would take years to determine the legal status of these children and in the meantime their adoptions and citizenship would remain in flux.[74] Even more troubling was when Ferrie admitted to *The Toronto Star* that she would bend rules to get the children to Canada as quickly as possible and implied it did not matter if her clients were not the best candidates for adoption because, "Isn't a marginal home better than death?"[75] Although Ferrie did not specify, she clearly meant that a marginal home in Canada, where the children could live unmolested by war in a country with a social security safety net, would be an improvement over their life in a war-torn orphanage, even if their new Canadian parents were not the embodiments of Ward and June Cleaver. Even though the final decision to approve adoptive homes was up to the provinces, Victoria Leach, the adoption coordinator for Ontario, feared that the media attention devoted to the plight of war orphans would cause public pressure to move faster than usual in signing off on homes selected by KYF or FFC.[76] If this happened, social workers worried that it was possible that the children would not be properly matched to the best caregivers and, as a result, would have difficulty settling into Canada—or worse, be subject to abuse.

Leach spent the 1970s investigating KYF for signs of illegal practices. She surveyed former and current KYF clients, FFC, and other private and public adoption agencies active in the United States and Europe to get their opinion on Ferrie and her work.[77] Leach also travelled to Vietnam and Bangladesh to see the situation on the ground. Most results of her investigation are not available due to privacy laws involving the case files of individual adoptees; however, since KYF remained in operation, it does not appear that

Leach found enough evidence to support her suspicion that Ferrie had breached Canadian immigration laws or that her practices had intentionally caused adoption breakdowns. Still, the Ontario government remained uncomfortable with international adoption being a welfare solution for developing countries and recommended that the Canadian government increase its foreign relief spending in international child welfare so as to help prevent abandonment and alleviate the needs of hungry and homeless children. In the meantime, while international adoptions persisted, child welfare representatives in several provinces implored government to create a new federal agency that would act as a central information system to monitor the international adoption process, develop Canadian standards, and ensure private agencies co-operated fully with all laws.[78] It should be noted that not all social workers sparred with the private agencies. Simpson recalls how two Montreal social workers, Betty Macleod and Grace Galley, volunteered their time to assist FFC and completed home studies for international adoptees outside of their regular work hours.[79]

The federal government had issues with FFC and KYF that went beyond the concerns of social workers. Diplomats in the Southeast Asian embassies and staff in the Department of External Affairs grew increasingly worried about the unsupervised work of the FFC and KYF women overseas.[80] They panicked whenever they learned that the women had met independently with foreign heads of state and government officials, because they feared these independent activities had the potential to affect Canada's image abroad and even alter Canada's foreign policy. Simpson recalled how government officials were appalled when FFC called its Phnom Penh orphanage "Canada House" because they were afraid Cambodians would think it was the non-existent Canadian embassy and show up for visas.[81] Diplomats seemed to agree that "there is no doubt that Ferrie and her colleagues had good intentions ... A well-intentioned foreign visitor cannot but feel pity ... particularly for children and war-affected women."[82] Good intentions, however, had the potential to create international incidents, and the idea that the women, whose legitimacy was being questioned at home, had free reign in these countries made the Department of External Affairs nervous. Officials monitored their activities closely, sending telegrams back and forth between local embassies and Canada. They were exceptionally annoyed when news arrived that Ferrie had resorted to a sit-in outside the private home of a Bangladeshi civil servant in order to get his attention.[83] Ferrie's radical behaviour caused External Affairs to distance itself from outward signs of support. When the Canadian Embassy in Dacca forwarded Ferrie's request for a plane to transport sick orphans to Canada, External Affairs, which had yet to confirm that Bangladesh Prime Minister Rahman supported this plan, refused. The department intended "to avoid any official CDN [Canadian] government activity in respect to Mrs. Ferries [*sic*] plans which could be interpreted by GOBD [Government of Bangladesh] as interfering in their internal affairs or running counter to their expressed views as to handling out of country adoptions."[84]

Operation Babylift

The social workers, diplomats, and adoption advocates continued to maintain cool relations until April 1975, when the predicted victory of communist forces in Vietnam and Cambodia led to a collaborative effort to evacuate the remaining children already screened to come to Canada.[85] The evacuation became known as Operation Babylift, the mass departure of approximately 2,600 infants and children to adoptive homes in Canada, the United States, and other Western nations in the two weeks before the People's Army of Vietnam and the National Liberation Front captured Saigon. This effort was the ultimate child-saving gesture and a last-ditch attempt to protect children from the supposed evils of communism. It was assumed that, under the new regime, foreign adoptions would be suspended and, in the postwar chaos, orphans would not be anyone's priority, especially those whose physical features showed American parentage. Although this event sparked co-operation, the aftermath illuminated the controversy still surrounding international adoption.

As most of her fellow citizens were evacuating South Vietnam, Bronstein arrived in Saigon hoping to fast-track the remaining adoptions of FFC children in Vietnam and Cambodia. Under heavy fire from the Khmer Rouge's attacks on Phnom Penh, Bronstein evacuated the Cambodian children from Canada House along with their French Canadian caregivers, sisters Eloise and Anna Charet, and brought them to the FFC orphanages in Saigon. Some of the children were able to leave immediately for Canada, but the majority were delayed due to difficulties arranging for immediate exit and entry visas and transportation. To help FFC, KYF staff spent days phoning Canadian donors and were able to raise $76,000 for airfare to help bring the children out.[86] Money was not the only issue. Bombing had stopped most commercial flights, and friendly embassies were besieged by long lineups of foreigners and Vietnamese trying to leave the country.[87] Then, on 3 April 1975, American president Gerald Ford announced he would budget $2 million and provide military planes to fly the remaining children out of Vietnam. Following

Ford's announcement, the Canadian government offered to cover the cost of airfare for the rest of the adoptees destined for Canada.

When news about the airlifts hit the press, provincial child welfare agencies from coast to coast received hundreds of phone calls from Canadian families volunteering to adopt an airlift child. For its part, FFC assured the provincial authorities that it already had homes long picked out for the children scheduled to come to Quebec and there would be no spontaneous placements. Veronica Strong-Boag and Rupa Bagga show how meanwhile, in Ontario, "key decision making rested with civil servants" as social worker Leach coordinated arrangements for the arrival and medical care for the children arriving in Toronto on the one plane with yet-to-be placed adoptees.[88] Although Leach had initially been critical of adoptions from Vietnam, because of the practices of private agencies and the attention they took from adoptable children already in Canada, she felt it was important for social workers to closely supervise international adoptions. Working alongside Helen Allen, widely known for her newspaper column "Today's Child" promoting adoptable children, Leach turned Surrey Place, a community centre for developmentally delayed children, into a reception centre and health care facility for the as yet unplaced Babylift arrivals.[89]

Leach also worked hard to find acceptable parents. She had social workers contact couples across Ontario who had recently completed home studies or were already known to social workers as multi-ethnic adoptive families or through their previous adoptions of "mixed-race" or disabled children. One of the parents contacted was Gail Kilner of Sarnia, the biological mother of two children, who with her teacher husband had adopted two other children from within Canada, including an Aboriginal boy. They had also recently completed a new home study in anticipation of the possibility of adopting from overseas. Initially, difficult pregnancies had prompted Kilner to expand her family through adoption; yet, much like Simpson, her specific interest in international adoption stemmed from articles and documentaries about the plight of orphans in South Korea and Vietnam. Living in a border city, inundated with American news, Kilner recollects being aware that "things were getting pretty dangerous over in Vietnam and also being very aware of the fact that living conditions were getting pretty appalling and shortage of food was becoming very, very apparent. For the people in general and the children in particular."[90] In the spring of 1975, Kilner recalls, a social worker from Children's Aid contacted her just before the Toronto plane's arrival and explained they were looking for families who "have already looked into mixed racial children [or] who have already discussed the issue of living with children of another race."[91] Kilner remembers the social worker took this approach rather than an open call for adoptive parents because the Ontario government was "concerned people [would] respond emotionally to these children without having thought of the situation of living with an adopted child."[92] Not long after the initial conversation, the Kilners were called to say a Vietnamese boy about twenty months old was waiting for them at Surrey Place. Kilner adds that the social worker was so excited to match them that she even offered to personally babysit their other children while they went to pick up their new son, Trent. As it happened, the Kilners could not take Trent home for several months as he had to be treated for a severe parasitic infection in Toronto.

One day after President Ford's announcement, the first flight to leave Saigon, carrying 328 children and their adult escorts, crashed just after takeoff, killing 153 of the passengers. Bronstein had been scheduled to take a group of Cambodian children on that plane; at the last minute, however, Ernest Hébert, the Canadian chargé d'affaires in Vietnam, offered the use of a Canadian plane. The crash devastated the adoption community. Bronstein immediately rushed to the crash site to help survivors and identify the bodies of the children and her colleagues. She also hurried to inform waiting parents in Canada of the last-minute change of plan that saved their children from the crash, though for a few days there was confusion over which children had been on the flight, and newspapers incorrectly reported that 34 children destined for Canada had been killed, when in fact all those children had been on the plane arranged by Hébert.[93] As sad as the crash was, Bronstein reminded observers that

> every time I was there [in Vietnam and Cambodia] I had babies to bury. There were children dying all the time. And so this was a terrible crash and of course a number of children died, but at any one day in Saigon, the same amount of children die. We have been seeing it for so many years and everyone else has seen it once.[94]

The tragedy of the crash cast a shroud over the remaining airlifts and raised concerns about the hastiness of the departures that forced children to travel in cargo planes without the proper safety features. Unease also arose over the children's status: was it possible in the mad rush to leave that non-orphaned children had been taken?

In the days and weeks after Operation Babylift, criticism exploded throughout the United States and Canada. In California a class-action suit was launched on behalf of three Operation Babylift siblings who claimed they still had a living parent in Vietnam.[95] Further investigation by United States Immigration and Naturalization Services found that, out of the 1,667 children brought to the United States, 233 had insufficient documentation.[96] These discoveries raised questions and concerns about the potential carelessness of the amateur adoption workers that led to non-orphans—children temporarily placed in an orphanage or separated from their parents—being adopted prior to and during Operation Babylift. The children brought to Canada were not affected by this lawsuit, but the case caused Canadian immigration officials to review their paperwork, and Hébert, who arranged the last flight for the Canadian children destined for Toronto, was deposed in a provincial court. Hébert stood by the work of FFC and testified that he believed "the aforesaid group of 57 children left Vietnam legally for the purpose of adoption in Canada, with full knowledge and consent of the recognized Vietnamese government."[97] Despite Hébert's statement, it was apparent that in the heat of the moment mistakes had been made on all sides, which FFC excused as unavoidable due to the haste in which they had left Saigon. However, FCC insisted that no shortcuts had been taken that placed the children in any harm; rather, it retorted that the real danger had been the encroaching war and the arrival of the communists, from which the children had been protected.

The American lawsuit was eventually dismissed due to lack of evidence, but rumours about the airlifts persisted and introduced debates about the morality of international and interracial adoptions. Were the adoptions rescues or thefts? Was it wrong to raise a child outside his or her culture? Canada's Cold War ideology had changed between the time of the first adoptions from Hong Kong and the ones occurring during Operation Babylift. The simplified fairy tale of rescuing innocent children from the evils of communism was complicated by widespread public opinion about how harmful the American intervention had been in Vietnam. Additionally, the civil rights movement in Canada and the United States had been influential in raising awareness about racial discrimination and the history of white domination over marginalized minority groups. In the 1970s, leaders of the black and Aboriginal communities in Canada and the United States stated that the common practice of removing minority children to white homes was ethically and developmentally wrong. The process forced separation from a child's natural culture, which they argued had long-term effects on the child's identity and social and familial integration. Furthermore, no matter how well meaning the adopters were, critics believed adoption took the power away from the child—

first, by the act of adoption, in which they had no choice, and second, by rendering them a minority or outsider within their birth families and communities. Since it was normally white families adopting minority or "mixed-race" children, this adoption process reinforced the disenfranchisement of communities already living at the margins of society.[98]

This connection is implied in a cartoon featured in the Native American periodical *Akwesasne Notes*, published by the Mohawk Nation in 1975. The drawing by Keith Bendis featured a middle-aged white American couple contemplating an assortment of Vietnamese children displayed as if for sale in a store. Signs on the display read "Vietnam Orphan Souvenirs," "Remember Your Stay in Vietnam Forever," and "Limited Supply."[99] The wife, pointing to a child on the top shelf, says to her husband, "That one would look nice in the den." That this image accompanied an article entitled "Another Native People Lose Their Children" suggests that the editors of *Akwesasne Notes* saw their own marginalization and disenfranchisement and the removal of their children to non-Aboriginal homes as mirroring the exploitation of the Vietnamese. This cartoon reinforces Sollinger's arguments about children from the developing world becoming commodified through the process of international adoption.[100] Representatives from FFC or KYF would most likely

"Vietnam Orphan Souvenirs," 1975. Courtesy of Ken Bendis.

have read the cartoon differently. Whether they agreed or disagreed with the portrayal of adoption as a market transaction, they would have added the caveat that at least the children were *alive* to be commodified.

The argument as to whether the Babylift children faced an immediate threat in postwar Vietnam and were better off in Canada was questioned by other Canadians who had been active in the anti-war movement or in foreign relief. Nancy Pocock, a VOW member, saw Babylift as another form of Western exploitation. "The orphans were there all the time," she claimed. "We've been killing them with Canadian-made arms. I don't think it's a good idea to bring them over. Think of the culture shock.[101] Unsurprisingly, Claire Culhane was vehemently opposed to the adoptions and noted the irony of Americans helping the same children whom they orphaned in the first place. She asked the Canadian Minister of Immigration to "(a) attempt to return the children to their departure areas; and (b) to forward the largest possible sums of aid to cover medical, housing, food, clothing needs of remaining children who are suffering partially as a result of the arms sales we have profited from so richly in the past two decades."[102] FPPI's representative in South Vietnam, Elizabeth Brown, had been highly critical of the increased number of orphanages in Saigon because she agreed with research by Dr. Anna Freud and Dr. Tiffany Burlingham that found that children, especially in wartime, did better in a home setting, under the supervision of adults, rather than in institutional care. Yet, interestingly, she would not go so far as to recommend international adoption as a means to find a home. Brown believed removing a child from Vietnam just so he or she could have a family was equally problematic. Out of all available solutions, Brown considered that of FFPI—helping families in crisis keep their children through foster plan sponsorships—the best compromise.[103]

The adoption advocates from KYF and FFC responded to their critics by acknowledging that under ideal circumstances a child should not have to cross borders to find a family and that resources should be dedicated to encourage birth mothers to keep their babies or find adoptive homes within their own nations. In wartime, however, they argued, these choices were unaffordable luxuries. In a televised interview with Barbara Frum, Bronstein explained that her agency adopted the children who they were convinced would have the hardest time living in postwar Vietnam: older children, sick children, handicapped children, and especially "mixed-race" children. No matter how benevolent the North Vietnamese were, Bronstein was convinced that "half-black kids are going to have a hell of a time trying to live in that country, as well as half-white. I mean they are walking American examples."[104]

She also disagreed with claims that it was wrong to remove children from their birthplace, because, in these circumstances, "I can't really say that babies have a culture at that age and certainly they don't get this in an orphanage."[105] Frum was quite dismissive of Bronstein's explanations and concluded that the effort that went into Operation Babylift should have been redirected into projects that showed Canada in a better light. Interestingly, Frum herself was an adoptive mother, a point that was not brought out in the interview. In the 1960s, she and her husband had adopted an Aboriginal boy named Matthew.[106]

In the aftermath of Operation Babylift, Canadian participation in international adoption changed. As a result of the discontent over current procedures and their potential negative effects on Canada's foreign policies and reputation, the Department of External Affairs created a new federal agency in 1977, the National Adoption Desk. This bureau was to act as a central registry for international adoption information, coordinating and tracking requests from Canadians wishing to adopt internationally and forwarding the requests to the appropriate provincial and federal departments. Ideally, this change was supposed to eradicate or, at the very least, control private agencies, and it was seen as a welcome intervention by some social workers serving in child welfare agencies in all provinces except Quebec, which refused to participate on the basis that the new measures infringed on its right to manage child welfare provincial.[107] Despite their hope that the Adoption Desk would end the need for private agencies, FFC and KYF persisted in their work, and prospective adoptive parents continued to depend on their services. It appears that, having been at the forefront of international adoption in Canada for so long, FFC and KYF could offer their clients confidence, experience, and a personal touch, a combination not available from either the provincial adoption services or the Adoption Desk. As advocates for parents and children, the founders did more than just help with paperwork; they were themselves living commitments to the principles of international adoption. Furthermore, as adoptive mothers themselves, they could offer practical advice and emotional support. FFC agreed to work with the Adoption Desk and invited the director, Derek White, to visit FFC's new orphanage in India.[108] Meanwhile, Ferrie felt the added layer of bureaucracy only further slowed the waiting period to bring children to Canada and appealed to Trudeau to close the Adoption Desk. Her request was ignored, and rumours about the legitimacy of Ferrie's practices continued to plague KYF. Hoping for less scrutiny, Ferrie relocated her family and agency across the border to Michigan in 1978.[109] FFC continued to make recommendations to change the Adoption Desk's configuration, but it did not fight against it as KYF did, perhaps because it knew it was free to operate as usual in its home base in Quebec.

The voices of the one group that might truly settle the debate about the legitimacy of this adoption process were not captured during the Babylift controversy. Beyond the adults' interpretations of their tears and smiles, the adoptive children themselves were almost invisible in the public record. As they grew older, however, their personal experiences were shared with researchers and the media. One of the first examples was a 1998 study that interviewed over 100 international adoptees brought to Canada in the 1960s, 1970s, and 1980s, which concluded that the children grew up to be relatively well adjusted.[110] The majority felt a strong sense of belonging and self-esteem and were comfortable with their ethnic identities. Some of the children had experienced discrimination and racism, but it was inconclusive if this was related to their adoption or if their experience was on the same level as non-adopted non-white immigrant children. One response that was surprising to the researchers was that almost half of the children thought of themselves as Canadian ethnically, an assertion that could be interpreted negatively or positively, depending on one's stance on transnational adoption.[111] The researchers' conclusion reinforced Bronstein's claims that international adoption had been in the children's best interest and they did not suffer negative consequences. The study revealed that the children, now grown, "felt they had been loved and wanted by their adoptive families, and they were secure in their ethnic and racial identities."[112]

More recently, the Babylift children that were brought to Canada have organized and spoken about their experiences. In 2005, thirty years after they were was airlifted to Toronto, two participants of Operation Babylift—Trent Kilner and Thanh Campbell—were introduced to each other; inspired by their own meeting, they attempted to reunite the other adoptees evacuated from Vietnam on their flight. With the help of several Ontario newspapers publicizing Kilner and Campbell's story, three years later they had tracked down 44 of their 57 flight mates and invited them to a reunion in Toronto. (Bronstein organized a similar reunion for FFC's adoptees in 2001.) "It was a grand moment," Kilner recalled. "We learned so much [about] what had been a mystery all our lives … It was an instant bonding experience."[113] At the reunion Kilner met another Babylift arrival from his flight, Lia Pouli, whom he later married. For other adoptees, things were not as sunny. At the reunion some adoptees shared stories of unhappy family life or their struggle with disabilities and illness. It was discovered that a few of

Reunion of Thanh Campbell, Trent Kilner, and Victoria Leach, 2005.
Photographer Lucas Oleniuk, *Toronto Star.*

the adoptees, who would now have been in their thirties, were deceased. "I mean when we first heard about it, it kind of shocked us," Kilner admitted, "but you know it's not surprising. Not all of us were going to have happy endings."[114] According to Kilner's recollections, there were adoptees at the reunion who expressed anger or resentment at Operation Babylift. "They were willing to join us in the reunion and be there," he explained, "but they felt they should have been left alone. So you know I can understand both sides. I'm all for it [international adoption] but you know it's a hit or miss I guess."[115] The reunion included Surrey Place staff, nurses, doctors, the pilots, and Allen and Leach, the social workers who had accompanied them on their flight. Leach was pleased to see the children grown up and doing well. "They will always be part of my good memories, but it fills me with great joy to know they have their own families now," she stated in reference to other adoptees now having their own children.[116]

The Toronto Babylift reunion led to an unexpected chapter in Campbell's life, when he was reunited with his biological brothers and father in 2008. After reading about the reunion in *The Hamilton Spectator*, a journalist from Vietnam contacted Campbell, asking if she could publish his story in a Vietnamese paper. Two days after it was published, the journalist contacted

Campbell again saying a reader wanted to make contact. Campbell agreed and received an email from a man claiming to be Campbell's brother, who explained that their father had recognized Campbell as his lost son from a baby photo reprinted in the Vietnamese article. Unlike most Babylift children, Campbell had arrived in Canada with some personal records, including a birth certificate, which he had assumed was forged simply to allow him to leave the country. When the names matched, Campbell began to wonder: "Maybe they are my parents, maybe these are my papers—what do I do? And then someone said well the only way you can really prove is through DNA." He wavered about moving forward, but ultimately decided to have a paternity test performed: "I had two boys at the time and I said if one of my boys was missing, I'd want to know. You know, here's a dad who's been missing his son and I'd want to know."[117] A DNA test confirmed Campbell's father was indeed Nguyen Thanh Minh, a retired teacher in Ho Chi Minh City. For 30 years Minh had searched for the son that he and his wife had given up temporarily to an orphanage, along with their two older sons, for safekeeping during the war. When Minh went to reclaim his children after the war, he found his youngest son missing from the orphanage and was told he had most likely been adopted.[118] Campbell admits to being "dumbfounded" by the turn of events. "You know like how did they find me? How is that even possible ... that my life is being affected by forces I don't even know? It was just phenomenal."[119] Sadly, he learned, his birth mother had died in 1987. Campbell accepted these revelations with grace, and along with his wife, children, and adoptive father William Campbell, visited his birth family in Vietnam. Campbell's experience suggests that not all Babylift children were orphans in the traditional sense of the word. His story also echoes Dubinsky's insistence that, buried under all the global politics and drama of international adoption, there are real children whose feelings and experiences need to be understood and remembered separately from broader theories or opinions about international adoption.[120]

International adoption continues to remain a controversial act in Canada and abroad, especially as it expanded throughout the 1980s and became viewed less as a matter of child saving and more as a means to supplement a domestic adoption market that has few healthy white infants available for adoption. Still, it is important to recognize that the roots of the controversy in Canada began not with concerns about the children's best interests or international relations but with the government's disbelief that a group of mothers could know better than professional social workers or diplomats. Despite this criticism, the founders of FFC and KYF overcame public scrutiny,

Thanh Campbell holds a baby photo of himself taken during Operation Babylift, 2005. Photographer Lucas Oleniuk, *Toronto Star*.

lack of state support, and personal challenges to fulfill their maternalistic and internationalist vision. The movement and placement of an estimated 700 children with Canadian families in the 1970s is an important testament to maternal internationalism being a powerful force to reckon with at home and abroad.

Conclusion

This study comes to a conclusion in 1975, amid shifts in international relations, sites of activism, and women's lives. Détente, a thaw in Cold War rivalries begun in the 1960s, continued to percolate. New international treaties between the Soviet Union and the United States in 1972 and 1975 limited the manufacture of nuclear weapons and froze the missile stockpiles at their current numbers. This move reduced the fear of a global nuclear war and allowed the two superpowers to pursue more amiable relations, which in turn led to renewed trade between the East and the West. The Sino–Soviet split in 1969 also helped improve relations between the Americans and the Chinese, which had been stalled since the Communist Revolution. Historians argue that this temporary stability was spawned by a mutual need to recover from the economic burden of the arms race and the domestic turmoil caused by regime changes in the USSR and the civil rights movement, counterculture, and Vietnam War in the United States.[1] This calmer climate existed until 1979, when, just months after the Americans and Soviets signed another Strategic Arms Limitation Treaty, thereby reinforcing their commitment to curtail the building of nuclear weapons, the eruption of the Revolution in Iran and the Soviet invasion of Afghanistan triggered a need for both countries to rearm. The end of détente resulted in ten more years of Cold War tension and foreign interventions in civil conflicts, thus prompting a new wave of Cold War activism. Many of the women and organizations profiled in this study continued to be active after 1975; however, as the Cold War evolved, interpretations of what peace and security meant changed. During this new stage of the war, some activists took the opportunity to retire or change direction; others were made redundant.

Civil defence as a solution to the threat of nuclear weapons never recovered from the public skepticism and criticism it faced in the 1960s. After Pearson cut the Emergency Measures Organization's budget in 1968, the nationwide program became localized and dedicated to assisting in the aftermath of natural disasters and major transportation accidents, a role it often undertook alongside the Red Cross.[2] Coinciding with the end of détente, a new agency, Emergency Planning Canada, was created to handle future war or peacetime crises. However, despite a renewed threat of nuclear war, civil defence's public presence lacked the intensity it had had between 1957 and 1963. Under the new system, employees in the state-run health and welfare fields remained a critical part of emergency planning, but there was no recruitment or training of an auxiliary volunteer workforce. The agency's information bureau continued to promote emergency planning in the home, including the recommendation that families build a fallout shelter. As in the past, private family shelters remained an unpopular means of protection.[3]

Even if the government had been looking to build an army of volunteers to assist in its civil defence project, it would not have found the same reserve of support available from women's organizations. Since the 1960s, membership had declined in Canada's long-standing women's organizations, including NCWC, IODE, and FWIC. Women were not joining these liberal feminist and staunchly nationalist organizations in the same numbers they had in the early postwar period, and these groups were no longer the only public spaces in which women could interact and organize. In the 1970s and 1980s, women found more opportunities in formal politics and unions. When they did join same-sex organizations, they tended to choose the new wave of women's liberation and civil rights groups rather than the organizations favoured by their mothers and grandmothers.

WILPF and VOW struggled to remain relevant in a less publically engaged era of the Cold War in Canada. WILPF continued to be active in the disarmament cause throughout the 1970s and 1980s, though it had even fewer members than it had had during the 1950s when it was under attack during the Red Scare or during the 1960s when its activism was overshadowed by VOW. A 1980 memo from the WILPF Vancouver branch to the international office read, "The passing of long-time members has reduced the Vancouver Branch to a very small group, with no young women to replace them. But the 'faithful few' have carried on."[4] Internationally, WILPF continued to function and became part of a renewed international women's peace movement in the 1980s. WILPF participated in the thirteen-year-long Greenham Common Peace Camp, which brought worldwide attention to the renewed disarmament cause and women's commitment to peace as mothers and citizens.[5] Without the momentum surrounding the ban-the-bomb or anti–Vietnam War movements to ground its work, VOW also experienced a difficult transition post-1975. In 1976 VOW's membership hovered at approximately 500, far fewer than the 4,000 members and 10,000 newsletter subscribers VOW had had at the pinnacle of its popularity in 1962.[6] The organization argued that the drop in support was caused by the perception that nuclear weapons and militarism had become less of threat.

Kay Macpherson, VOW's third president, believed that competition from the women's liberation movement was also a factor in pushing the disarmament cause to the sidelines. "With the resurgence of the women's movement and the emphasis on the liberation of women in the late sixties," Macpherson stated, "… young intellectuals were effectively occupied in discovering themselves and the facts of their oppression. To raise one's consciousness as a woman became to them more urgent than peace, civil rights, foreign affairs or disarmament."[7] Since the late 1960s, women had been forming consciousness-raising groups across the country bent on changing the power structures in society that caused women's political, economic, and sexual oppression.[8] Within and parallel to this movement was organizing by women around other identity politics related to race, ethnicity, sexuality, and language rights. Macpherson encouraged VOW to embrace the new interest in women's liberation because she believed "a peaceful world would not be achieved in a society where women were oppressed and ignored."[9] VOW became one of the thirty-three national women's organizations to demand a Royal Commission on the Status of Women in Canada in 1967. VOW was also a founding member of the National Action Committee (NAC), a lobby group created in 1972 to ensure the government followed through with the recommendations made in the Royal Commission's report. Macpherson, who became president of NAC between 1977 and 1979, credits VOW's peace work for inspiring a new generation of feminists:

> What the peace movement did in the sixties was to appeal to women to join together for the first time in their lives to express their concern for peace and for the future of their children and to think and act independently in their (largely) middle-class conventional homes. This was the beginning of a revolution for many.[10]

While VOW might have been at the forefront of this revolution, the examples discussed throughout this study show that women had been expressing a concern for peace and a future for their children much earlier. Long before VOW existed, groups of women believed they must be the change they wished to see in the world, and their work should also be recognized as a precursor to the women's liberation movement.

Just as they had throughout the Cold War, the activists took divergent paths and held different perspectives on what would lead to women's liberation. The example that VOW members set as lobbyists and liberal feminists was only one possible route. Paralleling the women's liberation movement in Canada was an interest in women's rights globally that evolved out of the long-standing internationalist spirit in many women's organizations and the rising consciousness of women in post-colonial and developing nations who refused to remain on the margins of their nations or the global women's movement. In 1975 individual women, organizations, and governments from 100 nations assembled in Mexico City at an event organized in collaboration with the UN's International Women's Year. They met to discuss women's status in society and design a world plan of action to improve women's lives. One outcome of the conference was the establishment of the UN Decade for Women, a ten-year project dedicated to fact-finding and action to give women the resources to mobilize, implement gender equity in UN projects, and encourage member states to design their own plans to improve women's lives.[11] Women's equal status began to be seen more and more as the linchpin necessary to build peace and development. Over the next decade, without losing the focus on children, the UNA and Canadian relief organizations, including FPPI and USC, prioritized gender equity in their overseas relief and development projects. Although child welfare and child rights continued to be the focus of many projects, gender and women's rights became more prominent in development circles. There was recognition that, unless girls and women have access to education, health care, suffrage, and safe employment, all the larger goals—peace, human rights, sustainable living—are doomed. As women began to work for women, rather than just for children, the maternalistic spirit prevalent in the Cold War relief and development projects faded from the foreground.

The Canadian state and voluntary agencies continued to invest heavily in relief and development projects. After 1975, FPPI and USC expanded their foster parent programs to new areas affected by civil strife and poverty, most notably in Africa (Botswana, Lesotho, Upper Volta, Mali, Sierra Leone, Kenya, Senegal, and Swaziland) and Latin America and the Caribbean

(Columbia, Ecuador, Bolivia, and Haiti). Poverty, famine, and refugee crises directed where the agencies started new projects; the Cold War was no longer a critical motivator for action. USC ended its long-time relationship with South Korea in 1978, believing the unaccompanied children situation to be under control and the country no longer in need of USC's support. This decision angered peace activist and foster mother Goldie Josephy, who did not want her eight-year relationship with her teenage foster child, Myung Hi, to end and found it difficult to continue without the translation and banking services provided by USC. This is indicative of the strong emotional ties that existed between some long-distance mothers and their foster children, as well as the lack of consensus about the macro (South Korea's development) and micro (individual foster children's needs) goals of the charity. Josephy complained to Lotta Hitschmanova about USC's decision to withdraw without consulting Canadian foster parents and was appalled by the USC's offer to replace her South Korean foster child with one from Indonesia, "as though children were interchangeable artefacts."[12] Josephy took her complaints about USC to *The Globe and Mail*, the Department of External Affairs, and the Korean embassy in Ottawa, explaining her belief that "we have a moral right to (continue correspondence with the child)—otherwise our money was taken away under false pretenses. It has caused much pain for hundreds of parents, I am sure and even more for the children concerned, who have nobody else."[13] Even though South Korea's economy had improved, Josephy contended the state's newfound stability could not provide the same love and support that orphans received from their foster parents. Josephy's complaints appear to have fallen on deaf ears. Hitschmanova and USC had moved on to helping children who they thought were more at risk, and no one in the government—including Flora Macdonald, the first female secretary of state for External Affairs—was interested in the opinion of a veteran of the 1960s peace movement on this seemingly inconsequential development in a country that was no longer on Canada's foreign policy radar.

By the time of her battle with USC, Josephy had also ended her relationship with VOW. She could not reconcile the organization's new focus on women's liberation, particularly a woman's right to an abortion, with their previous peace activism. She asked how the same organization, once dedicated to protecting children from the bomb, could now be interested in ending children's lives. Josephy expressed her dismay in an open letter to NAC president and peace activist Laura Sabia, which stated, "I thought we were both in the 'peace movement' which surely exists in order to ensure the preservation of the human race, and that includes coming generations as well as our own. Without the children in the womb, the human race hasn't any future, so I will indeed carry on fighting the 'war on the womb.'"[14] After she withdrew from VOW, Josephy continued her peace and human rights work through an agency that she found better suited her politics and philosophy, Amnesty International. After 1975 Claire Culhane also stepped away from VOW, not for any apparent political disagreement, but because she found herself consumed by another social justice and feminist issue, prisoners' rights. Culhane spent the next two decades teaching women's studies to female prisoners and campaigning to reform Canada's penitentiaries.[15] Meanwhile, Hitschmanova remained the face and voice of USC until her death in 1990. After thirty-five years in the field of international development, with stints in the Middle East, Vietnam, and Australia, Elizabeth Brown retired in Toronto in 1979 at age seventy-seven.

Despite the continued controversy over the morality of international adoption in Canada and abroad, the movement continued to flourish. FFC remained an unrelenting advocate for international adoption, developing new programs in Guatemala and India and returning to work in Cambodia in 1990. As the number of children, especially infants, available for adoption declined domestically in the 1980s due to family planning, welfare programs, and the legalization of abortion, the majority of non-kin adoptions in Canada began to be arranged internationally. The scope of inter-country adoptions expanded beyond the handful of countries active in the Cold War and included India, Russia, Haiti, Romania, Jamaica, Peru, El Salvador, Brazil, Bolivia, Mexico, Guatemala, and the Philippines.[16] In the 1980s and 1990s, China became the number one source for international adoption by Canadians due to the country's high availability of infants, usually girl babies because of the Chinese cultural preference for boys. Although the motivation behind international adoptions after 1975 differed significantly from that of the earlier period, there remained similarities. Some adoption advocates and adoptive parents still considered themselves saviours, especially in the case of China, wherein they regarded their adoptions as saving children, particularly girls, from the communist state's one child policy. Rather than foreign policy influencing the adoptions, however, it was primarily the lack of adoptable infants locally that motivated most couples and individuals to adopt overseas after 1975.

The so-called maverick mothers also reached newfound legitimacy after Operation Babylift. In 1983 Naomi Bronstein and Sandra Simpson were honoured with the Order of Canada, an award given by the Governor General in recognition of a citizen's service to the nation. In reference to her award,

Bronstein remarked, "Now, I know I'm not Suzy Homemaker, but I've been doing this for 35 years, so my life doesn't seem amazing or astronomical to me. But I understand that to someone else listening, it is."[17] To Bronstein, her work was not remarkable, and, as demonstrated by this study, she was not alone in following her convictions. Over the years, other activist women featured for their activism in this study were similarly honoured with the Order of Canada: Bonnie Cappuccino, Thérèse Casgrain, Claire Culhane, Muriel Duckworth, Lotta Hitschmanova, Ursula Franklin, Kay Macpherson, and Hanna Newcombe.[18] Whatever issues the state might have had at one time about the validity of Franklin's scientific research on radiation or Culhane's accusations about Canada's complicity in Vietnam, their activism was recognized in hindsight and honoured as something Canada wanted to claim and celebrate as a part of its nationalism. Nor were many of Bronstein's peers "Suzy Homemakers," the tongue-in-cheek or derogatory label given to enthusiastic housewives concerned only with what happens inside the walls of their homes. Even if they never left their homes to engage in activism, thousands more Canadian women were active behind the scenes as letter writers, donors, civil defence wardens, foster mothers, babysitters, knitters, home nurses, and newsletter subscribers, whose support and labour made this a collective movement. Whether they contributed from the home, workplace, or voluntary organization, from major city or small town, for a few hours or several decades, their efforts influenced the direction of Canada's Cold War and contributed to a national movement of Canadian women committed to activism.

The goal of this study was to explore the different ways women responded to Cold War threats and fears and to understand what their activism represented. At all points between 1945 and 1975 there were multiple options—created by women—for women who wanted to work toward building a more secure country and world. They could follow the state's recommendation to invest in their health and safety by committing to the principles of civil defence, or they could challenge the notion that humans were meant to live in a world with nuclear weapons. They could send money, goods, and expressions of love overseas in hope of quelling the turmoil found in sites of Cold War conflict, or they could simply remove those most vulnerable from those nations and bring them to Canada. Civil defence, peace and disarmament, foreign relief, and international adoption were four intertwined areas of endeavour embarked upon by women in order to make Canada and the world safer. Although these different expressions of activism shared oppositional ideologies, they also had much in common. All of them represented a form of maternalism and showed a strong commitment to nationalism and internationalism.

If the activism recounted in this study confirms anything, it is that a strong sense of maternalism was present in women's motivation for change. This was most clearly demonstrated by Canadian women's protectiveness toward children, both their own and those whom they might never have known personally but whose faces and plights became iconic representations of what was wrong with the Cold War. Women's maternalism was also evident in the work they performed within their various projects. Caring and nurturing was central to their defence, peace, relief, and rescue work, through the administration of those skills as mothers, nurses, social workers, teachers, volunteers, and administrators of health and welfare projects. Cold War maternalism did not mean women were only capable in the domestic realm. Weaving maternal language and imagery into their activism was as strategic as it was sincere, giving them access to realms of public life—defence, diplomacy, and foreign affairs—that were usually out of bounds for women. As Macpherson stated regarding the idea that VOW's traditionally feminine image was a political asset, "What, after all, could be more pleasing than women raising their voices in hymns to peace, international understanding and goodwill towards most men?"[19]

Women did not engage in their activism solely through maternalistic representations of their gender. They came to their commitment to peace and security through other markers of their identities and personal histories as well. Even though the predicted third world war promised to be a war like no other, women's experiences in other wars were critical in shaping their reaction to the Cold War. Memories of the losses and suffering experienced during the Second World War inspired the first cohort of activists, who wanted to avoid ever experiencing that again. Similarly, images, if not direct experience, of the Korean and Vietnam wars inspired women who came of age in the 1950s and 1960s. Women's professional identities and expertise, particularly in the fields of nursing, education, and social work, were also important in motivating them to get involved and offered a means by which to support their causes through leadership, data collection, training, and knowledge sharing. For many of the women, religious traditions and spirituality informed their commitment to a life of service. Politics, region, age, class, and ethnicity also came into play, revealing the rich intersectionality of women's identities and helping shape a vision of postwar womanhood that went far beyond the ideals associated with Suzy Homemaker.

Being Canadian was also central to women's activism. This was expressed in numerous ways. Some women resented that their nation, previously a sanctuary, was now being threatened; others believed their country's wealth and stability gave them the opportunity to help those less fortunate and that their nation's postwar international reputation as a middle power gave them access to the world stage. This allowed Canada to aspire to a liberal form of internationalism, something interpreted in different ways within the various forms of activism. The women involved in civil defence perceived Canada's new level of engagement with other countries as being the cause of their predicament, but global insecurity forced them to look outward and remain aware of what was going on elsewhere in order to judge their own levels of safety. Within the peace movement, internationalism was embraced whole-heartedly as the key to peace; only with tolerance and cross-cultural understanding could the differences between nations and peoples be overlooked. Through confidence in the UN and foreign relief, internationalism was expressed as a responsibility to export people, resources, and ideas from Canada to uplift those whose standard of living was deemed insufficient. A more extreme version of this sentiment was seen in international adoption, where advocates came to deny that nationality, culture, and race were important in saving or raising a child, instead promoting their own country as the best place for these children to live. All of these different yet entwined versions of postwar global citizenship helped create the world these women wanted to live in and can be seen therefore as different approaches to ending the Cold War, whether the hope was for a stalemate or a victory for the West.

Between 1945 and 1975 there was an interconnected network of Canadian women acting as Cold Warriors and peacemakers in their homes, workplaces, and communities. Their activism was based on a tradition of gendered mobilization around issues of war and peace and the fear that a new kind of war lurked in the future. The examination of Canadian women's Cold War activism at home and abroad offers an opportunity to analyze the effects and evolution of the conflict from the perspective and activities of women, whose diverse responses were in some cases welcomed and in other cases undermined by the state. The addition of children's images, voices, and experiences wherever possible showed that even the bodies and minds of the youngest Canadians and their overseas counterparts could play a role in shaping Cold War culture. This demonstrates the pervasiveness of maternalism as a motivator, an attitude, and a key to women's political mobilization. Intertwined with this gendered identity was a strong commitment to fulfill the responsibilities of national and global citizenship. This analysis presents a wider lens through which to view Canada's Cold War policies and culture, and recognizes the importance of women's grassroots organizing and their influence on public opinion and state policy. For the thousands of women and children involved in this flurry of activism, their lives, families, and nations were forever changed by the hours worked, money raised, relationships built, and ideas stirred by attempts to mitigate their greatest Cold War fears.

Notes

Notes to Introduction

1 LAC, Goldie Josephy fonds, MG31, I4, Letters to the Editor 1975–77 series, vol. 3, "Goodbye Goldie," by Juliet O'Neil, undated newspaper clipping.
2 AO, Oral History Interviews, RG17-30-23, Goldie Josephy, Tape #1, 2 Dec. 1980.
3 Reg Whitaker and Gary Marcuse, *Cold War Canada: The Making of a National Insecurity State, 1945–1957* (Toronto: University of Toronto Press, 1994), 161–62.
4 Sarah Glassford, "'The Greatest Mother in the World': Carework and the Discourse of Mothering in the Canadian Red Cross Society during the First World War," *Journal of the Association for Research on Mothering* 10, no. 1 (2008): 219–32; Linda Quiney, "'Bravely and Loyally They Answered the Call': St. John Ambulance, the Red Cross, and the Patriotic Service of Canadian Women during the Great War," *History of Intellectual Culture* 5, no. 1 (2005): 1–19; Desmond Morton, *Fight or Pay: Soldiers' Families in the Great War* (Vancouver: University of British Columbia Press, 2004).
5 Ruth Roach Pierson, *"They're Still Women After All": The Second World War and Canadian Womanhood* (Toronto: McClelland and Stewart, 1986).
6 Barbara Roberts, *"Why Do Women Do Nothing to End the War?": Canadian Feminists-Pacifists and the Great War* (Ottawa: Canadian Research Institute for the Advancement of Women, 1985); Barbara Roberts, "Women's Peace Activism in Canada," in *Beyond the Vote: Canadian Women and Politics*, ed. Linda Kealey and Joan Sangster (Toronto: University of Toronto Press, 1989); Frances Early, "The Historic Roots of the Women's Peace Movement in North America," *Canadian Women's Studies* 7, no. 4 (Winter 1986): 43–48; Linda Kealey, *Enlisting Women for the Cause: Women, Labour and the Left in Canada, 1890–1920* (Toronto: University of Toronto Press, 1998).
7 Sharon Macdonald, "Drawing the Lines: Gender, Peace and War: An Introduction," in *Images of Women in Peace and War: Cross Cultural and Historical Perspectives*, ed. Sharon Macdonald, Pat Holden, and Shirley Ardener (London: Macmillan Education, 1987), 9.

8 Lawrence S. Wittner, "Gender Roles and Nuclear Disarmament, 1954–1965," *Gender & History* 12, no. 1 (Apr. 2000): 214.

9 Wayne Roberts, "Rocking the Cradle for the World: The New Woman and Maternal Feminism in Toronto, 1877–1914," in *A Not Unreasonable Claim: Women and Reform in Canada, 1880s–1920s*, ed. Linda Kealey (Toronto: Women's Press, 1979).

10 Julie Guard, "A Mighty Power against the Cost of Living: Canadian Housewives Organize in the 1930s," *International Labor and Working-Class History* 77, no. 1 (Spring 2010): 1–20; Denyse Baillargeon, *Babies for the Nation: The Medicalization of Motherhood in Quebec, 1910–1970*, trans. W. Donald Wilson (Waterloo, ON: Wilfrid Laurier University Press, 2009).

11 Seth Koven and Sonya Michel, eds., *Mothers of a New World: Maternalist Politics and the Origins of Welfare States* (New York and London: Routledge, 1993), 2.

12 Joan Sangster, "Radical Ruptures: Feminism, Labor, and the Left in the Long Sixties in Canada," *American Review of Canadian Studies* 40, no. 1 (Mar. 2010): 2.

13 Lisa Yaszek, "Stories 'That Only a Mother' Could Write: Midcentury Peace Activism, Maternalist Politics, and Judith Merril's Early Fiction," *National Women's Studies Association Journal* 16, no. 2 (Summer 2004): 72–73.

14 Koven and Michel, *Mothers of a New World*, 2.

15 Cynthia Cockburn, *From Where We Stand: War, Women's Activism and Feminist Analysis* (London and New York: Zed Books, 2007), 8.

16 Nancy Christie and Michael Gauvreau, eds., *Cultures of Citizenship in Post-war Canada, 1940–1955* (Montreal and Kingston: McGill-Queen's University Press, 2003); Magda Fahrni and Robert Rutherdale, eds., *Creating Postwar Canada: Community, Diversity, and Dissent, 1945–75* (Vancouver: University of British Columbia Press, 2008).

17 Roberts, "Women's Peace Activism in Canada," 279.

18 Adam Chapnick, *The Middle Power Project: Canada and the Founding of the United Nations* (Vancouver: University of British Columbia Press, 2005), 2.

19 A sample of the most prominent British and American scholars specializing in the international history of the Cold War includes John Lewis Gaddis, *The Cold War: A New History* (New York: Penguin, 2005); Lawrence Freedman, *The Cold War* (London: Cassels, 2001); Anne Applebaum, *Between East and West: Across the Borderlands of Europe* (New York: Pantheon Books, 1994); Martin Walker, *The Cold War* (Toronto: Stoddart, 1994); Melvyn P. Leffler and David S. Painter, eds., *Origins of the Cold War: An International History* (New York: Routledge, 1994); and S. J. Ball, *The Cold War: An International History* (London: Arnold, 1998).

20 Philip Buckner and R. D. Francis, eds., *Canada and the British World: Culture, Migration, and Identity* (Vancouver: University of British Columbia Press, 2006); Robert Bothwell, *Alliance and Illusion: Canada and the World, 1945–1984* (Vancouver: University of British Columbia Press, 2007); John Price, *Orienting Canada: Race, Empire, and the Transpacific* (Vancouver: University of British Columbia Press, 2011).

21 Ruth Compton Brouwer, *New Women for God: Canadian Presbyterian Women and India Missions, 1876–1914* (Toronto: University of Toronto Press, 1990); Ruth Compton Brouwer, *Modern Women Modernizing Men: The Changing Missions of Three Professional Women in Asia and Africa, 1902–69* (Vancouver: University of British Columbia Press, 2002).

22 Robert Bothwell, *The Big Chill: Canada and the Cold War* (Concord, ON: Irwin, 1998); John English and Norman Hillmer, eds., *Making a Difference: Canada's Foreign Policy in a Changing World Order* (Toronto: Lester, 1992); Greg Donaghy, ed., *Canada and the Early Cold War, 1943–1957* (Ottawa: Department of Foreign Affairs and International

Trade, 1988); Andrew Richter, *Avoiding Armageddon: Canadian Military Strategy and Nuclear Weapons, 1950–1963* (Vancouver: University of British Columbia Press, 2002); J. L. Granatstein and David Stafford, *Spy Games: Espionage and Canada from Gouzenko to Glasnost* (Toronto: Key Porter Books, 1990).

23 Emily S. Rosenberg, "Gender," in "A Round Table: Explaining the History of American Foreign Relations," *The Journal of American History* 77, no. 1 (June 1990): 116–24.

24 Cynthia Enloe, *Making Feminist Sense of International Politics* (Berkeley: University of California Press, 1990), 3.

25 Gary Kinsman, Dieter K. Buse, and Mercedes Steedman, eds., *Whose National Security? Canadian State Surveillance and the Creation of Enemies* (Toronto: Between the Lines, 2000); Steve Hewitt, *Spying 101: The RCMP's Secret Activities at Canadian Universities, 1917–1997* (Toronto: University of Toronto Press, 2002); Richard Cavell, ed., *Love, Hate, and Fear in Canada's Cold War* (Toronto: University of Toronto Press, 2004).

26 Whitaker and Marcuse, *Cold War Canada*, 364.

27 Franca Iacovetta, *Gatekeepers: Reshaping Immigrant Lives in Cold War Canada* (Toronto: Between the Lines, 2006).

28 Christabelle Sethna and Steve Hewitt, "Sex Spying: The RCMP and Women's Liberation Groups," in *Debating Dissent: Canada and the Sixties*, ed. Dominique Clément, Lara Campbell, and Gregory Kealey (Toronto: University of Toronto Press, forthcoming).

29 Elaine Tyler May, *Homeward Bound: American Families in the Cold War Era* (New York: Basic Books, 1988), 14.

30 Doug Owram, *Born at the Right Time: A History of the Baby Boom Generation* (Toronto: University of Toronto Press, 1996), 53.

31 Veronica Strong-Boag, "Home Dreams: Women and the Suburban Experiment in Canada, 1945–60," *Canadian Historical Review* 72, no. 4 (Dec. 1991): 474.

32 Joanne Meyerowitz, ed., *Not June Cleaver: Women and Gender in Post-war America, 1945–1960* (Philadelphia: Temple University Press, 1994).

33 Veronica Strong-Boag, "Canada's Wage-Earning Wives and the Construction of the Middle Class, 1945–60," *Journal of Canadian Studies* 29, no. 3 (Fall 1994): 6–7.

34 Owram, *Born at the Right Time*, 4.

35 Dominique Marshall, "The Language of Children's Rights, the Formation of the Welfare State and the Democratic Experience of Poor Families in Quebec, 1940–1955," *Canadian Historical Review* 78, no. 3 (1997): 409–41.

36 Mona Gleason, *Normalizing the Ideal: Psychology, Schooling, and the Family in Postwar Canada* (Toronto: University of Toronto Press, 1999); Mary Louise Adams, *The Trouble with Normal: Postwar Youth and the Making of Heterosexuality* (Toronto: University of Toronto Press, 1997).

37 Veronica Strong-Boag, *Finding Families—Finding Ourselves: English Canada Encounters Adoption from the Nineteenth Century to the 1990s* (Oxford: Oxford University Press, 2006); Veronica Strong-Boag, *Fostering Nation? Canada Confronts Its History of Childhood Disadvantage* (Waterloo, ON: Wilfrid Laurier University Press, 2011).

38 Strong-Boag, *Fostering Nation?* 4–6.

39 Dominique Marshall, "Humanitarian Sympathy for Children in Times of War and the History of Children's Rights, 1919–1959," in *Children and War: A Historical Anthology*, ed. James Marten (New York: New York University Press, 2002), 196.

40 United Nations, "Declaration on the Rights of the Child," 1959.

41 Everett M. Ressler, Neil Boothby, and Daniel J. Steinbock, *Unaccompanied Children: Care and Protection in Wars, Natural Disasters, and Refugee Movements* (New York: Oxford University Press, 1988), 12.

42 Cynthia Comacchio, Janet Golden, and George Weisz, eds., *Healing the World's Children: Interdisciplinary Perspectives on Child Health in the Twentieth Century* (Montreal and Kingston: McGill-Queen's University Press, 2008).

43 Karen Dubinsky, *Babies without Borders: Adoption and Migration across the Americas* (Toronto: University of Toronto Press, 2010), 5.

44 Ibid., 56.

45 Ibid., 12.

Notes to Chapter 1

1   Canada, Department of National Health and Welfare, Civil Defence Health Services, "Bea Alerte" poster series, 1950–59.

2   Jane Baker, "Planning for Emergency," *Globe and Mail*, 6 Feb. 1962, 11.

3   *Civil Defence Bulletin* 52 (June 1956), 29.

4   CTA, Former City of Toronto (FCT) fonds 200, series 361, sub-series 1, file 965, 140516-4, folio 4, pamphlet, *Your Branch Disaster Committee—Where Do You Find Them?*

5   "Role of Women," *Civil Defence Bulletin* 3 (July 1951): 9–10.

6   Laura McEnaney, *Civil Defense Begins at Home: Militarization Meets Everyday Life in the Fifties* (Princeton, NJ: Princeton University Press, 2000), 70.

7   Barbara Moon, "What You Can Do about Fallout," *Maclean's*, 4 May 1963, 56.

8   *Flowers or Ashes* (Toronto: Metropolitan Toronto Civil Defence Organization, 1957), film.

9   Ruth Roach Pierson, *"They're Still Women After All": The Second World War and Canadian Womanhood* (Toronto: McClelland and Stewart, 1986), 220.

10 David McConnell, *Plan for Tomorrow ... Today! The Story of Emergency Preparedness Canada, 1948–1998* (Ottawa: Emergency Preparedness Canada, 1998), 3.

11 Anne Fisher, "Civil Defence in Canada, 1939–1965: Garnering Public Support for War and Nuclear Weapons through the Myth of Protection" (MA thesis, Lakehead University, 1999), 13–16.

12 McConnell, *Plan for Tomorrow*, 6–7.

13 Jeffrey A. Keshen, *Saints, Sinners, and Soldiers: Canada's Second War* (Vancouver: University of British Columbia Press, 2004), 37.

14 Melanie Oppenheimer, "Controlling Civilian Volunteering: Canada and Australia during the Second World War," *War and Society* 22, no. 1 (Oct. 2004): 27–50.

15 Kenneth Rose, *One Nation Underground: The Fallout Shelter in American Culture* (New York: New York University Press, 2001), 4.

16 Kenneth Hewitt, "'When the Great Planes Came and Made Ashes of Our City ...': Towards an Oral Geography of the Disasters of War," *Antipode* 26, no. 1 (1994): 3.

17 Gaddis, *The Cold War*, 7–47 (see introd., n. 19).

18 Rose, *One Nation Underground*, 4.

19 Gaddis, *The Cold War*, 65–67.

20 LAC, Canadian Council on Social Development (CCSD) fonds, MG28, I10, vol. 106, file 785, Civil Defence, Welfare Centres, Areas, Detachments, 1952–63, Harvey Adams, "Civil Defence and Your Life," reprinted from *Saturday Night*, 1958, 1.

21 Ibid.

22 Canada, Department of National Health and Welfare, Emergency Measures Organization, "Survival in Likely Target Areas," *Blueprint for Survival No. 5* (Ottawa: Queen's Printer, 1962).

23 Costia Nikitiuk, "Emergency and Organizational Legitimacy: The Dilemma of Emergency Planning in B.C.," *BC Studies* 38 (Summer 1978): 48.

24 McConnell, *Plan for Tomorrow*, 22–24.

25 Sir John Hodsoll, "Self-Help," *EMO National Digest*, Dec. 1966, 14.

26 McConnell, *Plan for Tomorrow*, 29, 52.

27 CTA, FCT fonds 200, series 361, sub-series 1, file 962, box 140516-1, folio 1, "Canadian Defence Planning," 24 July 1948.

28 Ibid., letter to Mayor McCallum from Miss Isobel Heideman, 6 Dec. 1948.

29 Ibid.

30 Ibid., folio 4, minutes of the Executive Administrative Council Meeting, 6 Dec. 1950.

31 Ibid., folio 1, minutes and Invitations for the Citizen's Committee Meeting, 8 Dec.1948.

32 Ibid., minutes of the Executive Administrative Council Meeting, 15 Dec. 1948.

33 Ibid., file 977, box 140517-1, folio 1, memo to Mr. F.G. Gardner, Q.C., Chairman, and Members of the Metropolitan Toronto Council from Donald Summerville, Controller Elect, Chairman, Metropolitan Toronto Civil Defence Organization, 30 Dec. 1958.

34 "Quebec Update," *Civil Defence Bulletin* 44 (Mar.–Apr. 1955): 13–15.

35 LAC, CCSD fonds, MG28, I10, vol. 106, file 785 Civil Defence, Advisory Committee 1951–57, list of nominees for Advisory Civil Defence Welfare Committee, 13 Oct. 1953.

36 Laura Severs, "A Woman Who Made Things Happen," *Edmonton Journal*, 21 Mar. 2005.

37 Judith Fingard, "Women's Organization: The Heart and Soul of Women's Activism," in *Mothers of the Municipality: Women, Work and Social Policy in Post-1945 Halifax*, ed. Judith Fingard and Janet Guildford (Toronto: University of Toronto Press, 2005), 26.

38 Canada, Department of National Health and Welfare, Civil Defence Planning Group, *Civil Defence Health Services Manual No. 7*, 1952, 14.

39 Deanna Toxopeus, "1951 Agreement between the Red Cross and St. John Ambulance: A Case Study of the Effect of Civil Defence on Canada's Health Care System" (MA thesis, Carleton University, 1997), 1.

40 CTA, Larry Becker fonds 70, series 340, sub-series 9, file 3, box 233554, folio 3, "Emergency First Aid," St. John's Ambulance Nucleus by R. A. Mustard, MD, Toronto, for the Civil Defence Organization, Department of National Health and Welfare, 1953.

41 Evelyn A. Pepper, "Hospital Experience Programme for Selected Home Nursing Trainees," *EMO National Digest*, Aug. 1962, 15–17.

42 "Self Help Rescue," *Bulletin* (Welfare Services) 10, 11 Mar. 1958, 3–4.

43 Canada, Department of National Health and Welfare, Civil Defence Health Services, *What the Home Nursing Auxiliary Should Know about Civil Defence* (Ottawa: Queen's Printer, 1957), 11.

44 Kathryn McPherson, *Bedside Matters: The Transformation of Canadian Nursing, 1900–1990* (Don Mills, ON: Oxford University Press, 1996), 246.

45 CTA, FCT fonds 200, series 474, file 49, box 143147, folio 1, Evelyn A. Pepper, "Orientation to Disaster Nursing," Précis 9.01 Nov. 1962, Emergency Public Health Services Manual, June 1963, Canadian Civil Defence College, Arnprior, ON.

46 Thelma Green, "Some Newer Aspects of Civil Defence," *Civil Defence Bulletin* 61 (Jan. 1957): 22.

47   Ibid.
48   CTA, FCT fonds 200, series 474, file 49, box 143147, folio 1, Morgan Martin, MD MSC, "Preparation for Psychological Aspects of Nuclear Disaster," Précis 6.19 Oct. 1962 Emergency Public Health Services Course Manual, June 1963, Canadian Civil Defence College, Arnprior, ON.
49   LAC, CCSD fonds, MG28, I10, vol. 106, file 785, Civil Defence Training Courses 1952–67 Background Material Operation Lifesaver, Calgary, 21 Sept. 1955.
50   Canada, Department of National Health and Welfare, Emergency Welfare Services Division, *Emergency Feeding Manual* (Ottawa: Queen's Printer, 1965), 74.
51   CTA, FCT fonds 200, series 474, file 49, box 143147, folio 1, Esther Robertson, "Nursing Responsibilities for Mothers and Children under Emergency Conditions" Précis 9.08 Nov. 1962, Course Manual, June 1963, Canadian Civil Defence College, Arnprior, ON.
52   Ibid.
53   "Notice," *Civil Defence Bulletin* 46 (June 1955): 7.
54   CTA, Municipality of Metropolitan Toronto (MMT) fonds 220, series 100, file 3315, Metro Toronto Emergency Measures Organization 1957–58, box 46700-5, folio 5, report from Miss Margaret Douglas to Commissioner of Public Welfare, 2 May 1956, 3.
55   LAC, CCSD fonds, MG28, I10, vol. 106, file 785 Civil Defence, Advisory Committee 1951–57, Canadian Welfare Council, Civil Defence Advisory Committee Meeting Minutes, 17 Jan. 1956.
56   John Morgan, "The Welfare Aspects of Civil Defence," *Welfare*, Dec. 1950, 15.
57   LAC, National Council of Women of Canada (NCWC) fonds, MG, I25, vol. 129, file 2, NCW Annual Meeting Minutes, 11 June 1962.
58   DCA, MG 01/VI/((313.3M1-N) Prime Minister's Office (PMO) Numbered Series, Federal Government Executive, The Prime Minister of Canada, Requests and Appeals, National Council of Women 1957–63, letter from Diefenbaker to NCW, 3 Sept. 1961.
59   LAC, CCSD fonds, MG28, I10, vol. 106, file 785, Civil Defence Training Courses 1952–67, letter from Miss Frances Montgomery, Emergency Welfare Division, Department of National Health and Welfare to George Caldwell, Associate Director, Family and Child Welfare, 1 Aug. 1967.
60   Edith Walker, "Address to Federal Civil Defence Welfare Planning Committee," *Civil Defence Bulletin* 20 (Jan. 1953): 6.
61   Ibid.
62   *Bulletin* (Welfare Services) 20, n.d., ca. 1960–62, 4.
63   CTA, MMT fonds 220, series 100, file 3315, Metro Toronto Emergency Measures Organization 1957–58, box 46700-5, folio 5, letter to Curry and Miss Dunn from Miss E. Songhurst, Miss Jean Graham, and Miss Douglas, 1 May 1957.
64   Ibid.
65   LAC, CCSD fonds, MG28, I10, vol. 107, file 785, Civil Defence, Welfare Services, 1951–57, Point of Discussion, Relief Requests for Families, n.d., 1–2.
66   Guy Oakes, *The Imaginary War: Civil Defence and American Cold War Culture* (New York: Oxford University Press, 1994), 53.
67   Nevil Shute, *On the Beach* (New York: Ballantine Books, 1957).
68   "Nevil Shute Provides a Case for Disarmers," *Globe and Mail*, 22 Dec. 1959, 7.
69   DCA, MG01/VI/(601.68 PA) PMO Numbered Series, Social Welfare; Associations, Clubs, and Societies; Women's Organizations, National Council of Women, 1957–63, letter from Mrs. E. J. McClearly to John Diefenbaker, 22 Nov. 1957.
70   "Schools and Emergency Measure against Nuclear Attack," *EMO National Digest*, Apr. 1954, 20.

71 J. H. Pollard, *Emergency Measures in Elementary and Secondary Schools in the Metropolitan Toronto Area* (Toronto: Metropolitan Toronto EMO, 1961), 9.

72 Owram, *Born at the Right Time*, 116 (see introd., n. 30).

73 *Civil Defence Bulletin* 2 (June 1951): 9.

74 *Civil Defence Bulletin* 31 (Jan. 1954): 3.

75 "The Fourth 'R' Radiation Added to School Studies," *Toronto Daily Star*, 1 Nov. 1961.

76 Archer Productions, *Duck and Cover*, 1951.

77 Hugh R. Partlow, "Operation Turtle," *Civil Defence Bulletin* 48 (Aug. 1955): 20.

78 Hunter, Jennifer Lynn, "Is It Even Worthwhile Doing the Dishes? Canadians and the Nuclear Threat, 1945–1963" (PhD diss., McGill University, 2004), 295–96.

79 Sidney Katz, "How Nuclear Fears Affect Children Even in Peacetime," *Maclean's*, 15 June 1963, 23, 38.

80 DCA, MG01/VI(141) Prime Minister's Office (PMO) Numbered Series, 1957–63, Federal Civil Defence Plans and Organizations: 1957–Dec. 1961, #041039.

81 Alma Laabs and Virginia Hathaway, "Teacher Tips on Mental Hygiene Aspects of Civil Defence," *Civil Defence Bulletin* 22 (Mar. 1953): 6.

82 "Schools and Emergency Measures against Nuclear Attack," *EMO National Digest*, Apr. 1964, 20.

83 Katz, "How Nuclear Fears Affect Children," 38.

84 Pollard, *Emergency Measures*, 9–10.

85 Bothwell, *The Big Chill*, 13–14 (see introd., n. 22).

86 Whitaker and Marcuse, *Cold War Canada*, 4 (see introd., n. 3).

87 Frank K. Clarke, "'Keep Communism Out of Our Schools': Cold War Anti-Communism at the Toronto Board of Education, 1948–1951," *Labour/Le Travail* 49 (Spring 2002): 102.

88 Ibid.

89 Kristina Llewellyn, "Gendered Democracy: Women Teachers in Post-war Toronto," *Historical Studies in Education* 18, no. 1 (2006): 10–11.

90 LAC, Helen Melnyk-Marko fonds, MG30, D380, vol. 1, The Alert Service, *Alert Service*, Jan. 1965.

91 Ibid., Marjorie Lamb, "Communist Influence on Thought and Action in Canada," *Alert Service*, 27 Apr. 1966.

92 Reg Whitaker and Steve Hewitt, *Canada and the Cold War* (Toronto: James Lorimer, 2003): 91–93, 103–5, 165–69.

93 LAC, Helen Melnyk-Marko fonds, MG30, D380, vol.1, *The Alert Service*, 1 Mar. 1962.

94 Ibid.

95 LAC, Imperial Order Daughters of the Empire (IODE) fonds, MG28, I17, vol. 14, file 29, Minutes, World Affairs Committee 1950–67, and vol. 26, file 5, World Affairs Committee, n.d., ca. 1960–69, minutes, IODE World Affairs Committee, 18 Oct. 1965.

96 Noma Taylor, "The Role of Women in Civil Defence," *EMO National Digest*, June 1961, 13.

97 Pepper, "Hospital Experience Programme," 15.

Notes to Chapter 2

1 "How to Survive: Life in a Fallout Shelter," *CBC Newsmagazine*, CBC TV, 17 Sept. 1961.

2 "Signs Ban-Bomb Petition after Week in Shelter," *Toronto Daily Star*, 18 Sept. 1961, 1.

3 Canada, Department of National Defence, Emergency Measures Organization, *Survival Planning Guide for Municipalities* (Ottawa: Queen's Printer, 1964).

4 F. F. Worthington, "The Role of Women in Civil Defence," *Civil Defence Bulletin* 33 (Mar. 1954): 2.

5 McEnaney, *Civil Defense Begins at Home*, 77 (see chap. 1, n. 6).

6 Mary Louise Adams, "Youth, Corruptibility, and English-Canadian Postwar Campaigns against Indecency, 1948–1955," *Journal of the History of Sexuality* 6, no. 1 (July 1995): 93.

7 Quoted in Mona Gleason, "Psychology and the Construction of the 'Normal' Family in Postwar Canada, 1945–60," *Canadian Historical Review* 78, no. 3 (Sept. 1997): 447.

8 Strong-Boag, "Home Dreams," 474 (see introd., n. 31); Gleason, *Normalizing the Ideal* (see introd., n. 36); Adams, *The Trouble with Normal* (see introd., n. 36).

9 Mona Gleason, "Disciplining Children, Disciplining Parents: The Nature and Meaning of Advice to Canadian Parents, 1945–1955," *Social History/Histoire sociale* 29, no. 57 (1996): 189.

10 Gleason, "Psychology and the Construction of the 'Normal' Family," 443.

11 "Minister Replies to Housewife's Queries on What to Do in an Emergency," *Civil Defence Bulletin* 50 (Oct.–Nov. 1956): 8–10.

12 Ibid.

13 Valerie J. Korinek, "'It's a Tough Time to Be in Love': The Darker Side of *Chatelaine* during the Cold War," in *Love, Hate, and Fear in Canada's Cold War*, ed. Richard Cavell (Toronto: University of Toronto Press, 2004), 160.

14 Canada, Department of National Defence, Emergency Measures Organization, *Survival Planning Guide for Municipalities* (Ottawa: Queen's Printer, 1964), chap. 33, n.p.

15 Ibid.; "Role of Women," *Civil Defence Bulletin* 3 (July 1951): 9–10; Worthington, "The Role of Women in Civil Defence," 2.

16 *Bulletin* (Welfare Services) 52 (June 1956): 30.

17 Canada, *Survival Planning Guide*, chap. 33, n.p.

18 *Flowers or Ashes* (Toronto: Metropolitan Toronto Civil Defence Organization, 1957), film.

19 LAC, CCSD fonds, MG28, I10, vol. 106, file 785, Department of National Health and Welfare, "The Relation of Welfare Services to Warden Services" Federal Civil Defence College Precis WL/13, Apr. 1953, 6–7.

20 Ibid., Civil Defence Training Courses 1952–67, minutes of the Civil Defence Welfare Centre Administration conference, June 1953.

21 Ibid.

22 *The House in the Middle* (Washington: National Paint, Varnish, and Lacquer Association, 1954), film.

23 Canada, Department of National Defence, Emergency Measures Organization, *11 Steps to Survival*, step 5, "Have Fourteen Days Emergency Supplies" (Ottawa: Queen's Printer, 1969), n.p.

24 Quoted in Gerard J. De Groot, *The Bomb: A Life* (Cambridge, MA: Harvard University Press, 2005), 285.

25 Canada, Department of National Health and Welfare, Civil Defence Information Services, *Personal Protection under Atomic Attack* (Ottawa: Queen's Printer, 1951), 41–42.

26 Canada, Department of National Health and Welfare, Emergency Welfare Services Division, *Emergency Feeding Manual* (Ottawa: Queen's Printer, 1965), 74.

27 Taylor, "The Role of Women in Civil Defence," 14 (see chap. 1, n. 95).

28 Canada, Health Canada, *Canada's Food Guides from 1942 to 1992* (Ottawa: Queen's Printer, 2003), 10–12.

29 Taylor, "The Role of Women in Civil Defence," 14.

30 Canada, *Personal Protection under Atomic Attack*, 42.

31 Barbara Moon, "What You Can Do about Fallout," *Maclean's*, 4 May 1963, 11.

32 Ibid., 12.

33 DCA, MG01/VI(141) PMO Numbered Series, 1957–63, Civil Defence, Federal Civil Defence Plans and Organizations, Shelters Nov. 1961–62, #41815.

34 Ibid., Defence Research, Atomic Research, Radioactive Fallout, 1957–61, letter to Diefenbaker from "A housewife who prays," 17 Oct. 1961.

35 The issue had been debated in Parliament as early as 1954, when Brooke Claxton, Minister of National Defence in St. Laurent's government, insisted that radiation levels were low enough not to be a threat to Canadians. Hunter, "Is It Even Worthwhile Doing the Dishes?" 78, 114 (see chap. 1, n. 78).

36 Ontario, Civil Defence Committee, *Survival under Atomic Attack*, 1950, 4, CTA, fonds 70, series 340, sub-series 9, file 3, Atomic Bombs, Shelters, and War 1950–86, box 233554, folio 3.

37 John Hersey, *Hiroshima* (New York: Vintage Books, 1946), 54, 76.

38 "The Hiroshima Maidens," *Assignment*, CBC Radio, 8 Aug. 1957; Rodney Barker, *The Hiroshima Maidens: A Story of Courage, Compassion, and Survival* (New York: Viking, 1985).

39 UBCSC, Women's International League for Peace and Freedom (WILPF) fonds, box 1, file 1-3, "Some Preliminary Considerations on the Results of the Life History Survey," International Symposium on the Damage and After-Effects of the Atomic Bombing of Hiroshima and Nagasaki, 1977.

40 Lance W. Roberts, Rodney A. Clifton, and Barry Ferguson, *Recent Social Trends in Canada, 1960–2000* (Montreal: McGill-Queen's University Press, 2005), 74.

41 Owram, *Born at the Right Time*, 3–4 (see introd., n. 30).

42 Ibid., 5.

43 Canada, Department of National Health and Welfare, Civil Defence Planning Group, *Your Survival in an H-Bomb War If You Do Not Live in a Target Area* (Ottawa: Queen's Printer, 1956).

44 McConnell, *Plan for Tomorrow*, 52 (see chap. 1, n. 9).

45 Canada, Department of National Health and Welfare, Emergency Measures Organization, "Survival in Likely Target Areas," *Blueprint for Survival No. 5* (Ottawa: Queen's Printer, 1962), 19.

46 *EMO National Digest*, Oct. 1961, 12; DCA, MG01/VI(141) PMO Numbered Series, 1957–63, Civil Defence, Federal Civil Defence Plans and Organizations: 1957–Dec. 1961, letter from Diefenbaker and Curry, 29 Sept. 1961.

47 *EMO National Digest*, Aug. 1962, 20.

48 "Bomb Shelters for Sale," *Assignment*, CBC Radio, 6 Nov. 1958.

49 "Minutes of Proceedings on Civil Emergency Planning," *EMO National Digest*, Aug. 1964, 17.

50 Canada, Department of National Defence, Emergency Measures Organization, *11 Steps to Survival*, step 4, "How to Take Shelter," 1969.

51 DCA, MG01/VI(141) PMO Numbered Series, 1957–63, Civil Defence, Federal Civil Defence Plans and Organizations, Shelters Nov. 1961–62, letter from mother, Chicoutimi, to Diefenbaker, 14 Nov. 1961.

52 Ibid., letter to Diefenbaker, 16 Nov. 1961.

53 Christina McCall Newman, "Can You Protect Your Family from the Bomb?" *Chatelaine*, Apr. 1963, 31.

54 *Toronto Daily Star*, 16 Nov. 1961.

55 Ibid.

56 Ruth J. Martin, "Use of Fallout Shelters Is Called into Question," *Ottawa Citizen*, 12 Oct. 1961.

57 DCA, MG01/VI(141) PMO Numbered Series, 1957–63, Civil Defence, Federal Civil Defence Plans and Organizations, Shelters 1958–Nov. 1961, letter to George Pearkes, 8 Oct. 1959.

58 Ibid.

59 "Exercise Tocsin B: 1961," *CBC Radio News Special*, CBC Radio, 13 Nov. 1961.

60 Frances Hill, "Unthinkable and Insane," *Ottawa Citizen*, 4 Oct. 1961.

61 Ibid.

62 "Signs Ban-Bomb Petition after Week in Shelter," *Toronto Daily Star*, 18 Sept. 1961.

63 DCA, MG01/VI(141) PMO Numbered Series, 1957–63, Civil Defence, Federal Civil Defence Plans and Organizations: 1957–Dec. 1961, #041189.

64 Ibid., Tocsin B 1961, Nov. 1961–62, letter to Diefenbaker, 16 Nov. 1961.

65 Goldie Josephy, letter to the editor, *Ottawa Citizen*, 5 May 1961.

66 "Dief Raps Attacks on Survival Test: 'Communists Use Same Argument,'" *Toronto Daily Star*, 15 Nov. 1961.

67 Whitaker and Hewitt, *Canada and the Cold War*, 119–21 (see chap. 1, n. 92).

68 *Windsor Star*, 29 Dec. 1961.

69 Canada, *Debates, House of Commons*, Session 1962, vol. 3, 23 Mar. 1962, 2129.

70 David Spurgeon, "Shelters Only Hope for 2,000,000 If War Comes, Warns EMO," *Globe and Mail*, 3 Nov. 1961, 8; "Minutes of Proceedings on Civil Emergency Planning," *EMO National Digest*, Aug. 1964, 9, 11.

71 "Major Part of Canada Menaced from Cuba," *Globe and Mail*, 23 Oct. 1962, 11.

72 "What Do I Do? Cuba Crisis Increased EMO Calls," *Globe and Mail*, 25 Oct. 1962, 5.

73 Ibid.

74 Nikitiuk, "Emergency and Organizational Legitimacy," 58–62 (see chap. 1, n. 22).

75 Statistic based on a survey of 197 letters to Prime Minister Diefenbaker (#040866–#041690) from the DCA, MG01/VI(140) PMO Numbered Series, 1957–63, Civil Defence, Federal Civil Defence Plans and Organizations, General. Of the 197 letters, 47 came from married women, 7 from women's organizations, 7 from women who did not identify themselves as wives or mothers, 10 from mixed-gender groups, 12 from married men, 71 from men who identified themselves as husbands or fathers, and 35 from men representing organization or businesses. The letters that could be identified by province showed the majority came from Ontario (76), followed by British Columbia (35), Quebec (29), Alberta (11), Manitoba (8), Saskatchewan (6), Nova Scotia (3), and New Brunswick (2), divided fairly evenly between rural, suburban, and urban areas.

Notes to Chapter 3

1 LAC, Voice of Women (VOW) fonds, MG28, I218, vol. 1, file 23, report from 5th Annual Meeting, May 1965.

2 Barbara Moon, "What You Can Do about Fallout," *Maclean's*, 4 May 1963, 56.

3 "VOW in Ottawa: Federal Action Urged on Fallout," *Globe and Mail*, 23 July 1963.

4 Gordon Dewar, "Wasted Efforts," *Ottawa Journal*, 31 July 1963.

5 "VOW Still Concerned about Radiation," *Calgary Albertan*, 30 May 1964.

6 LAC, VOW fonds, MG28, I218, vol. 1, file 23, report from 5th Annual Meeting, May 1965; UBCSC, WILPF fonds, box 3, file 3-9, letter from Sheila Young, WILPF, to World Health Organization, 15 Apr. 1963.

7 "Teeth Calm Strontium Fear," *Globe and Mail*, 18 Mar. 1966.

8 Ursula Franklin, interview, 6 July 2010.

9 Early, "The Historic Roots," 44 (see introd., n. 6).

10 Jodi York, "The Truth about Women and Peace," in *The Women and War Reader*, ed. Lois Ann Lorentzen and Jennifer Turpin (New York: New York University Press, 1998), 21.

11 Roberts, "Women's Peace Activism in Canada," 279 (see introd., n. 6).

12 Marion Douglas Kerans, *Muriel Duckworth: A Very Active Pacifist* (Halifax: Fernwood, 1996), 60.

13 Ursula Franklin, quoted in Michelle Swenarchuk, introduction to *The Ursula Franklin Reader: Pacifism as a Map*, by Ursula Franklin (Toronto: Between the Lines, 2006), 8.

14 Whitaker and Hewitt, *Canada and the Cold War*, 104 (see chap. 1, n. 92).

15 Dorothy Thompson, "What Kind of Peace?" *Globe and Mail*, 13 Aug. 1945, 6.

16 Women's International League for Peace and Freedom, "Constitution," section B, 1919.

17 Roberts, "Why Do Women Do Nothing to End the War?" 3–4 (see introd., n. 6).

18 Gertrude Carman Bussey and Margaret Tims, *Pioneers for Peace: Women's International League for Peace and Freedom, 1915–1965* (London: WILPF British Section, 1980), 187.

19 Ibid., 177.

20 UBCSC, WILPF fonds, box 3, file 3-10, brief to the Canadian government, 28 Oct. 1950.

21 Ibid., letter from Sheila Young, WILPF corresponding secretary, to Lester Pearson, 21 Mar. 1956, and Vancouver branch report to Annual International Executive Meeting, 1958.

22 Ibid., letter from Sheila Young to Diefenbaker, 9 Sept. 1957.

23 Whitaker and Marcuse, *Cold War Canada*, 364–83 (see introd., n. 3). Interestingly, the authors call the Congress the only active peace movement during the 1950s, ignoring the work of WILPF and the Canadian Congress of Women.

24 Joan Sangster, *Dreams of Equality: Women on the Canadian Left, 1920–1950* (Toronto: McClelland and Stewart, 1989), 192.

25 UBCSC, WILPF fonds, box 3, file 3-10, letter to international executive of WILPF, Geneva, from Sheila Young, 10 July 1952.

26 Roberts, "Women's Peace Activism in Canada," 295 (see introd., n. 6).

27 Catherine Foster, *Women for All Seasons: The Story of the Women's International League for Peace and Freedom* (Athens, GA: University of Georgia Press, 1989), 25–26.

28 UBCSC, WILPF fonds, box 2, files 2-8, Jean C. Cole, "Report of the Nations—Canada," 12th International Congress of the WILPF, Paris, 4–8 Aug. 1953.

29 Ibid., box 3, file 3-10, pamphlet, *An Appeal to All Parents: Too Many Backyards Are Turned into Battlegrounds—We Urge You to Disarm Your Children*, 1948 and 1952.

30 LAC, VOW fonds, MG28, I218, vol. 2, file 17, President's Report, 1965, 4–5.

31 Ibid., vol. 1, file 17, 1st Annual Meeting, Toronto, 16–17 June 1961, 3.

32 "Two Radioactivity Tests Carried Out by Scientist," *Globe and Mail*, 8 Nov. 1962.

33 Gaddis, *The Cold War*, 62–66 (see introd., n. 19).

34 Cyndy Hendershot, *I Was a Cold War Monster: Horror Films, Eroticism and the Cold War Imagination* (Bowling Green, OH: Bowling Green State University Popular Press, 2001).

35 Gaddis, *The Cold War*, 64–65 (see introd., n. 19).

36 Ann Sherif, *Japan's Cold War: Media: Literature and the Law* (New York: Columbia University Press, 2009), 156.

37 Roberts, "Women's Peace Activism in Canada," 296 (see introd., n. 6).

38 Baillargeon, *Babies for the Nation* (see introd., n. 10); Guard, "A Mighty Power," 1–20 (see introd., n. 10).

39 Roberts, "Women's Peace Activism in Canada," 296 (see introd., n. 6).

40 Robert Duffy, "Green Denies Report Canadian Bases Used," *Globe and Mail*, 12 May 1960.

41 Lotta Dempsey, "Private Line," *Toronto Daily Star*, 17 May 1960.

42 LAC, VOW fonds, MG28, I218, vol. 1, file 1–4, a collection of these letters from May to Oct. 1960.

43 Ibid., letter from Margo Gamsby, Clarkson, ON, to Lotta Dempsey, 1 June 1960.

44 Lotta Dempsey, "Private Line," *Toronto Daily Star*, 21 May 1960.

45 Ibid.

46 LAC, VOW fonds, MG28, I218, vol. 1, file 1, letter from Mavis Wiley, Downsview, ON, to Dempsey, 17 May 1960.

47 Ibid., file 2, letter from Mrs. Eleanor Thomson, Onaping, ON, to Josephine Davis, 24 June 1960.

48 See chapter 2 of Christine Ball's "A History of the Voice of Women" (PhD diss., University of Toronto, 1994), 78–133, for a detailed description of the founding of VOW.

49 LAC, VOW fonds, MG28, I218, vol. 1, file 17, minutes of 1st Annual Meeting, Toronto 16–17 June 1961, 5.

50 Ibid., vol. 13, file 4, Meg Sears and Kay Macpherson, "A History of the Voice of Women" (1974), 2.

51 The biographies of the founding members were derived from information in the 1961 members file, LAC, VOW fonds, MG28, I218, vol. 1, file 5; Ball, "A History of the Voice of Women," 90–98.

52 LAC, VOW fonds, MG28, I218, vol. 1, file 5, form letter to potential VOW supporters from Davis, 24 July 1960.

53 Ibid., vol. 3, file 29, conference report, April 1971.

54 Ibid., vol. 13, file 4, Meg Sears and Kay Macpherson, "A History of the Voice of Women," 1.

55 Ester Reiter, interview, 10 May 2010.

56 Robert Bothwell, Ian Drummond, and John English, *Canada since 1945*, rev. ed. (Toronto: University of Toronto Press, 1996), 231–33.

57 Lotta Dempsey, "The Leaders Listened!" *Toronto Daily Star*, 16 June 1960.

58 "Green Backs 'Voice of Women' Plan," *Montreal Gazette*, 16 June 1960.

59 Ibid.

60 LAC, VOW fonds, MG28, I218, vol. 1, file 5, letter from Maryon Pearson to VOW, 30 July 1960.

61 Ibid., file 5, letter from Olive Diefenbaker to VOW, 8 Aug. 1960.

62 A more detailed account of VOW's history can be found in the following personal and academic accounts: Kay Macpherson, *When in Doubt, Do Both: The Times of My Life* (Toronto: University of Toronto Press, 1994); Thérèse Casgrain, *A Woman in a Man's World*, trans. Joyce Marshall (Toronto: McClelland and Stewart, 1972); Roberta Lexier, "Linking the Past with the Future: Voice of Women in Regina," *Saskatchewan History* 56, no. 2 (2004): 24–34; Maryanne Cotcher, "A National Organization in a

Prairie City: The Regina Voice of Women, 1961–1963," *Saskatchewan History* 56, no. 1 (2004): 21–29; Candace Loewan, "Mike Hears Voices: Voice of Women and Lester Pearson, 1960–1963," *Atlantis* 12, no. 2 (Spring 1987): 24–30; Frances Early, "'A Grandly Subversive Time': The Halifax Branch of the Voice of Women in the 1960s," in *Mothers of the Municipality: Women, Work, and Social Policy in Post-1945 Halifax*, ed. Judith Fingard and Janet Guildford (Toronto: University of Toronto Press, 2005), 253–80.

63 LAC, VOW fonds, MG28, I218, vol. 1, file 23, minutes for 5th Annual Meeting, May 1965, 4.

64 Akira Iriye, *Cultural Internationalism and World Order* (Baltimore: Johns Hopkins University Press, 1997), x.

65 LAC, VOW fonds, MG28, I218, vol. 2, file 29, "Subjective Postmortem of the Indochinese Conference Held in Vancouver," 1971, by Lydia Sayle.

66 *VOW Newsletter* 3 (1960): 7; UWA, Jo Davis fonds 3.2.2, letters received from others, and letters to Davis from Helen Hinde, Scarborough, 14 Nov. 1960, and Shirley Cook, Toronto, 10 Nov. 1960.

67 Lucille Marr, "'If You Want Peace, Prepare for Peace': Hanna Newcombe, Peace Researcher and Peace Activist," *Ontario History* 84, no. 4 (1992): 266–72. Lucille Marr's biography of Newcombe reveals an interesting twist to her story. During her five years with the CPRI, she claims to have felt consistently left out of decision making by Institute founder Norman Alcock, so Newcombe and her husband left in 1967 to found the Peace Research Institute–Dundas out of their home, where they continued to publish the journal and started new research on the voting patterns at the UN.

68 LAC, VOW fonds, MG28, I218, vol. 1, file 8.

69 Sharon Anne Cook, Lorna R. McLean, and Kate O'Rourke, eds., *Framing Our Past: Canadian Women's History in the Twentieth Century* (Montreal: McGill-Queen's University Press, 2001), 250.

70 Ball, "A History of the Voice of Women," 480–81.

71 LAC, VOW fonds, MG28, I218, vol. 13, file 4, Meg Sears and Kay Macpherson, "A History of the Voice of Women," 5.

72 Kay Macpherson, "Persistent Voices: Twenty-Five Years with Voice of Women," *Atlantis* 12, no. 2 (Spring 1987): 67.

73 Ester Reiter, interview, 10 May 2010.

74 LAC, VOW fonds, MG28, I218, vol. 13, file 4, Meg Sears and Kay Macpherson, "A History of the Voice of Women," 4.

75 LAC, VOW fonds, MG28, I218, VOW, vol. 2, file 17, "VOW and the Communist Smear: Some Thoughts from the National President as a Consequence of Many Recent Conversations," Jan. 1965.

76 Ibid., vol. 7, file 17, "Why VOW?" pamphlet by Alberta VOW, 1963–64.

77 Owram, *Born at the Right Time*, 45 (see introd., n. 30).

78 Valerie J. Korinek, *Roughing It in the Suburbs: Reading Chatelaine Magazine in the Fifties and Sixties* (Toronto: University of Toronto Press, 2000), 307.

79 Macpherson, "Persistent Voices," 61.

80 LAC, VOW fonds, MG28, I218, vol. 7, file 17, *What How Why*, VOW pamphlet, 1963.

81 "Mrs. Hill and Her Four Reasons," *Ottawa Journal*, n.d., reprinted in *VOW Newsletter* 3 (1960): 2.

82 Ibid.

83 LAC, VOW fonds, MG28, I218, vol. 1, file 7, letter from Josephine Davis to Thérèse Casgrain, 23 Sept. 1961.

84 Ibid., file 18, annual report 2nd Annual Meeting, Sept. 1962, 1.

85 Ibid., file 8, letter from Peggy Hope-Simpson, Halifax, to Josephine Davis, 24 Nov. 1962.

86 Ursula Franklin, interview, 6 July 2010.

87 Macpherson, "Persistent Voices," 61.

88 Muriel Duggan, "As I See It ...," *VOW Newsletter* 6–8 (1961): 13.

89 Macpherson, "Persistent Voices," 61.

90 LAC, Goldie Josephy fonds, MG31, I4, vol. 3, Letters to the Editor 1975–77, "Goodbye Goldie" by Juliet O'Neil, undated newspaper clipping.

91 Michael Josephy and David Josephy, interview, 7 June 2005.

92 AO RG17-3-0-2, Oral History Interviews, Goldie Josephy interview, archivist Roger Nickerson, tape #2, 2 Dec. 1980.

Notes to Chapter 4

1 Robert Conley, "Faith Put in U.N., Not Shelters," *New York Times*, 1 Dec. 1961, 1.

2 Doris Anderson, "Gesture of Sanity and Faith," *Chatelaine*, Feb. 1962, 1.

3 Ibid.

4 Michael Carroll, "Canada and the Financing of the United Nations Emergency Force, 1957–1963," *Journal of the Canadian Historical Association* 13 (2002): 217–34.

5 Brenda Smith, "Paying for the UN," letter to the editor, *Globe and Mail*, 5 Dec. 1961, 6.

6 This figure was calculated by adding each year's donations and returns from the various projects listed in the annual reports between 1955 and 1975 published by UNICEF Canada.

7 AO, Local Council of Women fonds, F805-2-0-5, *The Councillor* 1962, 1963, "Report from UN Association in Canada—Women's Section," by Mrs. G. E. M. Livingstone, *The Councillor: Official Bulletin of the Local Council of Women of Toronto*, Mar. 1963.

8 LAC, United Nations Association (UNA) fonds, MG28, I202, box 45, file 5, Annual Meetings 1962, Public Relations Study, Toronto UNA, July 1962, 1–2.

9 Ibid., vol. 384, file 44, Annual Reports and Annual Audited Reports of the Unitarian Service Committee, 196, and Annual Report, 1961, Year End Review, 1.

10 Dominique Marshall, "The Cold War, Canada, and the United Nations Declaration of the Rights of the Child," in *Canada and the Early Cold War, 1943–1957*, ed. Greg Donaghy (Ottawa: Department of Foreign Affairs and International Trade, 1988), 185.

11 Marshall, "The Language of Children's Rights," 409–41 (see introd., n. 35).

12 *Seeds of Destiny* (Washington: Defense Department, United States Army War Department, 1946), film.

13 Ibid.

14 Laura Briggs, "Mother, Child, Race, Nation: The Visual Iconography of Rescue and the Politics of Transnational and Transracial Adoption," *Gender and History* 15, no. 2 (Aug. 2003): 179.

15 Ibid., 182.

16 Sean Kennedy, *The Shock of War: Civilian Experiences, 1937–1945* (Toronto: University of Toronto Press, 2011), 10.

17 *Seeds of Destiny.*

18 Chapnick, *The Middle Power Project*, 3 (see introd., n. 18).

19 Grant Dexter, *Canada and the Building of Peace* (Toronto: Canadian Institute of International Affairs, 1944).

20 "Children Assisted: Campaign to Aid Europe's Destitute," *Toronto Telegram*, 10 Jan. 1948.

21 No figures are given for the support for UNRRA; however, Jeff Keshen describes it as a "healthy majority" in "One for All or All for One: Government Controls, Black Marketing and the Limits of Patriotism, 1939–1947," *Journal of Canadian Studies* 29 (Winter 1994): 119.

22 Susan Armstrong-Reid and David Murray, *Armies of Peace: Canada and the UNRRA Years* (Toronto: University of Toronto Press, 2008), 9.

23 Brouwer, *New Women for God*, 3 (see introd., n. 21).

24 From *Toronto Star Weekly* 1944, quoted in Mary Kinnear, *Woman of the World: Mary McGeachy and International Cooperation* (Toronto: University of Toronto Press, 2004), 159.

25 Ibid., 174.

26 Ibid., 253, 260.

27 See Brown's letters to her brothers 13 Oct. 1943 to 24 Aug. 1944 in *The Army's Mister Brown: A Family Trilogy, 1941–1952*, ed. Harcourt Brown (Parry Sound, ON: Olympic Printing, 1982), 117–22.

28 Armstrong-Reid and Murray, *Armies of Peace*, 147.

29 Elizabeth Brown's personal account in Brown, *The Army's Mister Brown*, 136.

30 AO, Joshua Brown fonds, F1176, series C-3, box 5, file 17, draft of unpublished auto-biography, 1950s.

31 LAC, CCSD fonds, MG28, I10, vol. 106, file 785 Civil Defence, Advisory Committee 1951–57, Minutes from the Civil Defence Welfare Services Advisory Committee Meeting, 15 Sep. 1956, 4; Advisory Civil Defence Welfare Committee Nominees, 13 Oct. 1953.

32 LAC, VOW fonds, MG28, I218, vol. 2, file 10, Voice of Women International Co-operation Year Travel Mission, Personal Profiles, 1963. Ostry was also a key social worker in the migration of Jewish refugee children to Canada after the Second World War.

33 Ressler, Boothby, and Steinbock, *Unaccompanied Children*, 12 (see introd., n. 41).

34 Armstrong-Reid and Murray, *Armies of Peace*, 197.

35 Ibid., 200, 220.

36 Hansi Kennedy, "Memories of Anna Freud," *American Imago* 53, no. 3 (1996): 205–9.

37 Anna Freud and Dorothy Tiffany Burlingham, *War and Children* (New York: Medical War Books, 1943), 11.

38 Ibid., 12.

39 Irene Kahn Atkins, "Seeds of Destiny: A Case History," *Film and History* 11, no. 2 (May 1981): 28.

40 *Seeds of Destiny*.

41 *Seeds of Destiny*.

42 Atkins, "Seeds of Destiny," 31.

43 Ibid. When UNRRA folded in 1947, UNICEF inherited its remaining money.

44 Judith M. Spiegelman, *We Are the Children: A Celebration of UNICEF's First Forty Years* (Boston: Atlantic Monthly Press, 1986), 3–5.

45 LAC, UNA fonds, MG28, I202, UNA in Canada, box 54, file 8, Branch Officers, Correspondence 1946, memo to branch secretaries from National President James S. Thompson, 23 Sept. 1946.

46 Marr, "'If You Want Peace, Prepare for Peace,'" 265 (see chap. 3, n. 67).

47   These are a sample of talks hosted by the UNA in Toronto, advertised in *The Globe and Mail* on 15 Nov. 1950 and 17 May 1955. Smaller branches had a more difficult time attracting such well-known speakers.

48   LAC, UNA fonds, MG28, I202, box 45, file 5, Annual Meetings 1962, Public Relations Study, Toronto UNA, July 1962, 1.

49   A sample of membership lists from the Edmonton branch in 1949, 1956, 1961–62, and 1971–72 is taken from various documents in the CEA, Bertha Lawrence fonds, MSS 688, boxes 1–4.

50   LAC, UNA fonds, MG28, I202, box 1, file 1, Affiliated Community Organization, Correspondence, 1965.

51   CEA, Edmonton Local Council of Women Clippings File, "Local Council Gives Annual Report," untitled newspaper clipping, 27 Jan. 1949.

52   LAC, NCWC fonds, MG, I25, vol. 128, file 3, 1949–1951, Annual Meeting Minutes, 1 June 1950.

53   Ibid. vol. 92, file 5, Standing Committees: Reports, Correspondence, "United Nations," Report, 1950–51.

54   Ibid.

55   Ibid.

56   Ibid., file 11, Resolutions 1947–1950, "Resolution," Ontario Provincial Council of Women, 26 Oct. 1949.

57   Ibid. vol. 95, file 9, United Nations Convention: Correspondence 1950–53, Press Release, 14 Sept. 1950.

58   AO, Local Council of Women fonds, F805-2-0-3, *The Councillor*, 1956–59, Mrs. W. A. Riddell, "International," *The Councillor: Official Bulletin of the Local Council of Women of Toronto*, Apr. 1958.

59   LAC, NCWC fonds, MG28, I25, vol. 128, file 3, 1949–1951, NCWC Annual Meeting Minutes, 1 May 1949, 29.

60   LAC, UNA fonds, MG28, I202, box 45, file 1, Annual General Meeting, 1958 Agenda, Minutes, Reports, Resolution from Montreal branch, 1958.

61   Ibid., box 44, file 24 Annual Meeting Report 1957, Report to Annual Meeting, 1957.

62   Ibid., box 45, file 4, Annual Meetings 1961, Annual General Meeting, 20–21 May 1960.

63   Ibid., box 54, file 8 Branch Officers, Correspondence 1946, Box List of Branch Presidents, 11 Sept. 1946.

64   Tarah Brookfield, "Modeling the UN's Mission in Semi-formal Wear: Edmonton's Miss United Nations Pageants of the 1960s," in *Contesting Bodies and Nations in Canadian History*, ed. Jane Nichols and Patrizia Gentile (Toronto: University of Toronto Press, forthcoming).

65   Lorraine Oak, interview, 8 Feb. 2010.

66   CEA, Bertha Lawrence fonds, MSS688, box 3, UNA in Canada, Hallowe'en for UNICEF for Children Everywhere, Planning Manual Produced by the National UNICEF Committee, Toronto, 1960.

67   Bertha Lawrence et al., *Canada in the Modern World* (Toronto: J. M. Dent & Sons, 1955), 223–24.

68   LAC, UNA fonds, MG28, I202, UNA in Canada, box 60, file 17, General Core, 1959, National Director, Willson Woodside.

69   "The UN Proves Its Worth with the Blue Chips Down," *Maclean's*, 1 Aug. 1950, 2.

70   Whitaker and Marcuse, *Cold War Canada*, 113 (see introd., n. 3).

71   CEA, Bertha Lawrence fonds, MSS688, Box 3, UNA in Canada, "National Directors Report" by Willson Woodside, 26 May 1963.

72 United Nations, "Declaration on the Rights of the Child," 1959.

73 CEA, Bertha Lawrence fonds, MSS688, box 1, UNA in Canada, to External Affairs Committee of the House of Commons from Kathleen E. Bowlby, National secretary, 1952.

74 Ibid.

75 Marshall, "The Cold War," 196.

76 CEA, Bertha Lawrence fonds, MSS688, box 1, UNA in Canada, to External Affairs Committee of the House of Commons from Kathleen E. Bowlby, National Secretary, 1952.

77 Ibid., press release, Department of Public Information, United Nations, New York, 15 July 1952.

78 This figure was calculated by adding each year's donations and returns from the various projects listed in the annual reports between 1955 and 1975 published by UNICEF Canada.

79 UCOA, UNICEF Canada Annual Reports 1955–75.

80 Ibid., Annual Report, 1961–62, Report of Executive Director, Mrs. Gordon Richards.

81 CEA, Bertha Lawrence fonds, MSS688, Box 1, UNA in Canada, letter from Kathleen E. Bowlby, National Secretary, national office, to all branch presidents and secretaries, 8 May 1952.

82 UCOA, UNICEF Canada Annual Report 1963–64, Report from Manitoba, 41.

83 CEA, Bertha Lawrence fonds, MSS688, box 1, UNA in Canada, UNICEF greeting cards press release, 17 Oct. 1952.

84 Ibid., press release, 18 Feb. 1953.

85 Alain Larocque, "'Losing Our Chinese': The St. Enfance Movement," Working Paper 49, Joint Centre for Asia Pacific Studies (June 1987), 6.

86 CEA, Bertha Lawrence fonds, MSS688, box 3, UNA in Canada, Report of the executive secretary for the UNA's National UNICEF Committee by Mary P. Carter, June 1960.

87 UCOA, UNICEF Canada Annual Report 1966–67, Report from Calgary, 37.

88 CEA, Bertha Lawrence fonds, MSS688, box 3, UNA in Canada, Hallowe'en for UNICEF for Children Everywhere, Planning Manual Produced by the National UNICEF Committee, Toronto, 1960.

89 Mrs. R. Phillion, letter to the editor, *Ottawa Citizen*, 16 Nov. 1965.

90 Lorraine Oak, interview, 8 Feb. 2010.

91 CEA, Bertha Lawrence fonds, MSS688, box 3, UNA in Canada, Hallowe'en for UNICEF for Children Everywhere, Planning Manual Produced by the National UNICEF Committee, Toronto, 1960.

92 Lorraine Oak, interview, 8 Feb. 2010.

93 Ibid.

94 CEA, Bertha Lawrence fonds, MSS688, box 3, UNA in Canada, Hallowe'en for UNICEF for Children Everywhere, Planning Manual Produced by the National UNICEF Committee, Toronto, 1960.

95 Ibid. box 2, UNICEF, *There May Be Tigers—Anecdotes about UNICEF from All Over the World*, booklet, August 1966, 37.

96 UCOA, UNICEF Canada Annual Report 1966–67, Report from Calgary, 37.

97 Ibid., Annual Report 1971–72, PEI Committee Report.

98 Ibid., Report of the Annual General Meeting, 1971–72, Report from Manitoba, 39.

99 Ibid., Annual Report 1964–65, Kate Aitken's report, 33.

100 LAC, Unitarian Service Committee (USC) fonds, MG28, I322, vol. 228, Human interest 1955–59, DLH, personal and misc.

101   URIA, FPPI records, series X-117, box 99, file 76 Canada: Minor Halliday and Associates Ltd. Conference report, Oct. 1972 –Feb. 1973, "Facts about Foster Parent Plan."
102   Ibid., Oct. 1972 –Feb. 1973, "Facts about Foster Parent Plan."
103   Tarah Brookfield, "Children as 'Seeds of Destiny': Nation, Race, and Citizenship in Postwar Foreign Relief Programs," in *Canadian Children's History Reader*, ed. Tamara Myers and Mona Gleason (Toronto: Oxford University Press, forthcoming).
104   UMA, Margaret Konantz fonds, MM1, box 4, file 5, Speeches, 1956–67, "The Moral Climate," speech by Konantz, panel discussion for 1967 Junior League Association Conference.
105   Ibid., file 4, Notes and Speech fragments, undated, untitled speech fragment.
106   Ibid., file 5, Speeches, 1956–67, "The Moral Climate," speech by Konantz, panel discussion for 1967 Junior League Association Conference.
107   "Manitoba's New Liberal Star Beaming Brightly: Konantz's Crew Raises Thunderous Applause," *Winnipeg Free Press*, 9 Apr. 1963.
108   UMA, Margaret Konantz fonds, MM1, box 4, file 5, Speeches, 1956–67, "Clasp the Hand" speech, undated.
109   UCOA, UNICEF Canada Annual Report 1964–65, 20.

Notes to Chapter 5

1   The names of foster children and foster parents in unpublished documents have been changed to protect their identity. LAC, USC fonds, MG28, I322, vol. 193, letter, 4 June 1968.
2   Ibid.
3   URIA, FPPI records, series X-117, box 99, file 72 Canada: *Gossip* magazine, 1949–50, 1952, clipping on *Gossip*'s cover boy, 24 May 1950.
4   Strong-Boag, *Fostering Nation?*, 61 (see introd., n. 37).
5   Robert Bothwell, "Eyes West: Canada and the Cold War in Asia," in *Canada and the Early Cold War, 1943–1957*, ed. Greg Donaghy (Ottawa: Department of Foreign Affairs and International Trade, 1988), 61.
6   Bothwell, *Alliance and Illusion*, 72–76 (see introd., n. 20).
7   David R. Morrison, *Aid and Ebb Tide: A History of CIDA and Canadian Development Assistance* (Waterloo, ON: Wilfrid Laurier University Press, 1998), 28–29.
8   Louis St. Laurent, "Consequences of the Cold War for Canada," speech to the Canadian Club in Toronto, 27 Mar. 1950, http://www.collectionscanada.ca/primeministers/h4-4015-e.html.
9   LAC, USC fonds, MG28, I322, vol. 384, file 44 Year End Review, Annual Reports and Annual Audited Reports of the Unitarian Service Committee, 1961.
10   Ibid., vol. 235, DLH Speeches, 1947, speech to Hamilton Synagogue, 7 Feb. 1947.
11   Ibid., vol. 52, film commentary "Tomorrow Is Too Late," 1953.
12   URIA, FPPI records, series X-117, box 96, file 51, Canada: Correspondence, 1961–63, letter from Tam Deachman to Gloria Matthews, FPPI New York, 17 June 1963.
13   Henry D. Molumphy, *For Common Decency: The History of Foster Parents Plan International, 1937–1983* (Warwick, RI: Foster Parents Plan International, 1984), 9–14.
14   Ibid., 313–16.
15   Nathan Dreskin, "If You Haven't Met Lotta Hitschmanova, It's Probably Because You Aren't Starving, Sick or Homeless in a Foreign Land," *Maclean's*, Sept. 1967, 69.

16 LAC, USC fonds, MG28, I322, vol. 250, article in *Maclean's*, 1967, letter from H. I. Bolster to Patricia Towers, *Maclean's*, 12 July 1967.

17 In USC folder containing complaints, three people mention how unappealing Lotta's voice sounds. They do not remark on her accent but call her voice "whiney" and not suitable for the radio. See for example one letter from 30 Sept. 1963. LAC, USC fonds, MG28, I322, vol. 250, Letters of Criticism 1956–67.

18 Ibid., vol. 384, file 56, Annual Reports and Annual Audited Reports of the USC, 1973, Year End Review, 31 Dec. 1973, 6.

19 Ibid.

20 Claude Sanger, *Lotta and the Unitarian Service Committee Story* (Toronto: Stoddard, 1986), 199.

21 LAC, USC fonds, MG28, I322, vol. 384, Annual Reports and Annual Audited Reports, 1946, 1960, and 1974.

22 Ibid., file 48, Annual Reports and Annual Audited Reports 1964, Year End Review, 31 Dec. 1965, 3.

23 Ibid., vols. 156, 165, 170, 176, 179, 191, 193, 300, 304. The sample was chosen by looking at 10 percent of 1,678 sponsorship files, organized by province, that were part of the USC archival collection.

24 URIA, FPPI records, series X-117, box 96, file 51, Canada: Communications for PLAN in Canada 1971, Foster Parents Plan of Canada, Communications Programme, Apr. 1971.

25 LAC, USC fonds, MG28, I322, vol. 250, article in *Maclean's* 1967, letter from H. I. Bolster to Patricia Towers, *Maclean's*, 12 July 1967.

26 URIA, FPPI records, series X-117, box 96, file 51 Canada: Communications Programme, Apr. 1971, Records of Foster Parents Plan, 1937–82, Communications for PLAN in Canada 1971.

27 Ibid., Canada: Correspondence, 1949–52, letter from Constance Gurd Rykert, 4 Nov. 1949; LAC, USC fonds, MG28, I322, vol. 193, 1969–70 report from Hitschmanova.

28 URIA, FPPI records, series X-117, box 99, file 75, Canada: Minor Halliday and Associates Ltd. Conference report, 1971–Sept. 1972, conference report, Minor Halliday and Associates Ltd. with FPPI.

29 The removal of children by both sides is still a highly contentious issue. Ressler, Boothby, and Steinbock, *Unaccompanied Children*, 31–36 (see introd., n. 41).

30 Quoted in Molumphy, *For Common Decency*, 91.

31 URIA, FPPI records, series X-117, box 96, file 51, Canada: Correspondence, 1949–52, "I Want a Blue Eye," advertisement from an unidentified Canadian newspaper, 1949.

32 Ibid., box 99, file 72, Canada: *Gossip* magazine, 1949–50, 1952, clipping on *Gossip's* cover boy, 24 May 1950.

33 Ibid., box 96, file 51, Canada: Correspondence, 1949–52, letter from Constance Gurd Rykert to Miss Sandra Jones, 1 May 1950.

34 Ibid., "I Want a Blue Eye," advertisement from an unidentified Canadian newspaper, 1949.

35 Ibid., letter from Constance Gurd Rykert to Miss Sandra Jones, 1 May 1950.

36 LAC, USC, MG28, I322, vol. 236, DLH Speeches, 1949, speech to unknown audience by Hitschmanova, 1949.

37 Ibid., vol. 384, file 33, Annual Reports and Annual Audited Reports of the Unitarian Service Committee, 1950, Annual Reports, Year End Review, 31 Dec.1950.

38 Ibid., vol. 52, Film Commentary, "With Loving Hands," USC film, 1956.

39 Ibid. vol. 384, file 33, Annual Reports and Annual Audited Reports of the Unitarian Service Committee, 1950, Year End Review, 31 Dec. 1950.

40 Lucille Marr, "'The Time for the Distaff and Spindle': The Ontario Mennonite Women's Circles and the Mennonite Central Committee," *Journal of Mennonite Studies* 17 (1999): 130–51.

41 LAC, USC fonds, MG28, I322, vol. 228, Human interest stories, Annual Review Material, 1960, Unitarian Newsletter (USA), Winter 1959–60.

42 Ibid., vol. 384, file 48 Annual Reports and Annual Audited Reports 1964, Year End Review, 31 Dec. 1965, 3.

43 Ibid., 7.

44 Bothwell, "Eyes West," 67.

45 Pierre Berton, "Seoul's the Saddest City in the World," *Maclean's*, 1 June 1951, 9–10, 48, 50.

46 Graham N. Smith, "Moss I Gather," *Winnipeg Tribune*, 11 Nov. 1957; LAC, USC fonds, MG28, I322, vol. 250, Letters of Criticism 1956–67.

47 CEA, Bertha Lawrence fonds, MSS688, box 1, United Nations Association in Canada 1952, memo to branch presidents and secretaries from Kathleen Bowlby, 8 Dec. 1952.

48 Ressler, Boothby, and Steinbock, *Unaccompanied Children*, 37–41 (see introd., n. 41).

49 Sanger, *Lotta*, 82.

50 Molumphy, *For Common Decency*, 108.

51 Christina Klein, *Cold War Orientalism: Asia in the Middlebrow Imagination, 1945–1961* (Berkeley: University of California, 2003), 10–12.

52 Price, *Orienting Canada*, 13 (see introd., n. 20).

53 LAC, USC fonds, MG28, I322, vol. 191, letter to USC, 28 Mar. 1968.

54 Ibid., vol. 304, letter, 19 Jan. 1972.

55 Ibid.

56 Ibid., vol. 193, letter from Hitschmanova, 23 May 1973.

57 Ibid., letter from Hee to King, 29 May 1973.

58 URIA, FPPI records, series X-117 donor countries, box 99, file 77, Canada: Minor Halliday and Associates Ltd. Conference report, 1975–76, Conference report, Minor Halliday and Associates Ltd. with FPPI, 12 July 1975.

59 LAC, USC fonds, MG28, I322, vol. 157, letter from Hitschmanova, 19 Oct. 1972.

60 Ibid., letter to Hitschmanova, 8 Jan. 1973.

61 Ibid., letter, 28 Dec. 1972.

62 Ibid., letter, 7 Mar. 1973.

63 Ibid., letter to Hitschmanova, 23 July 1973.

64 Ibid., letter, 8 Jan. 1975.

65 AO, Joshua Brown fonds, series C-2, box 3, Australia, FPPI, file 2, *The Australian* interview with Elizabeth Brown by Beverly Hay, 6 Jan. 1971.

66 This information was taken by comparing the records of 159 USC sponsorships between 1954 and 1975 in Korea, Hong Kong, France, and India. LAC, USC fonds, MG28 I322, vols. 156, 165, 170, 176, 179, 191, 193, 300, 304.

67 Ibid., vol. 157, letter to USC, 16 Oct. 1973.

68 Ibid., vol. 176, letter to USC, 1 Dec. 1971.

69 Ibid., vol. 157, letter to Hitschmanova, 14 Nov. 1964.

70 Ruth Compton Brouwer, "Ironic Interventions: CUSO Volunteers in India's Family Planning Campaign, 1960s–1970s," *Social History/Histoire sociale* 43, no. 86 (Nov. 2010): 282.

71 Linda Gordon, *The Moral Property of Women: A History of Birth Control Politics in America* (Urbana: University of Illinois Press, 2007), 284.

72 Molumphy, *For Common Decency*, 103–5.
73 Fang Qin, "'Revenge for Our Children!': The Stigmatization of Christian-Managed Orphanages in the Early 1950s in China" (paper presented at the George Washington Graduate Student Cold War History Conference, April 2007).
74 Sanger, *Lotta*, 163.
75 Bothwell, *Alliance and Illusion*, 274 (see introd., n. 20).
76 Ninette Kelly and Michael Trebilcock, *The Making of the Mosaic: A History of Canadian Immigration Policy* (Toronto: University of Toronto Press, 1998), 315, 328–29.
77 LAC, CCSD fonds, MG28, I10, vol. 205, file 2, ISS Canadian Committee Minutes 1960–63, SS Minutes, 12 Oct. 1962.
78 Angus McLaren and Arlene Tigar McLaren, *The Bedroom and the State: The Changing Practices and Politics of Contraception and Abortion in Canada, 1880–1997* (Toronto: Oxford University Press, 1997), 9–14.
79 Sanger, *Lotta*, 157–58.
80 K. C. Chan, "The Role of the Family Planning Association in Hong Kong's Fertility Decline," *Studies in Family Planning* 7, no. 10 (Oct. 1976): 285.
81 LAC, USC fonds, MG28, I322, vol. 111, 1968 Press Releases, 24th fund campaign, 5 Sept. 1968; Sanger, *Lotta*, 157–58.
82 Chan, "The Role of the Family Planning Association," 284.
83 URIA, FPPI records, series X-117, box 99, file 76, Canada: Minor Halliday and Associates Ltd. Conference report, Oct. 1972–Feb. 1973, pamphlet, *Facts about Foster Parents Plan*, 1971.
84 Sanger, *Lotta*, 122–24. USC did work closely with the Family Planning Association of India, which held vasectomy and tubectomy clinics, a practice that has since been criticized because of the lack of patients' informed consent.
85 Sample comments about sterilization and castration from USC complaint file, direct quote from *Ottawa Citizen*, 9 Dec. 1957; LAC, USC fonds, MG28, I322, vol. 250, Letters of Criticism 1956–67.
86 Molumphy, *For Common Decency*, 95; URIA, FPPI records, series X-117, box 99, file 76, Canada: Annual Reports: 1949, 1955–57, 1969–70; LAC, USC fonds, MG28, I322, vol. 384 Annual Reports and Annual Audited Reports of the Unitarian Service Committee, 1946–75.
87 Sanger, *Lotta*, 86.
88 Marianne Brown was not related to UNRRA worker and FPPI director Elizabeth Brown.
89 Marianne Brown, interview, 10 Jan. 2010.
90 Ibid.

Notes to Chapter 6

1 "Vietnam," *Weekend Magazine* 17, no. 21 (17 May 1967): 2.
2 Claire Culhane, "Canada in Vietnam," *Bias* 2, no. 8 (15 Jan. 1972): 3.
3 Claire Culhane, *Why Is Canada in Vietnam? The Truth about Our Foreign Aid* (Toronto: NC Press, 1972), 10, 13–14.
4 Culhane, "Canada in Vietnam," 33.
5 "Fasting Grandmother Camps at MPs' Door," *Globe and Mail*, 4 Oct. 1968.
6 Culhane, *Why Is Canada in Vietnam?*, 96.
7 "Grandmother Sticks to Ten-Day Fast," *Globe and Mail*, 10 Oct. 1968.

8 Mick Lowe, *One Woman Army: The Life of Claire Culhane* (Toronto: Macmillan Canada, 1992), 174–203.

9 Douglas Ross, *In the Interests of Peace: Canada and Vietnam, 1954–1973* (Toronto: University of Toronto Press, 1984), 327.

10 Ibid., 378–81.

11 Culhane, *Why Is Canada in Vietnam?*, 9.

12 Frances Early, "Canadian Women and the International Arena in the Sixties: The Voice of Women/La Voix des femmes and the Opposition to the Vietnam War," in *The Sixties: Passion, Politics and Style*, ed. Dimitry Anastakis (Montreal and Kingston: McGill-Queen's University Press, 2008), 26.

13 LAC, VOW fonds, MG28, I218, vol. 13, file 4, Meg Sears and Kay Macpherson, "A History of the Voice of Women," 2, 1974.

14 Early, "Canadian Women," 27.

15 Macpherson, *When in Doubt, Do Both*, 120–26 (see chap. 3, n. 62).

16 LAC, VOW fonds, MG28, I218, vol. 2, file 4, "The Future of Vietnam … Our Future," Vietnamese; American, and Canadian women in conference, Hart House, Toronto, 7 July 1969.

17 Ibid., vol. 30, file 11, Guidelines for volunteer participants by Sheila Young, n.d.

18 Ibid., vol. 3, file 23, clipping from *Oxbox Herald*, n.d., ca. 1968.

19 Benjamin Spock and Mitchell Zimmerman, *Dr. Spock on Vietnam* (New York: Dell, 1968).

20 LAC, VOW fonds, MG28, I218, vol. 7, file 17, *What How Why*, pamphlet, 1963.

21 Stan McDowell, "Fight Laws That Curb Rights, Spock Says," *Toronto Daily Star*, 5 Dec. 1970.

22 "Soldier Says Women, Children Lined Up: 'Calley Fired and Killed Them All'" *Toronto Daily Star*, 5 Dec. 1970; LAC, Goldie Josephy fonds, MG31, I4, vol. 9, Ottawa Committee for Peace and Liberation, Correspondence re: Dr. Spock's Speech, 1970.

23 LAC, Marion Scott fonds, MG30, D399, vol. 13, Vietnam Material, 1972, 1 of 2, Appeal of the Democratic Republic of Vietnam Committee for the Protection of Mothers and Children, Mothers around the World!!! Scientists, Physicians and Child Specialists! 31 Oct. 1972.

24 Ibid., Vietnam, 1968, 3 of 5; William Pepper, "Children of Vietnam," *Ramparts*, special issue, 1966.

25 Ressler, Boothby, and Steinbock, *Unaccompanied Children*, 67–68 (see introd., n. 41).

26 Ross, *In the Interests of Peace*, 5.

27 Quoted in Daniel C. Hallin, *The Uncensored War: The Media and Vietnam* (Berkeley: University of California Press, 1989), 3.

28 Peter Sypnowich, "Canada Awakens to the Agony of Viet Nam's Maimed Children," *Star Weekly*, 29 Apr. 1967, 2.

29 Ibid., 2.

30 Ibid., 4.

31 "Special Issue on Vietnam," *Maclean's*, Feb. 1968.

32 Sypnowich, "Canada Awakens," 2.

33 LAC, VOW fonds, MG28, I218, vol. 1, file 23, 1965 Annual Report.

34 Andrew Preston, "Balancing War and Peace: Canadian Foreign Policy and the Vietnam War, 1961–1965," *Diplomatic History* 27, no. 1 (Jan. 2003): 74.

35 Ibid.

36 Ibid., 81.

37 Bothwell, *Alliance and Illusion*, 317 (see introd., n. 20).

38 Sypnowich, "Canada Awakens," 4.

39 Frances Russell, "Sharp Has Argument with Voice of Women Executive," *Globe and Mail*, 20 Feb. 1969.

40 Ibid.

41 David S. Churchill, "An Ambiguous Welcome: Vietnam Draft Resistance, the Canadian State, and Cold War Containment," *Social History/Histoire sociale* 37, no. 73 (2004): 1.

42 "Flying Napalm Hits Women, Children—By Mistake," *Globe and Mail*, 8 June 1972; Denise Chong, *The Girl in the Photo: The Kim Phuc Story* (Toronto: Viking, 2001), 67–68.

43 Chong, *The Girl in the Photo*, 355.

44 LAC, VOW fonds, MG28, I218, vol. 30, file 11, "Don't Buy Dow Products," VOW advisory, n.d.

45 Kearns, *Muriel Duckworth*, 115–17 (see chap. 3, n. 12).

46 "Supplying the War Machine," *As It Happens*, CBC Radio, 27 Jan. 1975.

47 Culhane, *Why Is Canada in Vietnam?*, 121.

48 "Supplying the War Machine," *As It Happens*, CBC Radio, 27 Jan. 1975.

49 Churchill, "An Ambiguous Welcome," 4.

50 AO, Oral History Interviews, RG17-30-23, Goldie Josephy, Tape #1, 2 Dec. 1980.

51 LAC, VOW fonds, MG28, I218, vol. 3, file 29, Lydia Sayle, "A Subjective Postmortem of the Indochinese Conference Held in Vancouver 1971."

52 Ibid., Kay Macpherson, "Visit of the Indochinese Women to Canada, April 1971: An Assessment."

53 Steve Hewitt and Christabelle Sethna, "'Sweating and Uncombed': Canadian State Security, the Indochinese Conference, and the Feminist Threat," paper presented at the Canadian Historical Association Meeting, Vancouver, 2–4 June 2008.

54 LAC, VOW fonds, MG28, I218, vol. 3, file 29, Vancouver Conference by Anne Van Hetersen, VOW Calgary, 1971.

55 Ibid.

56 Ibid., "Sisters of Peace," clipping from an untitled Halifax newspaper, 16 Apr. 1971.

57 Ibid., *Toronto Women's Liberation Newsletter*, May 1971, Mary Bolton, "Sisterhood at the Conference."

58 Ibid., Conference Report 1971, 4.

59 Ibid., 5.

60 Ibid., Kay Macpherson, "Visit of the Indochinese Women to Canada, April 1971: An Assessment," 2.

61 Ibid.

62 Ibid., Toronto Women's Liberation Movement Newsletter May Issue, Judy Gill, "Impression of the Conference."

63 Molumphy, *For Common Decency*, 138 (see chap. 5, n. 13).

64 AO, Joshua Brown fonds, series C-1, box 2, Brown, Robert (1960–1964), file 18, letter from Ruth Crawford Mitchell to the Brown family, 22 Feb. 1964.

65 Ibid., series C-2, box 3, FPPI, file 9, letter from Sage to Brown, 1 Oct. 1962.

66 Ibid., series C-1, box 2, Brown, Quentin (1960–66), file 7, letter from Brown to family, 29 Oct. 1963.

67 Ibid., Brown, Robert (1965–67), file 19, letter from Brown to Bob and Betsy, 3 Nov. 1965.

68 Ibid., series C-2, box 3, FPPI, file 9, letter from Brown to Matthews, 3 Mar. 1968.

69 Molumphy, *For Common Decency*, 163 (see chap. 5, n. 13).

70 AO, Joshua Brown fonds, series C-2, box 3, Chaffe, Fred and Martha (1971–73), file 5, letter from Fred Chaffe to Brown, 6 Dec. 1971; file 9, letter from Guild to Brown, 18 Mar. 1972.

71 LAC, USC fonds, MG28, I322, vol. 48, Vietnam General 1970, Hitschmanova's Confidential Report on 1969 Survey to Vietnam.

72 Ibid.

73 Culhane, "Canada in Vietnam," 11.

74 LAC, USC fonds, MG28, I322, vol. 48, Vietnam General 1972, Hitschmanova, "Jottings from Vietnam," May 1973, 2.

75 Ibid.

76 "Widow Reports Aid to Hanoi Children," *Globe and Mail*, 4 Dec. 1968, 12.

77 LAC, VOW fonds, MG28, I218, vol. 30, file 11, Guidelines for volunteer participants by Sheila Young, n.d.

78 Ibid., vol. 14, file 9, Canadian Aid for Vietnam Civilians [CAVC], Children's Committee, Newsletter July 1967, 2.

79 Ibid., vol. 14, file 10, letter to United Auto Workers Union from Mona Armour, President, Ontario, 23 Jan. 1970.

80 Ibid., vol. 30, file 11, CAVC, Children's Committee Newsletter, July 1966–July 1969, 1.

81 Ibid., vol. 14, file 9, CAVC, Children's Committee July 1967; ibid., vol. 24, file 19, untitled clipping.

82 Zoya Stevenson, interview, 30 Aug. 2011.

83 Ibid.

84 Ibid.

85 LAC, VOW fonds, MG28, I218, vol. 24, file 19, clipping from *Pacific Tribune* article by Tom McEwen, n.d.

86 Ibid., vol. 14, file 10, letter to Lil Greene, VOW, from M. B. Evans, 23 Oct. 1972.

87 Casgrain, *A Woman in a Man's World*, 181 (see chap. 3, n. 62).

88 LAC, VOW fonds, MG28, I218, vol. 6, file 7, poster for the Ontario VOW Knitting Project for Vietnamese children, 20 May 1968.

89 Ibid., vol. 14, file 9, "Millions of stitches carry our love," undated letter.

90 Ibid., vol. 14, file 10, CAVC letter to the editor of VOW newsletter from Kay Inglis, 3 Feb. 1976.

91 Ibid., vol. 14, file 9, CAVC newsletter, July 1967.

92 Ibid.

93 Ibid., vol. 30, file 11, letter to Lil Greene from Nancy (Pocock?) 1 Dec. 1973.

94 Ibid.

95 Early, "Canadian Women," 30.

Notes to Chapter 7

Parts of this chapter were adapted from Tarah Brookfield, "Maverick Mothers and Mercy Flights: Canada's Controversial Introduction to International Adoption," *Journal of the Canadian Historical Association* 19, no. 1 (2009): 307–30.

1 "Sandra and Her Kids," *The Nature of Things*, CBC TV, 1983.

2 Mark Abley, "Mother Lode: Sandra Simpson Has Raised 32 Children," *Montreal Gazette*, 3 Oct. 1999.

3 "Sandra and Her Kids," *The Nature of Things*.

4 Strong-Boag, *Finding Families* (see introd., n. 37); Barbara Melosh, *Strangers and Kin: The American Way of Adoption* (Cambridge, MA: Harvard University Press, 2002); E. Wayne Carp, ed., *Adoption in America: Historical Perspectives* (Ann Arbor: University of Michigan Press, 2002).

5 Rickie Sollinger, *Beggars and Choosers: How the Politics of Choice Shapes Adoption, Abortion, and Welfare in the United States* (New York: Hill and Wang, 2001), 20–23.

6 Briggs, "Mother, Child, Race, Nation," 180 (see chap. 4, n. 14).

7 Karen Dubinsky, "Babies without Borders: Rescue, Kidnap, and the Symbolic Child," *Journal of Women's History* 19, no. 1 (Spring 2007): 142.

8 Dubinsky, "Babies without Borders," 148.

9 For example, see Margaret Mulrooney, ed., *Fleeing the Famine: North America and Irish Refugees, 1845–1851* (Westport, CT: Greenwood Publishing Group, 2003); Joy Parr, *Labouring Children: British Immigrant Apprentices to Canada, 1869–1924* (Montreal: McGill-Queen's University Press, 1980); Geoffrey Bilson, *The Guest Children: The Story of the British Child Evacuees Sent to Canada during World War II* (Saskatoon, SK: Fifth House, 1988).

10 Fraidie Martz, *Open Your Hearts: The Story of Jewish War Children in Canada* (Montreal: Véhicule, 1996), 18–19.

11 Irving Abella and Harold Troper, *None Is Too Many: Canada and the Jews of Europe, 1933–1948* (Toronto: Key Porter, 2000).

12 Sidney Katz, "The Redeemed Children," *Maclean's*, 10 Feb. 1962, 12.

13 Ibid., 43.

14 "Mailbag," *Maclean's*, 10 Mar. 1962, 2.

15 Charlotte Whitton, "What You Should Know about Child Adoption," *Chatelaine* (Apr. 1948): 26, 102.

16 Patti Phillips, "'Financially Irresponsible and Obviously Neurotic Need Not Apply': Social Work, Parental Fitness, and the Production of Adoptive Families in Ontario, 1940–1965," *Histoire sociale/Social History* 78 (Nov. 2006): 343–46.

17 Karen Dubinsky, "'We Adopted a Negro': Interracial Adoptions and the Hybrid Baby in 1960s Canada," in *Creating Postwar Canada: Community, Diversity, and Dissent, 1945–75*, ed. Magda Fahrni and Robert Rutherdale (Vancouver: University of British Columbia Press, 2008), 268–69.

18 Ressler, Boothby, and Steinbock, eds., *Unaccompanied Children*, 12 (see introd., n. 41).

19 LAC, CCSD fonds, MG28, I10, vol. 61, file 491, Adoption, General Information Requests 1956–63, letter to McCrea, 16 Apr. 1956.

20 Ibid., vol. 206, file 6, ISS International General Correspondence Data, letter to Murphy, 20 July 1959.

21 Kelly and Trebilcock, *The Making of the Mosaic,* 315, 328–29 (see chap. 5, n. 75).

22 SWHA, International Social Services (ISS) fonds, SW109, box 29, ISS Affiliate: Canadian Welfare Council, General 1963–67, Assessment of ISS Program, Canadian Welfare Council, 24 Apr. 1963.

23 Susan Pettiss, "What Happens When Kinfolk Are Scattered across Borders and Seas? International Social Services," *Canadian Welfare*, Nov. 1957, 177.

24 LAC, CCSD fonds, MG28, I10, vol. 205, file 3, ISS Canadian Committee Minutes and Material 1957–59, Memo from ISS to CWC re: Organization of Referral Services for Inquiries from Abroad, 20 Jan. 1953.

25 Pettiss, "What Happens," 180.

26 LAC, CCSD fonds, MG28, I10, vol. 168, file 3, Mou-Mur, Biography, "Miss Marion Murphy."

27 Ibid., vol. 205, file 1, ISS Canadian Committee Minutes 1959, memo, 14 Aug. 1957.

28 Ibid., vol. 205, file 1, ISS Canadian Committee Minutes 1959, letter to Johnson from Marshall, 28 Oct. 1957.

29 Ibid., vol. 204, file 11, ISS Canadian Committee Minutes 1958, minutes from the CWC-ISS Committee Meeting, 10 Mar. 1958.

30 Ibid., vol. 206, file 1, ISS Headquarters, Financial and Statistical Reports 1957–67, Florence Boester, "Report of ISS Far East Representative to ISS International Council," Jan. 1961.

31 Ibid., vol. 205, file 1, ISS Canadian Committee Minutes 1959, CWC-ISS Committee meeting minutes, 20 Nov. 1959.

32 SWHA, ISS fonds, SW109, box 11, Adoption Manual and Other Printed Material, "Communism Failed Her ... Will We?" n.d.

33 LAC, CCSD fonds, MG28, I10 , vol. 205, file 12, ISS Child Adoption Placement Services: Hong Kong, Korean and Foster Care Costs, 1966–69, and Canadian Welfare Council, Procedure in Hong Kong "Orphan Refugee" Adoptions, May 1964.

34 Joyce Ireland, "By Air from Hong Kong," *Canadian Welfare*, July–Aug. 1963, 155.

35 Ibid.

36 Paul R. Cherney, "The Abandoned Child in Asia," *Canadian Welfare*, Mar.–Apr. 1966, 82.

37 LAC, Adoption Desk fonds, RG29, vol. 3539, file 4122-1-3 pt. 2, Ontario Ministry of Community and Children Services, "Report on Adoption of Vietnamese Children," Sept. 1973, 7–8.

38 SWHA, ISS fonds, SW109, box 38, Country: Vietnam, Conference on the Special Needs of Children in Vietnam, Report of Eurasians under French, Marcelle Trillat, ISS France, 19 July 1971.

39 LAC, CCSD fonds, MG28, I10, vol. 204, file 8, ISS Board of Directors: International Council Executive Committee 1959–69, minutes, Directors' Meeting, ISS, Geneva, 14 Apr. 1966.

40 LAC, Adoption Desk fonds, RG29, vol. 3539, file 4122-1-3 pt. 2, Ontario Ministry of Community and Children Services, "Report on Adoption of Vietnamese Children," Sept. 1973, 9.

41 Sheila Gormely, "Canada Brings in 100 Babies from War-Torn Asian Lands," *Toronto Star*, 3 Feb. 1973, 4.

42 SWHA, ISS fonds, SW109, box 38, Country: Vietnam, ISS International Vietnam Administrative Files, 1964–65, Regulations on Adoption in South Vietnam provided by Mrs. Herbert Baumgartner, American Embassy, Family Law (Luat Gia Dinh) No. 1/59.

43 LAC, CCSD fonds, MG28, I10, vol. 206, file 10, ISS International General Correspondence Data re: Branches, Staffing the Committee 1966, Mrs. A. Raphael, "Report on the Work of ISS in Vietnam from July 1965 to Sept. 1966," 18 Oct. 1966, 4.

44 Cherney, "The Abandoned Child," 83–85.

45 Kirsten Lovelock, "Intercountry Adoption as a Migratory Practice: A Comparative Analysis of Intercountry Adoption and Immigration Policy and Practice in the United States, Canada and New Zealand in the Post W.W. II Period," *International Migration Review* 34, no. 3 (Fall 2000): 918.

46 LAC, CCSD fonds, MG28, I10, vol. 206, file 12, ISS International General Correspondence Data re: Branches, Staffing the Committee 1968, Memo to Directors of Child Welfare, from CWC-ISS, 6 June 1968.

47 SWHA, ISS fonds, SW109, box 10, file 1, Adjustment of Korean American Children in their American Adoptive Homes, Margaret Valk, "Adjustment of Korean American

Children in their American Adoptive Homes" (paper presented at the National Conference on Social Welfare, Apr. 1957).

48 SWHA, ISS fonds, SW109 ISS, box 22, Pearl Buck Foundation, "A Progress Report on Caring for the Amerasian—A Difficult Task," 1978.

49 Lolly Golt, "A Family Is a Child's Best Gift," *Weekend Magazine*, 20 Nov. 1971, 19.

50 Rosemary Taylor and Wende Grant, *Orphans of War: Work with the Abandoned Children of Vietnam, 1967–1975* (London: Collins, 1988), 95.

51 "Naomi Bronstein," *Dan Turner: For the People*, CBC TV, 31 Jan. 1983.

52 Golt, "A Family Is a Child's Best Gift," 20.

53 Pauline Grey, interview, 17 Feb. 2011.

54 Hans Talboom, interview, 3 Oct. 2010.

55 Roma Talboom, interview, 3 Oct. 2010.

56 Gormely, "Canada Brings in 100 Babies," 4.

57 AO, Community and Social Services, RG29-110, box 3, *Kuan Yin Foundation Newsletter*, 1976, 2.

58 "Helke Ferrie: Crusader for the World's Children," *Chatelaine*, Oct. 1978, 33.

59 "Naomi Bronstein," *Barbara Frum*, CBC TV, 5 June 1975.

60 Gormely, "Canada Brings in 100 Babies," 1.

61 "Adopted Lad Dies at 23," *Montreal Gazette*, 14 Apr. 1989, A3.

62 "Sandra and Her Kids," *The Nature of Things*.

63 Dorothy Sangster, "The Little Family That Grew and Grew," *Chatelaine*, Nov. 1990, 145.

64 Gormely, "Canada Brings in 100 Babies," 1.

65 Julie Medeiros, interview, 3 Oct. 2010.

66 *A Moment in Time: The United Colours of Bronstein*, Judy [Jackson] Films, 2001.

67 Thanh Campbell, interview, 24 Aug. 2010.

68 *A Moment in Time: The United Colours of Bronstein*, Judy [Jackson] Films, 2001.

69 "Naomi Bronstein," *Dan Turner: For the People*.

70 "Sandra and Her Kids," *The Nature of Things*.

71 LAC, Adoption Desk fonds, RG29, vol. 3539, file 4122-1-3 pt. 1, Betty Graham, Note for File by South Asia Division, Ontario Government Views of the Adoption of Bangalee children, 29 Sept. 1972.

72 SWHA, ISS fonds, SW109, box 10, Children: Independent Adoption Schemes, Holt, Harry, 1955–57, vol. 1, Pearl Buck, "The Children Waiting: The Shocking Scandal of Adoption," *Woman's Home Companion*, Sept. 1955, 129–32; and letter from Andrew Juras, Child Welfare Director, State of Oregon, to ISS, 4 May 1956.

73 LAC, Adoption Desk fonds, RG29, vol. 3539, file 4122-1-3 pt. 2, Minutes of the Meeting of Provincial and Territorial Representatives of Child Welfare Departments, June 1973, 8.

74 Ibid., pt. 1, Note for File by South Asia Division, Ontario Government Views of the Adoption of Bangalee children, 29 Sept. 1972.

75 Gormely, "Canada Brings in 100 Babies," 1.

76 "Children's Aid Accused of Delaying Adoption of 25 War Orphans," *Toronto Star*, 4 Oct. 1972, 97.

77 LAC, Adoption Desk fonds, RG29, vol. 3540, file 4122-1-3 pt. 9, Department of Health and Welfare, Doris Waltman, "An Examination of Adoption Policy and Services on Local, Inter-provincial and International Levels," 30.

78 Ibid., vol. 3539, file 4122-1-3 pt. 2, Minutes of the Meeting of Provincial and Territorial Representatives of Child Welfare Departments, June 1973, 8.

79   Sandra Simpson, interview, 5 Aug. 2010.
80   LAC, Adoption Desk fonds, RG29, vol. 3539, File 4122-1-3, pt. 1, memo from Mrs. D. Zarski, Director Welfare Services from Ramona J. Nelson, Consultant on Services to Children and Youth, 7 Feb. 1973.
81   Abley, "Mother Lode," A1.
82   LAC, Adoption Desk fonds, RG29, vol. 3539, file 4122-1-3 pt. 1, confidential memo via telex to EXTOTT GPS from James Bartleman, Acting High Commission, Bangladesh, 2 Feb. 1973.
83   Ibid.
84   Ibid., telex To BNGKK from EXTOTT, 13 Oct. 1972.
85   "Adoption Orders Inundate Officials," *Globe and Mail*, 5 Apr. 1975, 15.
86   "Confusion Surrounds Orphan Flight," *Globe and Mail*, 5 Apr. 1975, 14.
87   Taylor and Grant, *Orphans of War*, 143–49.
88   Veronica Strong-Boag and Rupa Bagga, "Saving, Kidnapping, or Something of Both? Canada and the Vietnam/Cambodia Babylift, Spring 1975," *American Review of Canadian Studies* 39, no. 3 (2009): 278.
89   Ibid.
90   Gail Kilner, interview, 7 Dec. 2010.
91   Ibid.
92   Ibid.
93   "Crashed Jet Had 34 Headed to Canada," *Globe and Mail*, 5 Apr. 1975, 1.
94   "Naomi Bronstein," *Barbara Frum*.
95   Taylor and Grant, *Orphans of War*, 229.
96   SWHA, ISS fonds, SW109, box 38, Country: Vietnam, Vietnam Claim Returns Baby Lift April '75. Article by Nancy Stearns in *Monthly Focus*, reprinted in the newsletter for the National Council of Organizations for Children and Youth, 1975.
97   LAC, Adoption Desk fonds, RG29, vol. 3539, file 4122-1-3 pt. 8, Provincial Court, in the matter of Thi Kieu Diem Nguyen et al., 9 Sept. 1975.
98   Rita J. Simon and Howard Altstein, *Adoption across Borders: Serving the Children in Transracial and Intercountry Adoptions* (Lanham, MD: Rowman and Littlefield, 2000), 40–41.
99   "Another Native People Lose Their Children," *Akwesasne Notes*, Early Summer 1975, 26–27. Thanks to Karen Dubinsky for sharing the cartoon by Keith Bendis featured with this article.
100 Sollinger, *Beggars and Choosers*, 20–23.
101 "The War Waifs: Should South Vietnamese Orphans Be Brought to Canada for Adoption?" *Toronto Star*, 12 Apr. 1975, B1.
102 MUA, Claire Culhane fonds, box 32, Correspondence 1975, letter from Culhane to Andras, 30 Apr. 1975.
103 AO, Joshua Brown fonds, series C-2, Australia, FPPI, box 3, file 2, Orphan Airlifts and the Tragedy That Is Vietnam, ISS, Australian Branch Newsletter #11, May 1975.
104 "Naomi Bronstein," *Barbara Frum*.
105 Ibid.
106 Strong-Boag, *Finding Families*, 113 (see introd., n. 37).
107 LAC, Adoption Desk fonds, RG29, vol. 3539, file 4122-1-3 pt. 2, report to Mrs. D. Zarski from Ramona Nelson and Derek White, Re: Function and Operation of the Federal Adoption Desk, A To Do List, 1975.
108 Ibid., pt. 12, letter from White to T. Hunsley, 27 Feb. 1978.

109 AO, Community and Social Services, RG29-110, box 3, Kuan Yin Foundation, letter from the KYF to Child Welfare Branch, Toronto, 20 Dec. 1979.
110 Anne Westhues and Joyce S. Cohen, "The Adjustment of Intercountry Adoptees in Canada," *Children and Youth Services Review* 20, nos. 1–2 (1998): 130.
111 Ibid.
112 Simon and Altstein, *Adoption across Borders*, 141.
113 Trent Kilner, interview, 17 Sept. 2010.
114 Ibid.
115 Ibid.
116 Jonathan Heath-Rawlings, "Two Orphans, Two Countries, One Quest," *Toronto Star*, 17 Apr. 2005.
117 Thanh Campbell, interview, 24 Aug. 2010.
118 John Burman, "Lost and Found: Orphan No. 32: Reunited with Family He Didn't Know He Had," *Hamilton Spectator*, 9 Feb. 2008.
119 Thanh Campbell, interview, 24 Aug. 2010.
120 Dubinsky, "Babies without Borders," 142–43.

Notes to Conclusion

1 Gaddis, *The Cold War*, 182–84 (see introd., n. 19).
2 Nikitiuk, "Emergency and Organizational Legitimacy," 61 (see chap. 1, n. 23).
3 McConnell, *Plan for Tomorrow*, 109–10 (see chap. 1, n. 10).
4 UBCSC, WILPF fonds, box 3, file 3-2, press release, 1980.
5 Cockburn, *From Where We Stand*, 174–76 (see introd., n. 15).
6 LAC, VOW fonds, MG28, I218, vol. 22, file 16, Membership Report.
7 Ibid., vol. 13, file 4, Meg Sears and Kay Macpherson, "A History of the Voice of Women," 1974, 15.
8 Nancy Adamson, "Feminists, Libbers, Lefties, and Radicals: The Emergence of the Women's Liberation Movement," in *A Diversity of Women: Ontario, 1945–1980*, ed. Joy Parr (Toronto: University of Toronto Press, 1995), 252–53.
9 LAC, VOW fonds, MG28, I218, vol. 13, file 4, Meg Sears and Kay Macpherson, "A History of the Voice of Women," 1974, 12.
10 Kay Macpherson, "The Seeds of the Seventies," *Canadian Dimension*, June 1975, 41.
11 Eleanor Mark, "The Women in Development Movement's Effect on Economic Policies of the United Nations, 1975–1985" (Ph.D. diss., Boston University, 2001), 25–26.
12 LAC, Goldie Josephy fonds, MG31, I4, "Unitarian Service Committee 1978–80: Correspondence with Korean Foster Child" series, vol. 9, letter to the editor, *Globe and Mail*, 14 Feb. 1980.
13 Ibid., letter to Flora MacDonald, secretary of state for External Affairs, 12 July 1980.
14 Ibid., "Letters to the Editor 1975–77" series, vol. 3, letter to the editor, *Toronto Sun*, 14 June 1977.
15 Culhane wrote three books on her work with prisoners: *Barred from Prison: A Personal Account* (Vancouver: Pulp Press, 1979), *Still Barred from Prison: Social Injustice in Canada* (Montreal: Black Rose Books, 1984), and *No Longer Barred from Prison: Social Injustice in Canada* (Montreal: Black Rose Books, 1991).
16 Westhues and Cohen, "The Adjustment of Intercountry Adoptees," 115 (see chap. 7, n. 110).

17   Misty Harris, "Mother to Thousands Coming for a Visit," *Edmonton Journal*, 8 May 2003.

18   As far as I know, no women from the civil defence movement were recognized.

19   LAC, VOW fonds, MG28, I218, vol. 13, file 4, Meg Sears and Kay Macpherson, "A History of the Voice of Women," 1974, 4.

Bibliography

Oral History

Brown, Marianne. 10 Jan. 2010
Campbell, Thanh. 24 Aug. 2010
Campbell, William. 25 Aug. 2010
Culhane, Dara. 25 June 2010
Franklin, Ursula. 6 July 2010
Grey, Pauline. 17 Feb. 2011
Josephy, David. 7 June 2005
Josephy, Michael. 7 June 2005
Kilner, Gail. 7 Dec. 2010
Kilner, Lia. 20 Jan. 2011
Kilner, Trent. 17 Sept. 2010
Medeiros, Julie. 3 Oct. 2010
Oak, Lorraine. 8 Feb. 2010
Reiter, Ester. 10 May 2010
Simpson, Sandra. Via email. July–Aug. 2010
Stevenson, Zoya. Via email. Aug.–Sept. 2011
Talboom, Hans. 3 Oct. 2010
Talboom, Roma. 3 Oct. 2010

Archival Collections

Archives of Ontario (AO)

Archives of Ontario Oral History Interviews
Deputy Minister of Community and Social Services (Subject Files)
Deputy Minister of Health, Emergency Measures Operation (Correspondence)
Grindstone Peace Cooperative fonds
Joshua Brown fonds
Local Council of Women fonds

City of Edmonton Archives (CEA)

Bertha Lawrence fonds
Edmonton Voice of Women Clippings File
Edmonton Local Council of Women Clippings File

City of Toronto Archives (CTA)

Former City of Toronto fonds
Larry Becker fonds
Municipality of Metropolitan Toronto fonds

Library and Archives Canada (LAC)

Adoption Desk fonds
Canadian Council on Social Development fonds
Duncan Cameron fonds
Goldie Josephy fonds
Helen Melnyk-Marko fonds
Imperial Order Daughters of the Empire fonds
Lil Greene fonds
Marion Scott fonds
National Council of Women of Canada fonds
Unitarian Service Committee fonds
United Nations Association fonds
Voice of Women fonds

McMaster University Archives (MUA)

Canadian Committee for World Refugee Year fonds
Claire Culhane fonds

UNICEF Canada Office Archives (UCOA)

UNICEF Annual Reports

University of British Columbia Special Collections (UBCSC)

Women's International League for Peace and Freedom fonds

University of Manitoba Archives (UMA)

Margaret Konantz fonds

University of Minnesota, Social Welfare History Archives (SWHA)

International Social Services fonds

University of Rhode Island Special Collections and University Archives (URIA)

Foster Parents Plan International records

University of Saskatchewan Library, Diefenbaker Centre Archives (DCA)

Prime Minister's Office (Correspondence)

University of Waterloo Archives (UWA)

Jo Davis fonds

York University Archives

Edith Ferguson fonds
Nancy Pocock fonds

Newspapers

Calgary Albertan
Edmonton Journal
Globe and Mail
Hamilton Spectator
Kitchener-Waterloo Record
Montreal Gazette
New York Times
Ottawa Citizen
Ottawa Journal
Toronto Daily Star / Toronto Star
Toronto Telegram
Windsor Star
Winnipeg Free Press
Winnipeg Tribune

Periodicals

Akwesasne Notes
Bias
Bulletin (Welfare Services)
Canadian Welfare
Chatelaine
Civil Defence Bulletin
EMO National Digest
Maclean's
Ramparts
Saturday Night
Star Weekly
Weekend Magazine
Welfare

Government Publications

Canada. *Debates, House of Commons*. Session 1962. Vol. 3, 23 Mar. 1962.
————. Department of National Defence, Emergency Measures Organization. *11 Steps to Survival*. Ottawa: Queen's Printer, 1969.
————. Department of National Defence, Emergency Measures Organization. *Survival Planning Guide for Municipalities*. Ottawa: Queen's Printer, 1964.
————. Department of National Health and Welfare, Civil Defence Health Services. "Bea Alerte" poster series. Ottawa: Queen's Printer. 1950–59.
————. Department of National Health and Welfare, Civil Defence Health Services. *What the Home Nursing Auxiliary Should Know about Civil Defence*. Ottawa: Queen's Printer, 1957.
————. Department of National Health and Welfare, Civil Defence Information Services. *Personal Protection under Atomic Attack*. Ottawa: Queen's Printer, 1951.
————. Department of National Health and Welfare, Civil Defence Planning Group. *Civil Defence Health Services Manual No. 7*. Ottawa: Queen's Printer, 1952.
————. Department of National Health and Welfare, Civil Defence Planning Group. *Your Survival in an H-Bomb War If You Do Not Live in a Target Area*, Ottawa: Queen's Printer, 1956.
————. Department of National Health and Welfare, Emergency Measures Organization. "Survival in Likely Target Areas," *Blueprint for Survival No. 5*. Ottawa: Queen's Printer, 1962.
————. Department of National Health and Welfare, Emergency Welfare Services Division. *Emergency Feeding Manual*. Ottawa: Queen's Printer, 1965.
————. Health Canada. *Canada's Food Guides from 1942 to 1992*. Ottawa: Queen's Printer, 2003.

Ontario Ministry of Community and Children Services. "Report on Adoption of Vietnamese Children." Sept. 1973.

Pollard, J. H. *Emergency Measures in Elementary and Secondary Schools in the Metropolitan Toronto Area.* Toronto: Metropolitan Toronto EMO, 1961.

Radio

"Bomb Shelters for Sale." *Assignment.* CBC Radio, 6 Nov. 1958.

"Exercise Tocsin B: 1961." *CBC Radio News Special.* CBC Radio, 13 Nov. 1961.

"The Hiroshima Maidens." *Assignment.* CBC Radio, 8 Aug. 1957.

"Supplying the War Machine." *As It Happens.* CBC Radio, 27 Jan. 1975.

Television

"How to Survive: Life in a Fallout Shelter." *CBC Newsmagazine.* CBC TV, 17 Sept. 1961.

"Naomi Bronstein." *Barbara Frum.* CBC TV, 5 June 1975.

"Naomi Bronstein." *Dan Turner: For the People.* CBC TV, 31 Jan. 1983.

"Sandra and Her Kids." *The Nature of Things.* CBC TV, 1983.

Films

Duck and Cover. Archer Productions, 1951.

Flowers or Ashes. Toronto: Metropolitan Toronto Civil Defence Organization. 1957.

The House in the Middle. Washington: National Paint, Varnish, and Lacquer Association, 1954.

A Moment in Time: The United Colours of Bronstein. Judy [Jackson] Films, 2001.

Sad Song of Yellow Skin. National Film Board, 1970.

Seeds of Destiny. Defense Department, United States Army War Department, 1946.

Streets of Saigon. National Film Board, 1973.

The Voice of Women: The First Thirty Years. Pineau Production, 1992.

Theses and Dissertations

Ball, Christine. "A History of the Voice of Women." PhD diss., University of Toronto, 1994.

Fisher, Anne. "Civil Defence in Canada, 1939–1965: Garnering Public Support for War and Nuclear Weapons through the Myth of Protection." MA thesis, Lakehead University, 1999.

Hunter, Jennifer Lynn. "Is It Even Worthwhile Doing the Dishes? Canadians and the Nuclear Threat, 1945–1963." PhD diss., McGill University, 2004.

Mark, Eleanor. "The Women in Development Movement's Effect on Economic Policies of the United Nations, 1975–1985." PhD diss., Boston University, 2001.

Toxopeus, Deanna. "1951 Agreement between the Red Cross and St. John Ambulance: A Case Study of the Effect of Civil Defence on Canada's Health Care System." MA thesis, Carleton University, 1997.

Books and Articles

Abella, Irving, and Harold Troper. *None Is Too Many: Canada and the Jews of Europe, 1933–1948*. Toronto: Key Porter, 2000.

Adams, Mary Louise. *The Trouble with Normal: Postwar Youth and the Making of Heterosexuality*. Toronto: University of Toronto Press, 1997.

———. "Youth, Corruptibility, and English-Canadian Postwar Campaigns against Indecency, 1948–1955." *Journal of the History of Sexuality* 6, no. 1 (July 1995): 89–117.

Adamson, Nancy. "Feminists, Libbers, Lefties, and Radicals: The Emergence of the Women's Liberation Movement." In *A Diversity of Women: Ontario, 1945–1980*, edited by Joy Parr, 252–80. Toronto: University of Toronto Press, 1995.

Applebaum, Anne. *Between East and West: Across the Borderlands of Europe*. New York: Pantheon Books, 1994.

Armstrong-Reid, Susan, and David Murray. *Armies of Peace: Canada and the UNRRA Years*. Toronto: University of Toronto Press, 2008.

Atkins, Irene Kahn. "Seeds of Destiny: A Case History." *Film and History*, 11 no. 2 (May 1981): 25–33.

Azoulay, Dan. "'Ruthless in a Ladylike Way': CCF Women Confront the Post-war Communist Menace." *Ontario History* 89, no. 1 (Mar. 1997): 23–52.

Baillargeon, Denyse. *Babies for the Nation: The Medicalization of Motherhood in Quebec, 1910–1970*. Translated by W. Donald Wilson. Waterloo, ON: Wilfrid Laurier University Press, 2009.

Ball, S. J. *The Cold War: An International History*. London: Arnold, 1998.

Barker, Rodney. *The Hiroshima Maidens: A Story of Courage, Compassion, and Survival*. New York: Viking, 1985.

Bilson, Geoffrey. *The Guest Children: The Story of the British Child Evacuees Sent to Canada during World War II*. Saskatoon, SK: Fifth House, 1988.

Bothwell, Robert. *Alliance and Illusion: Canada and the World, 1945–1984*. Vancouver: University of British Columbia Press, 2007.

———. *The Big Chill: Canada and the Cold War*. Concord, ON: Irwin, 1998.

———. "Eyes West: Canada and the Cold War in Asia." In *Canada and the Early Cold War, 1943–1957*, edited by Greg Donaghy. Ottawa: Department of Foreign Affairs and International Trade, 1988.

Bothwell, Robert, Ian Drummond, and John English. *Canada since 1945*. Rev. ed. Toronto: University of Toronto Press, 1996.

Briggs, Laura. "Mother, Child, Race, Nation: The Visual Iconography of Rescue and the Politics of Transnational and Transracial Adoption." *Gender and History* 15, no. 2 (Aug. 2003): 179–200.

Brookfield, Tarah. "Children as 'Seeds of Destiny': Nation, Race, and Citizenship in Postwar Foreign Relief Programs." In *Canadian Children's History Reader*, edited by Tamara Myers and Mona Gleason. Toronto: Oxford University Press, forthcoming.

———. "Maverick Mothers and Mercy Flights: Canada's Controversial Introduction to International Adoption." *Journal of the Canadian Historical Association* 19, no. 1 (2009): 307–30.

———. "Modeling the UN's Mission in Semi-formal Wear: Edmonton's Miss United Nations Pageants of the 1960s." In *Contesting Bodies and Nations in Canadian History*, edited by Jane Nichols and Patrizia Gentile. Toronto: University of Toronto Press, forthcoming.

Brouwer, Ruth Compton. "Ironic Interventions: CUSO Volunteers in India's Family Planning Campaign, 1960s–1970s." *Social History/Histoire sociale* 43, no. 86 (Nov. 2010): 279–313.

———. *Modern Women Modernizing Men: The Changing Missions of Three Professional Women in Asia and Africa, 1902–69.* Vancouver: University of British Columbia Press, 2002.

———. *New Women for God: Canadian Presbyterian Women and India Missions, 1876–1914.* Toronto: University of Toronto Press, 1990.

Brown, Harcourt, ed. *The Army's Mister Brown: A Family Trilogy, 1941–1952.* Parry Sound, ON: Olympic Printing, 1982.

Buckner, Philip, and R. D. Francis, eds. *Canada and the British World: Culture, Migration, and Identity.* Vancouver: University of British Columbia Press, 2006.

Buddle, Melanie. *The Business of Women: Marriage, Family, and Entrepreneurship in British Columbia, 1901–1951.* Vancouver: University of British Columbia Press, 2010.

Bussey, Gertrude Carman, and Margaret Tims. *Pioneers for Peace: Women's International League for Peace and Freedom, 1915–1965.* London: WILPF British Section, 1980.

Carp, E. Wayne, ed. *Adoption in America: Historical Perspectives.* Ann Arbor: University of Michigan Press, 2002.

Carroll, Michael. "Canada and the Financing of the United Nations Emergency Force, 1957–1963." *Journal of the Canadian Historical Association* 13 (2002): 217–34.

Casgrain, Thérèse. *A Woman in a Man's World.* Translated by Joyce Marshall. Toronto: McClelland and Stewart, 1972.

Cavell, Richard, ed. *Love, Hate, and Fear in Canada's Cold War.* Toronto: University of Toronto Press, 2004.

Chan, K. C. "The Role of the Family Planning Association in Hong Kong's Fertility Decline." *Studies in Family Planning* 7, no. 10 (Oct. 1976): 284–89.

Chapnick, Adam. *The Middle Power Project: Canada and the Founding of the United Nations.* Vancouver: University of British Columbia Press, 2005.

Chong, Denise. *The Girl in the Photo: The Kim Phuc Story.* Toronto: Viking, 2001.

Christie, Nancy, and Michael Gauvreau, eds. *Cultures of Citizenship in Post-war Canada, 1940–1955.* Montreal and Kingston: McGill-Queen's University Press, 2003.

Churchill, David S. "An Ambiguous Welcome: Vietnam Draft Resistance, the Canadian State, and Cold War Containment." *Social History/Histoire sociale* 37, no. 73 (2004): 1–26.

Clarke, Frank K. "'Keep Communism Out of Our Schools': Cold War Anti-Communism at the Toronto Board of Education, 1948–1951." *Labour/Le Travail* 49 (Spring 2002): 93–120.

Cockburn, Cynthia. *From Where We Stand: War, Women's Activism and Feminist Analysis.* London and New York: Zed Books, 2007.

Comacchio, Cynthia, Janet Golden, and George Weisz, eds. *Healing the World's Children: Interdisciplinary Perspectives on Child Health in the Twentieth Century.* Montreal and Kingston: McGill-Queen's University Press, 2008.

Cook, Sharon Anne, Lorna R. McLean, and Kate O'Rourke, eds. *Framing Our Past: Canadian Women's History in the Twentieth Century.* Montreal: McGill-Queen's University Press, 2001.

Cotcher, Maryanne. "A National Organization in a Prairie City: The Regina Voice of Women, 1961–1963." *Saskatchewan History* 56, no. 1 (2004): 21–29.

Culhane, Claire. *Barred from Prison: A Personal Account.* Vancouver: Pulp Press, 1979.

———. *No Longer Barred from Prison: Social Injustice in Canada.* Montreal: Black Rose Books, 1991.

———. *Still Barred from Prison: Social Injustice in Canada.* Montreal: Black Rose Books, 1984.

———. *Why Is Canada in Vietnam? The Truth about Our Foreign Aid.* Toronto: NC Press, 1972.

De Groot, Gerard J. *The Bomb: A Life.* Cambridge, MA: Harvard University Press, 2005.

Dexter, Grant. *Canada and the Building of Peace.* Toronto: Canadian Institute of International Affairs, 1944.

Donaghy, Greg, ed. *Canada and the Early Cold War, 1943–1957.* Ottawa: Department of Foreign Affairs and International Trade, 1988.

Dubinsky, Karen. *Babies without Borders: Adoption and Migration across the Americas.* Toronto: University of Toronto Press, 2010.

———. "Babies without Borders: Rescue, Kidnap, and the Symbolic Child." *Journal of Women's History* 19, no. 1 (Spring 2007): 142–50.

———. "'We Adopted a Negro': Interracial Adoptions and the Hybrid Baby in 1960s Canada." In *Creating Postwar Canada: Community, Diversity, and Dissent,*

1945–75, edited by Magda Fahrni and Robert Rutherdale. Vancouver: University of British Columbia Press, 2008.

Early, Frances. "Canadian Women and the International Arena in the Sixties: The Voice of Women/La Voix des femmes and the Opposition to the Vietnam War." In *The Sixties: Passion, Politics and Style*, edited by Dimitry Anastakis. Montreal and Kingston: McGill-Queen's University Press, 2008.

———. "'A Grandly Subversive Time': The Halifax Branch of the Voice of Women in the 1960s." In *Mothers of the Municipality: Women, Work, and Social Policy in Post-1945 Halifax*, edited by Judith Fingard and Janet Guildford, 253–80. Toronto: University of Toronto Press, 2005.

———. "The Historic Roots of the Women's Peace Movement in North America." *Canadian Women's Studies* 7, no. 4 (Winter 1986): 43–48.

English, John, and Norman Hillmer, eds. *Making a Difference: Canada's Foreign Policy in a Changing World Order.* Toronto: Lester, 1992.

Enloe, Cynthia. *Making Feminist Sense of International Politics.* Berkeley: University of California Press, 1990.

Fahrni, Magda, and Robert Rutherdale, eds. *Creating Postwar Canada: Community, Diversity, and Dissent, 1945–75.* Vancouver: University of British Columbia Press, 2008.

Fingard, Judith. "Women's Organization: The Heart and Soul of Women's Activism." In *Mothers of the Municipality: Women, Work, and Social Policy in Post-1945 Halifax*, edited by Judith Fingard and Janet Guildford. Toronto: University of Toronto Press, 2005.

Foster, Catherine Foster. *Women for All Seasons: The Story of the Women's International League for Peace and Freedom.* Athens, GA: University of Georgia Press, 1989.

Franklin, Ursula. *The Ursula Franklin Reader: Pacifism as a Map.* Toronto: Between the Lines, 2006.

Freedman, Lawrence. *The Cold War.* London: Cassels, 2001.

Freud, Anna, and Dorothy Tiffany Burlingham. *War and Children.* New York: Medical War Books, 1943.

Friedan, Betty. *The Feminine Mystique.* New York: Dell, 1964.

Gaddis, John Lewis. *The Cold War: A New History.* New York: Penguin, 2005.

Glassford, Sarah. "'The Greatest Mother in the World': Carework and the Discourse of Mothering in the Canadian Red Cross Society during the First World War." *Journal of the Association for Research on Mothering* 10, no. 1 (2008): 219–32.

Gleason, Mona. "Disciplining Children, Disciplining Parents: The Nature and Meaning of Advice to Canadian Parents, 1945–1955." *Social History/Histoire sociale* 29, no. 57 (1996): 187–209.

———. *Normalizing the Ideal: Psychology, Schooling, and the Family in Postwar Canada.* Toronto: University of Toronto Press, 1999.

———. "Psychology and the Construction of the 'Normal' Family in Postwar Canada, 1945–60." *Canadian Historical Review* 78, no. 3 (Sept. 1997): 442–77.

Gordon, Linda. *The Moral Property of Women: A History of Birth Control Politics in America.* Urbana: University of Illinois Press, 2007.

Granatstein, J. L., and David Stafford. *Spy Games: Espionage and Canada from Gouzenko to Glasnost.* Toronto: Key Porter Books, 1990.

Guard, Julie. "A Mighty Power against the Cost of Living: Canadian Housewives Organize in the 1930s." *International Labor and Working-Class History* 77, no. 1 (Spring 2010): 1–20.

Hallin, Daniel C. *The Uncensored War: The Media and Vietnam.* Berkeley: University of California Press: 1989.

Hendershot, Cyndy. *I Was a Cold War Monster: Horror Films, Eroticism and the Cold War Imagination.* Bowling Green, OH: Bowling Green State University Popular Press, 2001.

Hersey, John. *Hiroshima.* New York: Vintage Books, 1946.

Hewitt, Kenneth. "'When the Great Planes Came and Made Ashes of Our City ...': Towards an Oral Geography of the Disasters of War." *Antipode* 26, no. 1 (1994): 1–34.

Hewitt, Steve. *Spying 101: The RCMP's Secret Activities at Canadian Universities, 1917–1997.* Toronto: University of Toronto Press, 2002.

Iacovetta, Franca. *Gatekeepers: Reshaping Immigrant Lives in Cold War Canada.* Toronto: Between the Lines, 2006.

Iriye, Akira. *Cultural Internationalism and World Order.* Baltimore: Johns Hopkins University Press, 1997.

Kealey, Linda. *Enlisting Women for the Cause: Women, Labour and the Left in Canada, 1890–1920.* Toronto: University of Toronto Press, 1998.

Kelly, Ninette, and Michael Trebilcock. *The Making of the Mosaic: A History of Canadian Immigration Policy.* Toronto: University of Toronto Press, 1998.

Kennedy, Hansi. "Memories of Anna Freud." *American Imago* 53, no. 3 (1996): 205–9.

Kennedy, Sean. *The Shock of War: Civilian Experiences, 1937–1945.* Toronto: University of Toronto Press, 2011.

Kerans, Marion Douglas. *Muriel Duckworth: A Very Active Pacifist.* Halifax: Fernwood, 1996.

Keshen, Jeffrey A. "One for All or All for One: Government Controls, Black Marketing and the Limits of Patriotism, 1939–1947." *Journal of Canadian Studies* 29 (Winter 1994): 111–43.

———. *Saints, Sinners, and Soldiers: Canada's Second War.* Vancouver: University of British Columbia Press, 2004.

Kinnear, Mary. *Woman of the World: Mary McGeachy and International Cooperation.* Toronto: University of Toronto Press, 2004.

Kinsman, Gary, Dieter K. Buse, and Mercedes Steedman, eds. *Whose National Security? Canadian State Surveillance and the Creation of Enemies.* Toronto: Between the Lines, 2000.

Klein, Christina. *Cold War Orientalism: Asia in the Middlebrow Imagination, 1945–1961.* Berkeley: University of California, 2003.

Korinek, Valerie J. "'It's a Tough Time to Be in Love': The Darker Side of *Chatelaine* during the Cold War." In *Love, Hate, and Fear in Canada's Cold War,* edited by Richard Cavell. Toronto: University of Toronto Press, 2004.

———. *Roughing It in the Suburbs: Reading* Chatelaine *Magazine in the Fifties and Sixties.* Toronto: University of Toronto Press, 2000.

Koven, Seth, and Sonya Michel, eds. *Mothers of a New World: Maternalist Politics and the Origins of Welfare States.* New York and London: Routledge, 1993.

Larocque, Alain. "'Losing Our Chinese': The St. Enfance Movement." Working Paper 49, Joint Centre for Asia Pacific Studies, Toronto, 1987.

Lawrence, Bertha, L. C. Mix, C. S. Wilkie, and Edgar McInnis. *Canada in the Modern World.* Toronto: J. M. Dent and Sons, 1955.

Leffler, Melvyn P., and David S. Painter, eds. *Origins of the Cold War: An International History.* New York: Routledge, 1994.

Lexier, Roberta. "Linking the Past with the Future: Voice of Women in Regina." *Saskatchewan History* 56, no. 2 (2004): 24–34.

Llewellyn, Kristina. "Gendered Democracy: Women Teachers in Post-war Toronto." *Historical Studies in Education* 18, no. 1 (2006): 1–25.

Loewan, Candace. "Mike Hears Voices: Voice of Women and Lester Pearson, 1960–1963." *Atlantis* 12, no. 2 (Spring 1987): 24–30.

Lorentzen, Lois Ann, and Jennifer Turpin, eds. *The Women and War Reader.* New York: New York University Press, 1998.

Lovelock, Kirsten. "Intercountry Adoption as a Migratory Practice: A Comparative Analysis of Intercountry Adoption and Immigration Policy and Practice in the United States, Canada and New Zealand in the Post W.W. II Period." *International Migration Review* 34, no. 3 (Fall 2000): 907–49.

Lowe, Mick. *One Woman Army: The Life of Claire Culhane.* Toronto: Macmillan Canada, 1992.

Macdonald, Sharon. "Drawing the Lines: Gender, Peace and War: An Introduction." In *Images of Women in Peace and War: Cross Cultural and Historical Perspectives,* edited by Sharon Macdonald, Pat Holden, and Shirley Ardener. London: Macmillan Education, 1987.

Macpherson, Kay. "Persistent Voices: Twenty-Five Years with Voice of Women." *Atlantis* 12, no. 2 (Spring 1987): 60–72.

———. "The Seeds of the Seventies." *Canadian Dimension,* June 1975, 39–41.

———. *When in Doubt, Do Both: The Times of My Life.* Toronto: University of Toronto Press, 1994.

Marr, Lucille. "'If You Want Peace, Prepare for Peace': Hanna Newcombe, Peace Researcher and Peace Activist." *Ontario History* 84, no. 4 (1992): 263–81.

———. "'The Time for the Distaff and Spindle': The Ontario Mennonite Women's Circles and the Mennonite Central Committee." *Journal of Mennonite Studies* 17 (1999): 130–51.

Marshall, Dominique. "The Cold War, Canada, and the United Nations Declaration of the Rights of the Child." In *Canada and the Early Cold War, 1943–1957,* edited by Greg Donaghy. Ottawa: Department of Foreign Affairs and International Trade, 1988.

———. "Humanitarian Sympathy for Children in Times of War and the History of Children's Rights, 1919–1959." In *Children and War: A Historical Anthology,* edited by James Marten. New York: New York University Press, 2002.

———. "The Language of Children's Rights, the Formation of the Welfare State and the Democratic Experience of Poor Families in Quebec, 1940–1955." *Canadian Historical Review* 78, no. 3 (Fall 1997): 409–41.

Martz, Fraidie. *Open Your Hearts: The Story of Jewish War Children in Canada.* Montreal: Véhicule, 1996.

May, Elaine Tyler. *Homeward Bound: American Families in the Cold War Era.* New York: Basic Books, 1988.

McConnell, David. *Plan for Tomorrow ... Today! The Story of Emergency Preparedness Canada, 1948–1998.* Ottawa: Emergency Preparedness Canada, 1998.

McEnaney, Laura. *Civil Defense Begins at Home: Militarization Meets Everyday Life in the Fifties.* Princeton, NJ: Princeton University Press, 2000.

McLaren, Angus, and Arlene Tigar McLaren. *The Bedroom and the State: The Changing Practices and Politics of Contraception and Abortion in Canada, 1880–1997.* Toronto: Oxford University Press, 1997.

McPherson, Kathryn. *Bedside Matters: The Transformation of Canadian Nursing, 1900–1990.* Don Mills, ON: Oxford University Press, 1996.

Melosh, Barbara. *Strangers and Kin: The American Way of Adoption.* Cambridge, MA: Harvard University Press, 2002.

Meyerowitz, Joanne, ed. *Not June Cleaver: Women and Gender in Post-war America, 1945–1960.* Philadelphia: Temple University Press, 1994.

Molumphy, Henry D. *For Common Decency: The History of Foster Parents Plan International, 1937–1983.* Warwick, RI: Foster Parents Plan International, 1984.

Morrison, David R. *Aid and Ebb Tide: A History of CIDA and Canadian Development Assistance.* Waterloo, ON: Wilfrid Laurier University Press, 1998.

Morton, Desmond. *Fight or Pay: Soldiers' Families in the Great War.* Vancouver: University of British Columbia Press, 2004.

Mulrooney, Margaret, ed. *Fleeing the Famine: North America and Irish Refugees, 1845–1851.* Westport, CT: Greenwood Publishing Group, 2003.

Nikitiuk, Costia. "Emergency and Organizational Legitimacy: The Dilemma of Emergency Planning in B.C." *BC Studies* 38 (Summer 1978): 47–64.

Oakes, Guy. *The Imaginary War: Civil Defence and American Cold War Culture*. New York: Oxford University Press, 1994.

Oppenheimer, Melanie. "Controlling Civilian Volunteering: Canada and Australia during the Second World War." *War and Society* 22, no. 1 (Oct. 2004): 27–50.

Owram, Doug. *Born at the Right Time: A History of the Baby Boom Generation*. Toronto: University of Toronto Press, 1996.

Parr, Joy. *Labouring Children: British Immigrant Apprentices to Canada, 1869–1924*. Montreal: McGill-Queen's University Press, 1980.

Phillips, Patti. "'Financially Irresponsible and Obviously Neurotic Need Not Apply': Social Work, Parental Fitness, and the Production of Adoptive Families in Ontario, 1940–1965." *Histoire sociale/Social History* 78 (Nov. 2006): 329–61.

Pierson, Ruth Roach. *"They're Still Women After All": The Second World War and Canadian Womanhood*. Toronto: McClelland and Stewart, 1986.

Preston, Andrew. "Balancing War and Peace: Canadian Foreign Policy and the Vietnam War, 1961–1965," *Diplomatic History* 27, no. 1 (Jan. 2003): 73–81.

Price, John. *Orienting Canada: Race, Empire, and the Transpacific*. Vancouver: University of British Columbia Press, 2011.

Quiney, Linda. "'Bravely and Loyally They Answered the Call': St. John Ambulance, the Red Cross, and the Patriotic Service of Canadian Women during the Great War." *History of Intellectual Culture* 5, no. 1 (2005): 1–19.

Ressler, Everett M., Neil Boothby, and Daniel J. Steinbock. *Unaccompanied Children: Care and Protection in Wars, Natural Disasters, and Refugee Movements*. New York: Oxford University Press, 1988.

Richter, Andrew. *Avoiding Armageddon: Canadian Military Strategy and Nuclear Weapons, 1950–1963*. Vancouver: University of British Columbia Press, 2002.

Roberts, Barbara. *"Why Do Women Do Nothing to End the War?": Canadian Feminists-Pacifists and the Great War*. Ottawa: Canadian Research Institute for the Advancement of Women, 1985.

———. "Women's Peace Activism in Canada." In *Beyond the Vote: Canadian Women and Politics*, edited by Linda Kealey and Joan Sangster. Toronto: University of Toronto Press, 1989.

Roberts, Lance W., Rodney A. Clifton, and Barry Ferguson. *Recent Social Trends in Canada, 1960–2000*. Montreal: McGill-Queen's University Press, 2005.

Roberts, Wayne. "Rocking the Cradle for the World: The New Woman and Maternal Feminism in Toronto, 1877–1914." In *A Not Unreasonable Claim: Women and Reform in Canada, 1880s–1920s*, edited by Linda Kealey. Toronto: Women's Press, 1979.

Rose, Kenneth. *One Nation Underground: The Fallout Shelter in American Culture*. New York: New York University Press, 2001.

Rosenberg, Emily S. "Gender." In "A Round Table: Explaining the History of American Foreign Relations." *The Journal of American History* 77, no. 1 (June 1990): 116–24.

Ross, Douglas. *In the Interests of Peace: Canada and Vietnam, 1954–1973.* Toronto: University of Toronto Press, 1984.

Sanger, Claude. *Lotta and the Unitarian Service Committee Story.* Toronto: Stoddard, 1986.

Sangster, Joan. *Dreams of Equality: Women on the Canadian Left, 1920–1950.* Toronto: McClelland and Stewart, 1989.

———. "Radical Ruptures: Feminism, Labor, and the Left in the Long Sixties in Canada." *American Review of Canadian Studies* 40, no. 1 (Mar. 2010): 1–21.

Sethna, Christabelle, and Steve Hewitt. "Sex Spying: The RCMP and Women's Liberation Groups." In *Debating Dissent: Canada and the Sixties,* edited by Dominique Clément, Lara Campbell, and Gregory Kealey. Toronto: University of Toronto Press, forthcoming.

Sherif, Ann. *Japan's Cold War: Media: Literature and the Law.* New York: Columbia University Press, 2009.

Shute, Nevil. *On the Beach.* New York: Ballantine Books, 1957.

Simon, Rita J., and Howard Altstein. *Adoption across Borders: Serving the Children in Transracial and Intercountry Adoptions.* Lanham, MD: Rowman and Littlefield, 2000.

Sollinger, Rickie. *Beggars and Choosers: How the Politics of Choice Shapes Adoption, Abortion, and Welfare in the United States.* New York: Hill and Wang, 2001.

Spiegelman, Judith M. *We Are the Children: A Celebration of UNICEF's First Forty Years.* Boston: Atlantic Monthly Press, 1986.

Spock, Benjamin, and Mitchell Zimmerman. *Dr. Spock on Vietnam.* New York: Dell, 1968.

Strong-Boag, Veronica. "Canada's Wage-Earning Wives and the Construction of the Middle Class, 1945–60." *Journal of Canadian Studies* 29, no. 3 (Fall 1994): 5–25.

———. *Finding Families—Finding Ourselves: English Canada Encounters Adoption from the Nineteenth Century to the 1990s.* Oxford: Oxford University Press, 2006.

———. *Fostering Nation? Canada Confronts Its History of Childhood Disadvantage.* Waterloo, ON: Wilfrid Laurier University Press, 2011.

———. "Home Dreams: Women and the Suburban Experiment in Canada, 1945–60." *Canadian Historical Review* 72, no. 4 (Dec. 1991): 471–504.

Strong-Boag, Veronica, and Rupa Bagga. "Saving, Kidnapping, or Something of Both? Canada and the Vietnam/Cambodia Babylift, Spring 1975." *American Review of Canadian Studies* 39, no. 3 (2009): 271–89.

Swenarchuk, Michelle. Introduction to *The Ursula Franklin Reader: Pacifism as a Map,* by Ursula Franklin. Toronto: Between the Lines, 2006.

Taylor, Rosemary, and Wende Grant. *Orphans of War: Work with the Abandoned Children of Vietnam, 1967–1975.* London: Collins, 1988.

Walker, Martin. *The Cold War.* Toronto: Stoddart, 1994.

Westhues, Anne, and Joyce S. Cohen. "The Adjustment of Intercountry Adoptees in Canada." *Children and Youth Services Review* 20, nos. 1–2 (1998): 115–34.

Whitaker, Reg, and Steve Hewitt. *Canada and the Cold War.* Toronto: James Lorimer, 2003.

Whitaker, Reg, and Gary Marcuse. *Cold War Canada: The Making of a National Insecurity State, 1945–1957.* Toronto: University of Toronto Press, 1994.

Wittner, Lawrence S. "Gender Roles and Nuclear Disarmament, 1954–1965." *Gender & History* 12, no. 1 (Apr. 2000): 197–226.

Yaszek, Lisa. "Stories 'That Only a Mother' Could Write: Midcentury Peace Activism, Maternalist Politics, and Judith Merril's Early Fiction." *National Women's Studies Association Journal* 16, no. 2 (Summer 2004): 70–97.

Other Sources

Hewitt, Steve, and Christabelle Sethna. "'Sweating and Uncombed': Canadian State Security, the Indochinese Conference, and the Feminist Threat." Paper presented at the Canadian Historical Association Meeting, Vancouver, 2–4 June 2008.

Qin, Fang. "'Revenge for Our Children!': The Stigmatization of Christian-Managed Orphanages in the Early 1950s in China." Paper presented at the George Washington Graduate Student Cold War History Conference, Apr. 2007.

St. Laurent, Louis. "Consequences of the Cold War for Canada." Speech to the Canadian Club in Toronto, 27 Mar. 1950, http://www.collectionscanada.ca/primeministers/h4-4015-e.html.

United Nations. "Declaration on the Rights of the Child." 1959.

Index

Books in the Studies in Childhood and Family in Canada Series Published by Wilfrid Laurier University Press

Making Do:Women, Family, and Home in Montreal during the Great Depression by Denyse Baillargeon, translated by Yvonne Klein • 1999 / xii + 232 pp. / ISBN 0-88920-326-1 / ISBN-13: 978-0-88920-326-6

Children in English-Canadian Society: Framing the Twentieth-Century Consensus by Neil Sutherland with a new foreword by Cynthia Comacchio • 2000 / xxiv + 336 pp. / illus. / ISBN 0-88920-351-2 / ISBN-13: 978-0-88920-351-8

Love Strong as Death: Lucy Peel's Canadian Journal, 1833–1836 edited by J.I. Little • 2001 / x + 229 pp. / illus. / ISBN 0-88920-389-x / ISBN-13: 978-0-88920-389-230-x

The Challenge of Children's Rights for Canada by Katherine Covell and R. Brian Howe • 2001 / viii + 244 pp. / ISBN 0-88920-380-6 / ISBN-13: 978-0-88920-380-8

NFB Kids: Portrayals of Children by the National Film Board of Canada, 1939–1989 by Brian J. Low • 2002 / vi + 288 pp. / illus. / ISBN 0-88920-386-5 / ISBN-13: 978-0-88920-386-0

Something to Cry About: An Argument against Corporal Punishment of Children in Canada by Susan M. Turner • 2002 / xx + 317 pp. / ISBN 0-88920-382-2 / ISBN-13: 978-0-88920-382-2

Freedom to Play: We Made Our Own Fun edited by Norah L. Lewis • 2002 / xiv + 210 pp. / ISBN 0-88920-406-3 / ISBN-13: 978-0-88920-406-5

The Dominion of Youth: Adolescence and the Making of Modern Canada, 1920–1950 by Cynthia Comacchio • 2006 / x + 302 pp. / illus. / ISBN 0-88920-488-8 / ISBN-13: 978-0-88920-488-1

Evangelical Balance Sheet: Character, Family, and Business in Mid-Victorian Nova Scotia by B. Anne Wood • 2006 / xxx + 198 pp. / illus. / ISBN 0-88920-500-0 / ISBN-13: 978-0-88920-500-0

A Question of Commitment: Children's Rights in Canada edited by R. Brian Howe and Katherine Covell • 2007 / xiv + 442 pp. / ISBN 978-1-55458-003-3

Taking Responsibility for Children edited by Samantha Brennan and Robert Noggle • 2007 / xxii + 188 pp. / ISBN 978-1-55458-015-6

Home Words: Discourses of Children's Literature in Canada edited by Mavis Reimer • 2008 / xx + 280 pp. / illus. / ISBN 978-1-55458-016-3

Depicting Canada's Children edited by Loren Lerner • 2009 / xxvi + 442 pp. / illus. / ISBN 978-1-55458-050-7

Babies for the Nation: The Medicalization of Motherhood in Quebec, 1910–1970 by Denyse Baillargeon, translated by W. Donald Wilson • 2009 / xiv + 328 pp. / illus. / ISBN 978-1-5548-058-3

The One Best Way? Breastfeeding History, Politics, and Policy in Canada by Tasnim Nathoo and Aleck Ostry • 2009 / xvi + 262 pp. / illus. / ISBN 978-1-55458-147-4

Fostering Nation? Canada Confronts Its History of Childhood Disadvantage by Veronica Strong-Boag • 2011 / x + 302 pp. / ISBN 978-1-55458-337-9

Cold War Comforts: Maternalism, Child Safety, and Global Insecurity, 1945–1975 by Tarah Brookfield • 2012 / xiv + 292 pp. / illus. / ISBN 978-1-55458-623-3